The Slightest Philosophy

QUEE NELSON

This edition published by Dog Ear Publishing
4010 W. 86th Street, Ste H
Indianapolis, IN 46268
www.dogearpublishing.net

ISBN: 1-59858-378-6
Library of Congress Control Number:
This book is printed on acid-free paper.

Printed in the United States of America

To Catherine Kimball Varnum Beaman
1935-1977

CONTENTS

It seems evident, that men are carried, by a natural instinct or prepossession, to repose faith in their senses; and that, without any reasoning, or even almost before the use of reason, we always suppose an external universe, which depends not on our perception, but would exist, though we and every sensible creature were absent or annihilated. Even the animal creation are governed by a like opinion, and preserve this belief of external objects, in all their thoughts, designs, and actions.

It seems also evident, that, when men follow this blind and powerful instinct of nature, they always suppose the very images, presented by the senses, to be the external objects, and never entertain any suspicion, that the one are nothing but representations of the other. This very table, which we see white, and which we feel hard, is believed to exist, independent of our perception, and to be something external to our mind, which perceives it. Our presence bestows not being on it: our absence does not annihilate it. It preserves its existence uniform and entire, independent of the situation of intelligent beings, who perceive or contemplate it.

But this universal and primary opinion of all men is soon destroyed by the slightest philosophy, which teaches us, that nothing can ever be present to the mind but an image or perception, and that the senses are only the inlets, through which these images are conveyed, without being able to produce any immediate intercourse between the mind and the object. The table, which we see, seems to diminish, as we remove farther from it: but the real table, which exists independent of us, suffers no alteration: it was, therefore, nothing but its image, which was present to the mind. These are the obvious dictates of reason; and no man, who reflects, ever doubted, that the existences, which we consider, when we say, this house *and* that tree, *are nothing but perceptions in the mind, and fleeting copies or representations of other existences, which remain uniform and independent...*

By what argument can it be proved, that the perceptions of the mind must be caused by external objects, entirely different from them, though resembling them (if that be possible) and could not arise either from the energy of the mind itself, or from the suggestion of some invisible and unknown spirit, or from some other cause still more unknown to us?

...It is a question of fact, whether the perceptions of the senses be produced by external objects, resembling them: how shall this question be determined? By experience surely; as all other questions of a like nature. But here experience is, and must be entirely silent. The mind has never anything present to it but the perceptions, and cannot possibly reach any experience of their connexion with objects. The supposition of such a connexion is, therefore, without any foundation in reasoning. [1]

---David Hume, 1748

I do not see that we are farther along today than where Hume left us. The Humean predicament is the human predicament. [2]

---Willard van Orman Quine, 1969

"Philosophy informs us, that every thing, which appears to the mind, is nothing but a perception... whereas the vulgar confound perceptions and objects, and attribute a distinct continued existence to the very things they feel or see."

---David Hume

"External objects...are mere appearances, and are therefore nothing but a species of my representations."

"All bodies together with the space in which they are, must be considered nothing but mere representations in us, and exist nowhere but in our thoughts."

"The objects with which we have to do in experience are by no means things in themselves but only appearances."

"Appearances are not things, but rather nothing but representations, and they cannot exist at all outside our minds."

---Immanuel Kant

INTRODUCTION
The Postmodern Condition

On Bullshit is a serious philosophy book. At first glance, it might look offensive or flippant, but actually it's a rigorous philosophical analysis of an important concept which, unfortunately, just doesn't have any other name. Harry Frankfurt's careful analysis argues that 'bullshit' isn't, like *lying*, a kind of discourse that *intentionally opposes* the truth, but rather a kind of discourse that just *disregards* the truth. A casual reader might wonder why a philosopher would bother to work so hard to discover something so seemingly obvious. But anybody who's spent a lot of time in the postmodern world of the Sokal Hoax might appreciate Frankfurt's book. As he puts it, "one of the salient features of our culture is that there's so much bullshit."[3]

In fact, Frankfurt almost seems to have proved that postmodern philosophy is bullshit, by definition. To see how the argument might work, we might look at, for example, the postmodernism of Richard Rorty. Rorty, whom Harold Bloom called "the most interesting philosopher in the world,"[4] is also "arguably the most influential contemporary philosopher writing in English,"[5] and "one of the world's most influential living thinkers."[6] According to Rorty:

> We need to think of reason not as a truth-tracking faculty but as a social practice.[7]

> The notion of "accurate representation" is simply an automatic and empty compliment which we pay to those beliefs which are successful in helping us to do what we want to do.[8]

> There is no enclosing wall called "the Real." There is nothing outside language to which language attempts to become adequate.[9]

> The claim that we are responsible to reality is as hopeless as the idea that true sentences correspond to reality....we have no responsibilities except to fellow-players of what Sellars and Brandom call the game of giving and asking for reasons.[10]

> We cannot find a skyhook which lifts us out of mere coherence---mere agreement---to something like 'correspondence with reality as it is in itself.' ...Pragmatists would like to replace the desire for objectivity---the desire to be in touch with a reality which is more than some community with which we identify ourselves---with the desire for solidarity with that community.[11]

> We understand knowledge when we understand the social justification of belief, and thus have no need to view it as accuracy of representation.[12]

So, maybe we can make short work of postmodernism by proving that the fact that it's bullshit simply follows logically from the definitions of the terms involved. If postmodernism is a kind of discourse that pays little or no regard to the truth, and that's the very definition of the word 'bullshit,' then postmodernism is bullshit, by definition.

That's a pretty neat move. But, unfortunately, it doesn't settle the matter. Those who already feel that postmodernism is a crock will agree, of course. But postmodern philosophers will either deny that they disregard the truth, or else complain that if they do, then so does everybody else, and nothing can be done about it. They'll object that such a naive notion of "the Truth" obviously presupposes a vulgar realism that can't survive philosophical examination. Postmodernists see this *realist* notion of truth (truth as a conformity or correspondence between claims, beliefs, ideas or representations, on the one hand, and ready-made, mind-independent things in themselves, on the other) as "hopeless." For this and other reasons, Rorty feels compelled to "see truth, as in James's phrase, as 'what it is better for us to believe' rather than as 'the accurate representation of reality'."[13]

Some might imagine that the best cure for postmodern silliness is the same as for other kinds of flaky thinking: call the Bullshit Squad, i.e., the philosophy department, whose job it is to untangle logical fallacies and understand things like truth, reason, evidence, justification and knowledge. Unfortunately, postmodernists didn't get that way on account of ignoring the teachings of the philosophy department, but on account of sincerely imbibing them. The terrible truth is that postmodernism is what happens when honest, intelligent people read the canonical philosophers and believe them.

This isn't to say that the cure for postmodernism doesn't lie in the hands of philosophy. It does. But the blame lies there too. To halt the postmodern plague, the doctors need to be cured first. It's like one of those incredibly hardy hospital strains. The roots of postmodernism run so deep in philosophy that the condition can only be reversed by a radical surgery that cuts into the very heart of the canon to expose a shocking amount of diseased tissue.

Committed to saving the patient, I'll argue that the way to proceed is to combine abduction with naive realism. The tricky part of the operation, as everybody knows, concerns the threat of radical skepticism. But, of course, being the key to an effective cure, that's the best part.

First *Naiveté*

J. L. Austin once said that in philosophy it's usually all over by the bottom of page one. Something like this seems to hold also for philosophy as an academic subject, in that it's usually all over by the end of Philosophy 101, when every fresh crop of students must learn from the canonical texts that what you perceive when you eat your lunch aren't ready-made things in themselves existing independently of the mind, but, rather, mere representations of the mind, and to think otherwise, though it may seem commonsensical, is naive. In other words, once the students see what's wrong with "naive realism," epistemology can get rolling. Over the gates of history's first Academy was written, 'Let No Man Ignorant of Geometry Enter.' At the gates of Hell it's, 'Abandon Hope All Ye Who Enter Here.' The philosophy department could post a hybrid: 'Abandon Naive Realism All Ye Who Enter Here.'

This is an exaggeration, since it ignores moral and political philosophy, but in metaphysics and epistemology (the inner core of philosophy), it's been more or less the case for centuries. In 1989 John Heil published a survey in which he noted that "anti-realist tracts overwhelm both in number and sheer density a steady but comparatively modest realist output." He noted that "Australia, isolated and out of the loop evolutionarily, continues as a stronghold of realists and marsupials."[14] One of the latest books from Oxford University Press still assures us of "our epistemological situation in our state of philosophical enlightenment, where we have corrected our ordinary, naive view, and accepted that external items are not accessible to sense-perception."[15]

Of course, things are always worse in France, where philosophy seems to have gone all but raving mad. But in America too we scratch our heads since *Reading McDowell,* and Hilary Putnam, after decades of disparaging realism, nominally calls for the troops to retreat through a jungle of their own making, hacking their way back, if possible, to a "second naiveté." Putnam almost seems to credit William James with the discovery that two people on the Harvard campus can perceive the same building (a feat no doubt easier to perform the farther it occurs from campus). [16] To this day, the epistemology collection of your local bookstore is unlikely to offer more than a few *naifs* awash in a sea of sophisticated disparagers of the ordinary realism Hume and Berkeley attributed to "the vulgar" (a category they opposed to "the philosophers"). It's not unlike looking for atheists in the Religion section. The modern philosophy canon is the anti-realist canon; if twenty of the world's most popular epistemologists since Berkeley were made into baseball cards, you might not find a good champion of the vulgar in the pack.[17]

True, there will always be many working in the moral and political sub-specialties of philosophy who'll wonder if a determined attack on anything they'd think of as anti-realism isn't beating a dead horse, since nobody they eat lunch with seems to be talking about it. But these might be compared to the eighteenth-century *philosophes* who thought religion was through. Would that it were a dead horse, but as things stand today, it looks doubtful whether most of the world will ever get over it. This horse could use a lot more beating. Besides, even if it were to attain dead horse status some time in the future, as Charles Taylor observed, "in philosophy dead horses have a tendency to ride again."[18] Even to stampede whole continents. Entrenched in hoary, canonical texts, this horse will never die. Like Christianity, Judaism, Marxism, and Islam, it will live forever. Like oak root fungus, it can only be kept in check.

But there's another reason those off in the fields of moral and political philosophy need to care about postmodern epistemology, and that's because it has an unavoidable effect on their own specialties. At the very least it's indispensable to understand how it could happen that Richard Rorty could be "one of the world's most influential living thinkers"[19] while saying things like

> I do not think there are any plain moral facts out there in the world, nor any truths independent of language, nor any neutral ground on which to stand and argue that either torture or kindness are preferable to the other.[20]

Of course, another problem we will always suffer from, is that, to the extent any philosophy book truly succeeds in achieving what philosophy ought to achieve, which is "common sense methodized and perfected,"[21] then to that extent such a commonsensical book isn't saying anything that is too terribly shocking or disastrous. And that means it's unlikely to become a major canonical text, while the works of Hume and Kant, no less than *Das Kapital* and *Mein Kampf*, will indefinitely enjoy their sinecure as required reading for each new generation of freshly-scrubbed young minds.

At this point in history, things could go either way. On the one hand, a skeptical anti-realism, still more or less in the drivers' seat, might chronically dominate philosophy indefinitely, until the word 'Philosophy' eventually comes to denote some kind of strained intellectual religion incompatible with common sense. In that case, philosophy, once naively imagined to serve as a pesticide against humbug, might instead turn into fodder for a new dark age of especially hardy pests.

Or, things could go the other way, and a vulgar *naiveté* regain the upper hand, with marginalized arguments for common sense winning back enough of the limelight from Hume and Kant to retake the ivory tower. It's probably too late for France and Germany, but what needs to happen in the salvageable world is for philosophy to plainly admit that this parting of the ways between philosophy and common sense wasn't just a small technical error, but a momentous blunder and a fateful wrong turn. What philosophy owes to the vulgar isn't some belated and begrudging concessions, but a sincere and contrite apology and a promise to make amends for centuries of preposterous slander, libel, and defamation.

At the very least, it should be admitted to young philosophy students that they have a choice in the matter, and will not necessarily feel like atheists majoring in Divinity, should they refuse to abjure their vulgar common sense.

Of course, students must still be taught the canonical texts. There's no getting around that. Hume is considered more important and sophisticated than Reid. Kant and Hegel are considered more important and sophisticated than Austin. Madmen and villains are often considered more important and sophisticated than sensible, harmless people. But this means that in order to cling to their common sense in the teeth of such a formidable array as they must face, students have to hold out like stubborn teetotalers in a crowded saloon. We can only wonder if more than a minority of them will ever have the strength to stand their naive ground against the Greatest Minds in History. This book was written for these students, in hopes it may give them courage.

Above all else, right or wrong, at least I want to make this debate as plain and easy to understand as I possibly can. That's why I've tried to avoid the academic style, riddled with ambiguous jargon. That's a style tailor-made to talk yourself into preposterous notions you'd see right through immediately, if, instead, they were stated plainly. Besides, the subject is tricky enough without being made even more obscure by unnecessary cant.

I've also chosen to use the dialogue form, because a fellow student, Mark Engel, once said he thought all philosophy would be clearer if written in dialogue form, and I thought he had a point. My own suggestion for curing errors in philosophy was to require at least one concrete example per abstract claim, and so I've also tried to remember to take my own advice.

Non-professionals may find chapter one pedantic, and realists may find chapter three tiresome from their point of view. They should skip forward to the next chapter. One person's overkill is another's "not proved," and the first obligation of a philosophical argument is to satisfy its enemies, even if this means trying the patience of its friends. It's fun to preach to the choir, but the point is to save the damned.

Beat the Demon

The last chapter hopefully won't bore anybody. That's because it takes on the toughest monsters in philosophy's dungeon, including Descartes's Demon, the Evil Deceiver, Hume's Riddle, and the Disembodied Brain in the Vat. (They're even scarier than they sound.) In philosophy this is called the problem of *skepticism*.

In his book *Challenging Postmodernism: Philosophy and the Politics of Truth*, David Detmer lamented:

> A position that I find to be very frequently defended with explicit argumentation in popular culture is anti-realism, meaning either the doctrine that there is no such thing as "reality" (that is, there is no one way that "things are," or that "the world is"), or the more modest view that even if there is some way that "reality" or the world is, we cannot possibly know what this way is. The former thesis I will call "ontological anti-realism"; the latter I will term "epistemological anti-realism."[22]

The latter position, which Detmer proposed to call "epistemological anti-realism," is usually, in the philosophy department, called *external-world skepticism*. Or, more often, just plain *skepticism* for short. And, yet, it's easy to sympathize with Detmer's idiosyncratic label, because skepticism and anti-realism are so similar that even famous philosophers have a hard time telling them apart.[23] And no wonder. To over-simplify, skepticism is basically the claim that nothing about the world outside the mind can be known, and anti-realism is basically the claim that nothing actually existing in the world outside the mind can be perceived.

It would be vain to try to refute anti-realism without also refuting skepticism. This is because, while anti-realism wants to prove that houses and trees don't actually exist apart from the mind as independent things in themselves, skepticism, as we'll see, involves the claim that *it's no less probable a possibility* that (for some reason) they don't. So anybody who wants to argue that it's at least probable (that the very houses and trees we see and feel *do* actually exist as independent things in themselves outside the mind), must refute *both* anti-realism and skepticism. For this and other reasons, there's no dealing with one of these problems without dealing with the other at the same time.

Basically, the skeptic points out that, for all you know, you could just as well be living in a jelly pod in the world of *The Matrix*, or else be a disembodied brain floating in a vat of fluid, hooked up to the electrodes of a mad scientist's supercomputer which feeds you all your experiences. Maybe your memories are all false, implanted only a moment ago. Or perhaps your whole life is merely a dream. Or maybe, as Descartes once suggested, you're just a hapless spirit deluded by an evil demon who gets his jollies by fooling you into thinking this crazy world really exists outside your addled mind. The philosophical skeptic says, since it cannot be known that this isn't the case, therefore, no beliefs about an external world outside the mind are rationally justified.

Now, while it happens, sometimes, that anti-realism drives people to skepticism, actually, it often goes the other way. As Rorty once explained, "people become Pragmatists for the same reason they become idealists or verificationists: they hope to frustrate the skeptic."[24] If we can know nothing about any mind-independent, external world outside the mind, then, if we say the world is inside the mind, maybe then we can know about it! So, historically, it's been a dread of the demon that scared philosophers off the pedestrian realism of less enlightened folk. As David Armstrong put it:

> Phenomenalism is parasitic upon scepticism. The Phenomenalist raises the sceptical difficulties, and then appears as the heaven-sent deliverer from them.[25]

Obviously, this kind of radical, philosophical, epistemological skepticism is not to be confused with what ordinary people call "a healthy skepticism." This skepticism isn't the healthy kind.

But, the trouble is, we need to admit that maybe it should give us pause, if our favorite epistemology can't withstand this skeptical challenge. In fact, that's what makes skepticism a kind of philosophical test. So, while skepticism is a scourge, it's also a goad. Maybe we should even admit that, without the threat of radical skepticism, philosophy might be a stunted thing, like an economy without the pressure of free competition. But, on a darker note, we need to remember Rome, and see that history suggests a civilization which can't muster the wherewithal to answer a Pyrrhonist challenge may be a civilization at risk.

Unfortunately, most philosophers shy away from a serious confrontation with skepticism. As Anthony Rudd noticed:

> Strawson thinks we can properly respond to the skeptic, not with arguments but with a "Humean shrug." Rorty recommends that we should turn away from the tedious old conundrum about "the external world," and Davidson largely, though with some reservations, concurs with him; we shouldn't try to answer the skeptic, but simply tell him "to get lost." McDowell also thinks that we shouldn't "answer skeptical questions" but "ignore" them, though he does add that we need to do hard work to show "how it might be intellectually respectable" to do so.[26]

Sadly, it's rare for a philosopher to really take the skeptical bull by the horns. Instead, the typical response is a more or less facile dismissal. It usually seems like sour grapes, because usually it is. As Colin Howson rightly observed, "the problem is not solved, or even partially solved, by sanguine remarks."[27]

Besides, the same epistemologists who avoid mentioning the dreaded demon are still letting him intimidate their every move. While the word *skepticism* may hardly appear at all in their books, the specter invisibly haunts every page. What they really fear is what Rorty is honest enough to say plainly: "Nothing can refute the skeptic."[28]

Of course, it's not enough just to point out that the skeptical anti-realism at the heart of postmodern philosophy flies in the face of *common sense,* and leave it at that. This rightly fails to impress those who feel that "in a philosophical court the place for common sense is in the dock, or on occasion the witness-box, never the bench."[29] After all, Copernicus and Einstein went against common sense too.

Sometimes common sense turns out, actually, to be *wrong*. Besides, to think that it's okay to summarily dismiss postmodernism out of hand, merely on the grounds that it contradicts the conventional wisdom, looks an awful lot like you're embracing exactly the kind of philosophy you're pretending to be against.

On the other hand, if common sense is in the dock, maybe it could use some new attorneys. An innocent client should never be pled guilty. Besides, to embrace anti-realism, in a vain attempt to elude skepticism, is merely to climb into the vat and seal the lid. There's no reason to give up so easily. Where facile dismissals and Kantian revolutions have failed, something a lot more plodding and ordinary can beat the demon.

Only an earnest and searching heart can overcome the postmodern condition, because skepticism, to be beaten, must be faced honestly, and taken seriously. To pretend to ignore or dismiss it without a serious and careful examination is to forfeit the match and subject everything to a cynical and crippling fideism, and it just doesn't work to fold our cards and accept Hume's verdict that there's no alternative other than to base what we believe upon irrational dogmas we accept, despite a complete lack of evidence, in a capricious act of "blind submission."[30] Too long has reason cowered in Hume's shadow. Philosophy needs to exorcise this demon-haunted world.

"With all my heart, retain the word *matter*, and apply it to the objects of sense, if you please, provided you do not attribute to them any subsistence distinct from their being perceived....

My endeavours tend only to unite and place in a clearer light that truth, which was before shared between the vulgar and the philosophers: the former being of opinion, that *those things they immediately perceive are the real things:* and the latter, that *the things immediately perceived are ideas which exist only in the mind.* Which two notions put together, do in effect constitute the substance of what I advance."

---Bishop George Berkeley

CHAPTER 1

What Can Be Realism

"Naive Realism is the view of the great mass of civilized humanity," explained Oswald Kulpe's 1895 *Introduction to Philosophy*. "Naïve realism" is, as Ernst Mach put it in 1886, "The philosophical point of view of the average man."[1] Dickinson Miller, in his 1908 article "Naive Realism: What is It?" expressed it similarly: "By naive realism we mean the attitude of the ordinary mind towards the external world."[2]

This is what I mean to defend, *naive realism*. The only problem is that so many philosophers have been persuaded by the canon to reject it, that a few of them have offered various descriptions of naive realism that make it out to be something strange and implausible.[3] In other words, a few felt that, since so many philosophers seem to agree with Hume that "the slightest philosophy teaches us" that the vulgar realism of ordinary folks is untenable, therefore, it might be doing everybody a favor, not merely to label it "naive," but to go even farther, and offer helpful definitions designed to enlighten any newcomers in danger of not immediately seeing what's wrong with it.

This has led to a situation in which one or two philosophers who believe, more firmly than some, in the actual existence of ordinary people, have nevertheless questioned whether any Naive Realists actually exist.

But if the natural realism of untutored common sense isn't always exactly what its enemies might pretend it is, then what is it? This is pretty easy to find out. If you go to your plumber, and insist that the existence of light rays, eyeballs, and retinas proves that chairs are perceived "indirectly," rather than "directly," he might say, sure, fine, whatever. Have it your way. Inwardly, he may rightly suspect you of semantic quibbling. Just don't try telling him that you think that he cannot exist as a thing in himself independently of you, or that he's a mere appearance, and nothing in particular apart from your mind. Nor is he liable to look kindly upon you, if you tell him that his children are "mere representations" which "exist only in thought," or that there are "no such things" as pipe wrenches, or that the Moon is an intersubjective social construct, or that meteors and cannonballs, and even whole worlds, are actually made out of words by members of a linguistic community playing a language-game and "there is no ready-made world."[4]

But all this is merely negative. How can we say what naive realism is, in a more positive way? And dare we use the term "naive realism"? Fearing straw definitions of naive realism, the plumber's partisans may be pressured to give up a beloved epithet. Should this be considered necessary by those who think it wrong in principle to dispute with other people's definitions, a cue can be taken from Hume, who is to blame for so much, and, sticking with philosophy's tradition of tagging common sense with disapproving adjectives, take up the name Vulgar Realism. This name comes from Hume's epistemology, which convinced philosophy that only "the vulgar" could suffer under the "entirely unreasonable sentiment" which makes them "attribute a distinct continued existence to the very things they feel or see."[5]

In other words, Vulgar Realism is the claim that the very things you feel and see can, and often do, enjoy a distinct and continued existence, independently, apart from any mind. Or, to put the emphasis where it might do more good, we might reverse it and say: things in themselves actually existing and subsisting independently apart from the mind, often are, just as in Hume's own words, *the very things you feel and see.* Hume said:

> Men are carried, by a natural instinct or prepossession, to repose faith in their senses; and that, without any reasoning, or even almost before the use of reason, we always suppose an external universe, which depends not on our perception, but would exist, though we and every sensible creature were absent or annihilated.[6]

It would be hard to find a better definition than that. Realism is the vulgar, naive belief that "the very things we feel or see," pipe wrenches, tables, chairs, houses, trees, and flying cannonballs, comprise, just as Hume puts it, "an external universe, which depends not on our perception, but would exist, though we and every sensible creature were absent or annihilated."

This, then, is a defense of exactly that vulgar, naive realism Hume so famously discredited as an irrational prejudice.[7] This realism involves no particular innovations, nor a retreat from a mundane *naiveté,* nor is it particularly scientific, nor unscientific, nor well-articulated, nor even interesting. That's just the point. On the contrary, what's interesting is what has happened as a result of centuries of chronic denial of it. In other words, the claim is that there was never actually anything wrong with naive realism, and philosophy, precisely on account of continually disparaging it, has been off on a crazy wild goose chase for three hundred years.

What Realism Can't Be

Philosophers who reject a naive, vulgar realism sometimes call themselves "anti-realists" or "idealists." Unfortunately, sometimes they also call themselves other things, like "phenomenalists," "pragmatists," "irrealists," or even "realists" with some kind of qualifying adjective like "empirical," "scientific," or "internal." This can be confusing.

Originally, philosophers like George Berkeley who held that tables and chairs cannot exist outside the mind, called themselves, clearly enough, "idealists." Unfortunately, the word "idealist" has gone out of fashion. Lately, for example, the followers of Kant like to call him an "empirical realist," rather than an idealist. Kant usually called himself an idealist, but it's also a claim of Kant's that his "transcendental idealism" contains a brave new creature he named "empirical realism."

"Empirical realism," according to Kant, holds that, even though a cannonball isn't a mind-independent thing in itself, but "a mere appearance," a mere "representation" which "cannot exist at all outside the mind," still, if it *seems* real, if the mind experiences it *as if* it were external, then that is enough to call it *empirically* (i.e., experientially) "external," or "empirically real." In other words, the "empirically real" is the seemingly real; the "empirically external" is the seemingly external. As Kant explains it:

Since space is a form of that intuition we call outer...we can and must regard the beings in it as real; and the same is true of time. But this space and this time, and with them all appearances, are not in themselves things; they are nothing but representations and cannot exist at all outside our minds.[8]

External objects (bodies)...are mere appearances, and are therefore nothing but a species of my representations, the objects of which are something only through these representations. Apart from them they are nothing.[9]

Appearances are not things, but rather nothing but representations, and they cannot exist at all outside our minds.[10]

As we have just shown that the senses never and in no manner enable us to know things in themselves, but only their appearances...we conclude that all bodies together with the space in which they are, must be considered nothing but mere representations in us, and exist nowhere but in our thoughts.[11]

Your object is merely in your brain.[12]

The understanding itself is the lawgiver of Nature; save through it, Nature would not exist at all.[13]

If I remove the thinking subject, the whole corporeal world must at once vanish.[14]

This is reminiscent of Kant's predecessor Berkeley, who'd taken a similar position regarding ordinary objects:

With all my heart, retain the word *matter*, and apply it to the objects of sense, if you please, provided you do not attribute to them any subsistence distinct from their being perceived.

You talked often as if you thought I maintained the non-existence of sensible things: whereas in truth no one can be more thoroughly assured of their existence than I am...though indeed I deny they have any existence distinct from being perceived; or that they can exist out of all minds whatsoever.

I might as well doubt of my own being, as of the being of those things I actually see and feel.

My endeavours tend only to unite and place in a clearer light that truth, which was before shared between the vulgar and the philosophers: the former being of opinion, that *those things they immediately perceive are the real things:* and the latter, that *the things immediately perceived are ideas which exist only in the mind.* Which two notions put together, do in effect constitute the substance of what I advance.

Sensible things are all immediately perceivable; and those things which are immediately perceivable, are ideas; and these exist only in the mind. [15]

Berkeley, of course, is the paradigmatic idealist. In other words, he's basically the definitive case of what "realism" can't be. Yet he took the position that he had no objection to labeling tables and chairs "material," or "matter." Likewise, Kant said he had little objection to calling them "empirically real," or even "empirically external." Just so long as it remained understood that tables and chairs cannot actually exist outside of thought, or apart from the mind.

In other words, "empirical realism" bears something like the same relationship to realism, as mock turtle bears to turtle. "Empirical realism" isn't really, as it pretends, a kind of realism, but merely a coy and ironical euphemism for a kind of anti-realism even its author called "startling."[16]

Representative Realism

Besides Kant's "empirical realism," many philosophers have believed there to be various other "sophisticated" realisms that they hoped might find a happy dwelling place somewhere between the extremes of a vulgar *naivete*, or a full-blown Berkeleyan idealism. One popular candidate often nominated for the fence-straddling position is "representative realism." With its classical origins in Locke, Hobbes, and Galileo, "representative realism" is usually conceived as the idea that, for example, while a banana may look yellow, really it isn't yellow: the yellowness isn't in the banana, it's in you. Colors aren't properties of external objects, but "reside only in consciousness."

Locke said the banana has, true enough, that banana *shape*, and it is, true enough, really *out there* in *space* right where you think it is. But the banana's *color* isn't really out there in the banana. As Galileo explained it:

> I think that tastes, odors, colors, and so on... are no more than mere names so far as the object in which we place them is concerned, and that they reside only in the consciousness. Hence if the living creature were removed, all these qualities would be wiped away and annihilated. But since we have imposed upon them special names, distinct from those of the other and real qualities [extension, motion, etc.], mentioned previously, we wish to believe that they really exist as actually different from those. ...I think that if ears, tongues, and noses were removed, shapes and numbers and motions would remain, but not odors or tastes or sounds. ...many sensations which are supposed to be qualities residing in external objects have no real existence save in us... ...When the live body is taken away, heat becomes no more than a simple name.[17]

As Hobbes put it:

> Neither in us that are pressed, are they anything but diverse motions; (for motion produceth nothing but motion.) But their appearance to us is fancy, the same waking that dreaming. ...For if those colors, and sounds, were in the bodies, or objects which cause them, they could not be severed from them as by glasses, and in echoes by reflection, we see they are; where we know the thing we see, is in one place; the appearance, in another.[18]

In Locke's version, there are "primary qualities," like *shape* and location, which are really out there, and "secondary qualities," like *color*, that aren't. So your perceptions in some ways (primary qualities) represent or "resemble" things as they are in themselves, but in other ways (secondary qualities) they don't. Which almost seems to suggest that if you watch a black & white television with the sound off, you'll get a more faithful impression of things.

Although it may sound silly at first, this question about the *color* of things is in fact historically paradigmatic here, and it persists as a notorious dispute until this day. A traditional approach to it was once "crudely but vividly summarized" by Daniel Dennett as involving a fallacy of composition:

It seems that science has taught us that everything is some collection or other of atoms, and atoms are not colored. Hence nothing is colored; hence nothing is yellow. Shocking! Where did the yellow go? Sellars has for years been wondering where the yellow went…[19]

Scientific Realism

Dennett was talking about Wilfrid Sellars. Sellars once said "speaking as a philosopher I am quite prepared to say that the common sense world of physical objects in Space and Time is unreal---that is, that there are no such things."[20] And yet he called himself a "scientific realist." Philosophers who qualify their "realism" with the adjective *scientific* are sometimes concerned that a plainer realism might conflict with science. Galen Strawson, for example, felt that A. J. Ayer's attempt to reconcile "common-sense realism" with a "scientific" view of the world "can only seem to succeed by doing violence to one of the two viewpoints, the scientific."[21]

Strawson identified "scientific realism" primarily with "Lockean realism."[22] But some follow Kant in censuring Locke's "primary qualities" (like shape and spatial location) hardly less than his "secondary" ones (like colors). So there's disagreement among "scientific realists." But it's probably fair to say that "scientific realism," when the phrase appears in a philosophy book, typically suggests a commitment *only* to the actual existence of various allegedly "imperceptible" or "theoretical" objects or properties most at home in a Physics book, e.g., atoms, molecules, electrons, photons, quarks, gravitational forces, or superstrings. Or, whatever it is that ends up being settled upon, later, when physics finally comes to an end. If it ever does.

In other words, in the eyes of some philosophers, being a realist about atoms *conflicts with* being a realist about cannonballs, and they therefore call themselves "scientific realists" to express a prejudice in favor of the former over the latter type stuff.

To the untrained observer, this may sound like a person who thinks there's some kind of conflict between the actual existence of bricks and the actual existence of houses. But, however that may be, outside of the Physics department the actuality of oncoming freight trains is an easier call than the actuality of quarks. Few non-physicists are willing to bet the rent on quarks anyway. Probably this is because most people find it easier to believe in the intractable mind-independence of a medium-sized Physics professor than to have faith in whatever tiny "particles" or invisible "forces" this professor appears to endorse, judging by the seeming noises that issue forth from the supposed direction of his apparent body.

So, while the question of whether or not the theoretical entities of physics actually exist outside the theories of physics is primarily a question for physicists to worry about (just as other specialists likewise have their own narrow "realism" debates about the reality of various theoretical entities like ADHD or the GNP), to have serious doubts about ordinary medium-sized objects like *houses* and *trees* has traditionally been the job of the Philosophy department.

This is why it can be very misleading for a *philosopher* to label himself a "realist" merely because he grants to the pet particles of a theoretical future physicist a kind of respect he denies to his own house. Hilary Putnam once illustrated this fact, in a funny parable about the "Scientific Realist" who seduces the Innocent Maiden. His point was that it's bound to come as an unpleasant shock to the innocent *naif*, when once she finds out, as sooner or later she must, that this philosopher calling himself a "realist" is actually a shameless idealist when it comes to "her good old ice cubes and chairs." As Putnam so memorably put it, "Some will say that the lady has been had." [23]

Mock Realism Internalized

The weird thing is that Putnam was guilty of the very same crime preached against by his excellent parable of the Seducer. For example, while leading the opposition to realism for much of his career, he nevertheless chose to label his own philosophy "internal *realism*." Putnam's "realism" held that "there isn't a ready-made world," [24] because "we have no direct access to mind-independent things," and thus "we have no access to unconceptualized reality," and therefore "the mind never compares an image or word with an object, but only with other images, words, beliefs, judgments, etc." So, Putnam himself had powerfully contributed to the seductive suggestion that every philosopher was some sort of "realist," no matter how unblushingly anti-realist their claims.

In fact, it almost started to look like there was nothing in the world but just different kinds of "realists." There were Naive Realists (and who wants to be naive?), and then there were the Sophisticated Realists, such as the Empirical Realists, the Scientific Realists, and the Internal Realists.

But, if everybody's a realist, no matter what, then the word *realist* begins to collapse, robbed of sense. Worse, those who have the naive vulgarity to disagree with the outlandish claims of Berkeley, Hume, and Kant about cannonballs residing entirely in the mind, seem denied meaningful ownership of a name.

And, yet---wasn't it the idealists who had introduced the name "realism" as a handy label for the vulgar *naiveté* which they intended to oppose? In other words, we now seem to need a new word to do exactly the job that the old word 'realist' would have done happily, had it not been shamelessly appropriated by the same school that introduced it in the first place as a name for what they meant to deny.

The vulgar and naive were left nameless, breathless, and speechless. Even philosophers eventually began to protest. As Richard Fumerton complained, "Toy soldiers aren't soldiers and internal realism isn't realism." [25] It is, as Michael Devitt agreed, "a form of *anti-Realism*."[26]

Happily, Putnam "now confesses to having subscribed to a 'residue of idealism' in his "Internal Realism," which is "a label he now regards as unfortunate." [27]

"Direct Realism:" Straw Man, Red Herring

"It is customary," said D. M. Armstrong, "and I think useful, to classify philosophical theories of perception as direct realist, representative (representative realist), and phenomenalist."[28] To the extent that this classification is customary, it constitutes an example of Austin's complaint mentioned before that "in philosophy it's usually all over by the bottom of page one." The problem with Armstrong's tripartite scheme is that it seems to imply that to defend the mundane, commonsense realism of the philosophically untutored must essentially mean defending the claim that the perception of objects like tables and chairs is "direct."

Unfortunately, Armstrong is hardly alone. It's easy to find other philosophers who seem to think like this, for example, Strawson, Fumerton, and Ayer on various occasions.[29] In a more recent case, DeVries and Triplett's work on Sellars says, while explaining what "direct realism" is, that "a direct realist" is "sometimes tendentiously referred to as a naive realist."[30] Of course, if you happen to be a commonsensical person unsportingly labeled *naive*---merely on account of your unwavering faith in the actual existence and intractable mind-independence of locomotives---this seems pretty refreshing, you know, to have somebody notice that calling you *naive* for that, may be "tendentious." And of course it's a chivalrous gesture, to point that out, and certainly well intentioned.

But, the trouble is, it looks like it's suggesting that the ordinary, natural realism of untutored common sense which anti-realists have tendentiously labeled *naive realism* is better labeled *direct realism.* And that would be a problem, because calling it "direct" is even worse than calling it "naive." Where to label it "naive" or "vulgar" is merely to indulge in mildly prejudicial adjectives, to label it "direct" is to do something worse and commit a fallacy called the Straw Man.

First of all, it's nearly impossible to divide philosophers according to whether or not they think we can perceive tables and chairs "directly" (or "immediately") on the one hand, versus perceiving them "indirectly" (or "mediately") on the other. Are we supposed to imagine, for example, that "direct" realists deny the obvious intermediary role played by *eyeballs* and/or *light* in order to see tables and chairs? In other words, just *how* indirect does perception have to be, to be "indirect"? Do you have to go so far as to posit a full-blown *chair* in between yourself and an invisible, mind-independent we-know-not-what, in order to get yourself placed on the "indirect" side of the ledger? Or are mere *light rays* or *optic nerves* medium enough for mediacy? If a distant star viewed through a telescope is described as being perceived "indirectly," is that enough to make the perception of an apple "indirect"? What if you grab the apple and take a bite out of it? What if somebody throws the apple at you, and it hits you so hard it knocks you over? What if you get hit by a bus? What if a brain surgeon pokes you in the brain with a pencil? Obviously, "directness" is, in this sense, relative.

The thing is, it's easy to agree that a complex process is involved in sense perception, including, for example, in the case of vision, a role for light rays, retinas, lenses, rods, cones, optic nerves, and the visual cortex, at least, to say nothing of any other neural processes. And, of course, a complex situation can be divided into a number of pieces, if not completely arbitrarily, at least in more than one way. But this fact makes the question of the relative "directness" of sense perception a completely trivial one. Besides, realists and anti-realists have never really quarreled over any particular account of corneas, retinas, optic nerves, or light rays. So, viewing the realism debate like this, as if it were a dispute over how relatively "direct" the biological process of perception is, can't be the right way to understand the issue, because people who don't disagree about the process can't truly be having a very meaningful dispute about how relatively direct it is, since, when it comes to the question of how relatively direct perception is, they basically agree. So, how could this really be the issue?

Besides, there could hardly be a greater fan of the *immediacy* and *directness* of the visual perception of chairs than the definitive idealist, George Berkeley; and, yet, surely it would be hard for anyone to get further than Berkeley from either *realism* or *naiveté*. Indeed, Kant likewise insisted that our experience of tables and chairs is "immediate,"[31] especially since, for Kant, this "immediacy" was one of the main attractions of *idealism*.

In other words, it makes no sense to frame the realism/anti-realism debate as a dispute about the relative "directness" or "immediacy" of our perceptual access to tables and chairs, and neither can a naive realist be understood as a person who is necessarily concerned to establish that your visual sense-perception of tables and chairs is "direct" or "immediate."

The question isn't whether or not you can perceive tables and chairs "directly," or even how relatively directly, more or less, you can, or can't, perceive them. The question is whether or not that chair you're sitting on right now, however more or less "directly" or "immediately" you suppose you perceive it, is, in your opinion, a ready-made thing in itself existing, persisting and subsisting independently, outside of thought and apart from the mind. In other words, the question is whether you consider that chair, this page you're reading, and the ground beneath your feet, to be things in themselves which would probably not be affected too severely if every last *mind* in the universe were suddenly annihilated.

In truth, the deeper controversy isn't about the relative directness of perception. It's a dispute about things like the mind-independence, substantiality, knowability, color, subsistence, meaning, reference, priority, objectivity, relativity, mentality, materiality, publicity, externality, identity, subjectivity and social construction of your chair. It's about questions like whether you are in the room, or the room is in you. It's about whether and how two different persons can perceive the *same* chair. It's about what it might mean to say that *gold* could have existed in the world without any minds to notice that gold, or name it. It's about the belief that there is, at bottom, finally some fact of the matter, some real objective truth, about Lizzie Borden, Alger Hiss, the grassy knoll, O.J. Simpson, Monica Lewinsky, and the planet Jupiter---some true, objective, mind-independent, external reality which just *is what it is*---in spite of what anybody thinks, and no matter what the meaning of 'is' is.

The Irrelevance of Representationalism

What's the upshot of all this for representationalism? What if somebody says that we don't "directly" perceive the world because instead what we perceive "directly" or "immediately" are "representations?" After all, not only Kant, but a lot of other philosophers say this, or things apparently *like* this, though in the proposition as it stands they might substitute, in the place of the term "representations," another word like "percepts," "qualia," "ideas," "appearances," "impressions," "presentations," "sense-contents," or "sense-data."

But what *are* these things? Here we enter into a perilous morass. Charles Taylor argued that "the sense datum is an impossible entity."[32] Many if not most would probably agree that it's at least notoriously unclear what elusive terms like "representation," "sense-datum," and "sense-quale" refer to.[33] For some philosophers, it seems such words denote private mental entities, and are in some sense the furniture of the mind, while for others they can be rather mind-independent. Alternatively, they can serve as a relation or bridge, which straddles the divide between mind and world. Some, however, wish to eliminate the middleman, and therefore simply identify "representations" with ordinary tables and chairs. In the usage of other philosophers, the reference is not to tables and chairs, but perhaps to something like light rays and sound waves. For some they might be flavors and colors. Or the electrical impulses that travel along the pathways of the human nervous system.

The intended reference may even be to what (if anything) gets doubled when you cross your eyes or hear an echo. Strange as this may sound, some philosophers interpret a "sense-datum" as a weird creature comprising only the visible *surfaces* of all the objects comprised in a single glance, so that, for example, it would *not* include the back side, or the red innards, of an uncut watermelon.

As DeVries and Triplett find themselves concluding, "the basic idea of sense-data...is quite neutral, taking no stand about the nature of sense-data."

> Are they mental entities? Are they particular individual things, or are they events? Are they to be located within the person, perhaps as physical states of sensory organs or neurophysiological interactions between those organs and the brain? Can they be, at least in the case of successful or veridical perception, ordinary physical objects?[34]

There is precious little agreement over meanings in this area. Is a "sense-content" the same thing as a "representation"? Are "qualia" the same as "impressions?" Are "presentations" also "percepts?" Ambiguity is rampant. If we say "colors are sensations," does that mean that the word 'red' merely refers to a state of mind? Or does it refer to electromagnetic radiation within a particular range of wavelengths, or to a persistent tendency of an external object to reflect sunlight at noon on Earth within a given range, or a persistent tendency to stimulate a particular type of retinal cone cell in normal humans? When you look at those famous drawings of the Necker cube and the duck-rabbit, is there a change---or a continuity---in the "sense-datum" when the interpretive flip is performed?

The fact that no two philosophers seem to be able to agree on how to interpret this stuff has driven some to despair. Daniel Dennett threw in the towel:

> When your kite string gets snarled up, in principle it can be unsnarled, especially if you're patient and analytic. But there's a

point beyond which principle lapses and practicality triumphs. Some snarls should just be abandoned. Go get a new kite string. It's actually cheaper in the end than the labor it would take to salvage the old one, and you get your kite airborne again sooner. That's how it is, in my opinion, with the philosophical topic of qualia, a tormented snarl of increasingly convoluted and bizarre thought experiments, jargon, in-jokes, allusions to putative refutations, "received" results that should be returned to sender, and a bounty of other sidetrackers and time wasters.[35]

Happily, those involved in the debate between realism and anti-realism can just cut to the chase. For us, the only thing that really matters about the untamed animals in any representationalist menagerie (call them what you will) is basically just two things: first, can they exist independently of us, outside the mind, and secondly, are things like *trees* and *cannonballs* supposed to be nothing but. It's basically answering these two questions "no" and "yes," respectively, that offends common sense. Since it's tough to avoid making the answer to the first question (mind-independent?) seem to be "no" by definition, it's typically the second question (trees nothing but?) that separates the sheep from the goats.

In other words, while it's hard to object to the claim that we can perceive an oncoming freight train only by means of data we have gathered by means of our senses, it's a whole other thing to start claiming that an oncoming freight train *is nothing other than* a bundle of sense data, or that when we say "oncoming freight train" we, by those words, *cannot possibly mean, or refer to,* anything more substantial than a swarm of sensations, a congeries of perceptions, a mental conception, a modification of our sensibility, or a state of mind.

So, the representationalist's creatures, while very hazardous, do not *necessarily* lead to anti-realism, if handled with extreme caution. Barry Maund, for example, proposes an approach, which, he hopes, can reconcile a reformed representationalism with "natural realism."

> The right way to present the representative thesis is to say that the perceiver does not perceive physical objects except by being aware of intermediaries. One does not perceive the intermediaries at all.[36]

Richard Fumerton had offered similar advice:

> If I were a sense-datum theorist, I would no doubt insist that one not speak of *perceiving* sense-data. Certainly, on the view I am defending, it would be a mistake to speak of perceiving anything but a physical object and its properties.[37]

The overall lesson here is that we need to view the handling of representationalist reifications as a technical sideshow. The debate between realism and anti-realism isn't ultimately a disagreement about the actual existence, outside our theories, of "sense-data" or "mental representations." It's a disagreement about the actual existence, outside our theories, of rocks and trees.

Again, the question isn't whether or not you can perceive rocks and trees directly, or even how relatively directly, more or less, you can, or can't, perceive them. The question is whether or not you believe that water and gold and rocks and trees, *however* more or less "directly" or "immediately" you want to say you perceive them, can be things in themselves existing and subsisting independently of us, things which would still exist and be what they are and little bothered if no *mind* had ever evolved on Earth or anywhere else.

All suddenly about his body wound,
That hand or foot to stir he strove in vain:
God help the man so wrapt in Error's endless train

...For he, that once hath missed the right way,
The further he doth go, the further he doth stray. [1]

---Edmund Spenser

CHAPTER 2

The Same Waking that Dreaming

So what? Who cares? As Hume once said, "the errors in religion are dangerous; those in philosophy only ridiculous." [2]

Unfortunately, history has not been kind to that claim. John Maynard Keynes rendered a wiser verdict. As an academic economist active in a world of "practical" men who imagined themselves free from academic questions, Keynes observed the opposite to be the case:

> The ideas of economists and political philosophers, both when they are right and when they are wrong, are more powerful than is commonly understood. Indeed, the world is ruled by little else. Practical men, who believe themselves to be exempt from any intellectual influences, are usually the slaves of some defunct economist. Madmen in authority, who hear voices in the air, are distilling their frenzy from some academic scribbler of a few years back. [3]

Not only do "academic" beliefs have consequences, even the idea that they *don't* have consequences has consequences. Sometimes people hate to admit that such beliefs make any practical difference, because they're afraid admitting this fact might lead to censorship. But what is that, after all, except a perfect example of such beliefs having, as a matter of fact, practical implications?

There's no escaping from philosophical questions, since even to denounce the whole subject as bunk, is to take a position within it (and a very traditional one at that), and to refuse to say anything at all about it, would be to side with Cratylus, one of philosophy's founding fathers. But the most wretched of these is the so-called "pragmatist" who dismisses philosophy as impractical, showing by this, one of the most mainstream doctrines in philosophy today (handed down from Hume no less), that he is anything but *free* from it. Likewise, Isaac Newton, if he could visit us today, would smile to see that people who never heard of him, and consider themselves quite independent of any seventeenth century philosophers, nevertheless have the word "gravity" often on their lips, and would think it silly to doubt its existence.

Arguments which are poured out even from the highest ivory towers eventually trickle down. For good or ill, they make their way at last into the remotest nooks and crannies. A Cambodian guerrilla deep in a steaming jungle carries a paperback copy of Rousseau, and the next thing you know, a million people are dead. It's painful, now, to read Fichte and Hegel. It may take centuries, but what was once a puddle of ink from a lonely pen can end in a river of blood. The logical and practical consequences of our "merely philosophical" beliefs are impossible to banish or ignore.

Let's try to imagine, merely as an example, as a thought experiment, what it might mean to be an innocent person on trial some day in the future, standing before an unfriendly jury steeped from birth in the postmodern doctrine that "the claim that we are responsible to reality" is "hopeless," and that *truth* cannot possibly be anything more than "an automatic and empty compliment which we pay to those beliefs which are successful in helping us to do what we want to do."[4]

At any rate, there's really no escape from epistemology, any more than from moral dilemmas, since these are of course questions everybody answers in some way or another. Even the most stubbornly anti-philosophical person who---say---refused to act upon any principle higher than blind animal instinct, or who refused to embrace any belief besides the conventional wisdom, would not thereby succeed in escaping from epistemology. As a matter of fact, he'd be occupying one of the most orthodox positions in it.

Trying to be less "epistemological" and more "pragmatic" cannot, as the (epistemological) doctrines of Hume and Rorty pretend, be a way to do an *end-run* around a skeptical dead end. If Hume's skepticism were right, then Hume and Rorty's advice telling us to just

17

ignore it and be "pragmatic" (Rorty) or just thoughtlessly follow custom, nature, and habit (Hume) would be impossible. If we can tell whether or not what we're doing is, as an empirical matter of fact, pragmatic, or customary, or habitual, or even natural, then Hume's skepticism is false, because it says we can't discern *any* matter of empirical fact whatsoever, even as a *probability*. That's the supposed dead end. That's the whole reason why we supposedly need the end-run. If this skeptical dead end were real, then nobody could ever tell whether or not what they're doing is even *probably* practical, because to know this is to know what Hume calls an empirical "matter of fact and existence."

Of course, Hume and Rorty may have overestimated skepticism. The demon they think reason can't refute might be perfectly refutable after all. So, there might be no real dead end there at all, but just a *mirage*. But, in that case, the sideways end-run into the postmodern quagmire was unnecessary and wrongheaded.

To say all this more clearly: everybody is already *trying* to be pragmatic, even a kid who blows himself up in order to get into Heaven. What's wrong with him isn't that he's insufficiently pragmatic, or that he's chosen an impractical method of transportation. What's wrong with him is that he believes things that aren't actually true. And the problem with postmodern philosophy, is that educated people no longer think it worthwhile to articulate the reasons and evidence we have that belie what that kid believes, because we're all much too sophisticated now to fall for a corny *naiveté* that imagines we'll get anywhere that way. There is, as we keep hearing every day, and from every camp, no use reasoning with people.

There are some very serious problems in the world that cannot be solved independently of philosophy. Nor have these problems arisen independently of philosophy, as it is the purpose of this chapter to show.

Postmodern Hopelessness

So, what is "postmodern" philosophy anyway? And why is it called that? If we want to get a handle on postmodern philosophy, we want to get a handle on Hume and Kant. They are Modern philosophers (Modern as opposed to Ancient or Medieval), but the thing to understand is that the *post* prefix does not mean *anti*. Far from it. *Post* means *after*, but the connotation here is something closer to *since*. It's helpful to understand that when *post-Modern* first appeared in the late nineteenth century, it echoed an expression then current in philosophy, "post-Kantian"---which dated back at least to the 1850s and referred to what is now usually called "German Idealism."[5] In fact, it might be easiest to fully grasp the deeper connotations here if we think of driving under the influence as *post-beer* driving. Likewise, a *post-Modern* philosopher is a philosopher operating under the influence of Modern philosophers. Modern philosophers like, for example, Descartes, Locke, Leibniz, Berkeley, Hume, Kant, and Hegel.

I especially pick on Hume and Kant because they're the most influential. They are, you might say, something like the Moses and Christ of philosophy now. "There is virtually no philosophy that has come since, in the two hundred years since Kant died, that has not in some way been influenced by Kant," said Oxford's Adrian Moore.[6] Kant is, said John Herman Randall, "without question the most influential modern philosopher."[7] But there's another sense in which we could say Hume, "the most important philosopher ever to have written in English,"[8] is even more influential than Kant. Not only because Hume was the most important influence on Kant ("the Prussian Hume"), but, also, because while there certainly are English-speaking philosophers who don't like Kant, you'll hear more disparagement of Moses from theologians than of Hume from professional philosophers.

Admittedly, Hume was undeniably great. There are passages of his to die for, and, truth be told, he's charming. This is why even those who hate Hume love him, where the opposite is the case with Kant. But this is also why, even if he isn't the "founder" of the line of thought that leads to the postmodern dead end, again and again, it's Hume who really clinches the deal.

Hume's contemporary opponent was Thomas Reid, the Scottish "philosopher of common sense." Reid was fairly influential in the American colonies, and Tom Paine's famous 1776 pamphlet "Common Sense" was published just a few years after Reid, in 1764, published his *Inquiry into the Human Mind on the Principles of Common Sense*. But, it's a testament to Hume's eventual dominance that "from the time of their eighteenth century editions, Reid's collected works remained out of print until 1967."[9]

Reid rejected the hazardous turn philosophy had taken with idealism:

> The theory of ideas, like the Trojan horse, had a specious appearance both of innocence and beauty; but if those philosophers had known that it carried in its belly death and destruction to all science and common sense, they would not have broken down their walls to give it admittance. [10]

Reid was right. Abandon hope all ye who abandon a naive, vulgar realism. That way lies madness. A whirlwind tour through the phenomenal fields of philosophy since Hume will help to prove this claim. Please fasten seat belts.

Farewell to Reason

First of all, we can just glance around at what postmodern philosophy is up to lately. Thomas Kuhn, no *naif,* authored one of the most (some say *the* most) often cited philosophy books in recent history. In it, he argued that scientists who believe different theories cannot both observe the same things. For example, at the time of the Copernican revolution Kepler and Tycho Brahe perhaps "did not see the same thing in the east at dawn," because "after a revolution scientists work in a different world."[11]

> Proponents of competing paradigms must fail to make complete contact with each other's viewpoints. [12]

> Practicing in different worlds, the two groups of scientists see different things when they look from the same point in the same direction. [13]

"In these matters neither proof nor error is at issue,"[14] said Kuhn. "Paradigm change cannot be justified by proof."[15]

> We may, to be more precise, have to relinquish the notion, explicit or implicit, that changes of paradigm carry scientists and those who learn from them closer and closer to the truth. [16]

Chemists could not…simply accept Dalton's theory on the evidence, for much of that was still negative. Instead, even after accepting the theory, they still had to beat nature into line, a process which, in the event, took almost another generation. When it was done, even the percentage composition of well-known compounds was different. The data themselves had changed.[17]

The man who continues to resist after his whole profession has been converted has *ipso facto* ceased to be a scientist.[18]

What better criterion than the decision of the scientific group could there be?[19]

This is important, because it is one of the most interesting aspects of anti-realism that it tends to lead to this sort of doctrine. If the objects you seem to see are really nothing more than mere representations in the mind, then two people who interpret things differently can't be seeing the same thing.

Indeed, it would seem that two people who *don't* interpret things differently can't be seeing the same thing either. If "the things with which we have to do in experience" can never be more than "mere representations in us" and "perceptions in the mind," then, unless you think you're a mind-reader, it seems impossible to understand how you could perceive something which has anything to do with what another person perceives.

Another question which naturally arises is: "with no ready-made world as a touchstone, how can there be criteria of truth and rightness?"[20] For example, if everything we perceive is a "mere appearance" or "mere perception of the mind," then what's the difference between merely imaginary things, and things which really exist?

One anti-realist answer to this, has been to say that the criteria for something's having a right to be considered true, objective, or real is basically provided by the agreement of other minds with one's own.

Our knowledge is sound and good, within the limits of appearance, within the limits of our experience. No doubt the entire world as we know it is appearance, but it is not a mere illusion, because the forms of this appearance are universal and necessary. They apply to all minds constructed as ours are. They are not merely the groundless fancies of an *individual's* mind; which is what is meant by illusion.[21]

As Rorty explained, when accused of being Orwellian:

> There is no procedure called 'turning to the facts'…there is no procedure of 'justification in light of the facts' which can be opposed to concilience of one's own opinion with those of others.[22]

But, what might be the implications of this doctrine when faced with the fact that most people believe with reckless abandon in ghosts, miracles, magic, supernatural spirits, and Lord knows what else? Of course, these are prime examples of things once imagined by a few vulgar innocents to be something a person might be allowed to disagree with, rather than canonize as the highest arbiters of what is, as a matter of fact, real *vs.* imaginary, or true *vs.* false.

But that's not the only trouble. If you're supposed to rely, not upon the groundless fancies of your own mind, but upon your agreement with other minds, then it seems you have a deeper problem. How are you supposed to have a reason to think any *other minds* exist, since, as Thomas Reid complained, according to anti-realism "what I call a father, a brother, or a friend, is only a parcel of ideas in my own mind."[23] In other words, anti-realism threatens to collapse into the philosophy that dare not speak its name. Solipsism.

Anxious to head off charges of solipsism,[24] anti-realists over the years have experimented with the idea of some sort of collective, social construction of an "intersubjective" world, in which different persons might be able to ride on the same bus.

"If one reinterprets objectivity as intersubjectivity or as solidarity," Rorty suggested, "then one will drop the question of how to get in touch with 'mind-independent and language-independent reality.'"[25] It is for this reason that Rorty proposes

> to replace the desire for objectivity---the desire to be in touch with a reality which is more than some community with which we identify ourselves---with the desire for solidarity with that community."[26]

As Donald Davidson put it:

> The ultimate source (not ground) of objectivity, is in my opinion, intersubjectivity. If we were not in communication with others, there would be nothing on which to base the idea of being wrong, or, therefore, of being right, either in what we say or in what we think.[27]

Of course, the whole point of making the opinions of others play the role of truth-arbiter was so that the realist's uncertain world of mind-independent cannonballs wouldn't have to. But how *can* you be "in communication with others," if what you call "others" are really nothing more than "mere representations" in your own mind? Again, as Kant put it:

> External objects (bodies)...are mere appearances, and are therefore nothing but a species of my representations, the objects of which are something only through these representations. Apart from them they are nothing.[28]

> All bodies together with the space in which they are, must be considered nothing but mere representations in us, and exist nowhere but in our thoughts.[29]

So, the problem remains. If your friend's *body* is a mere appearance, then, surely, what you think you *hear* when your friend speaks is likewise "a mere appearance," i.e., "nothing but a species of your own representations." And as for his supposed "thoughts," therefore, what could these be? They too would ultimately be nothing but your own thoughts. This usually goes by the name of "the Problem of Other Minds."

Are You on the Bus?

Solutions supposed to solve the problems of anti-realism seem only to multiply the problems. How can two persons with two minds ride on the *same* bus, if buses "must be considered nothing but mere representations in us," which can "exist nowhere but in our thoughts?"[30] Bad enough not to be able to say, if the bus is in you, how you can be in the bus. But, curiouser and curiouser, if your friend is in you, and his bus is in him, how can you be in the same bus that supposedly exists in his thoughts alone, and is apart from his mind, nothing? What does your bus have to do with his bus? You can't even *see* his bus, so how can you be riding in it? Are you riding an invisible bus?

Some want off this bus. As even Putnam began to complain, "for a phenomenalist...two people can't literally share a percept." So, "how could truth be shared if reality couldn't be shared?"[31] And yet, what other choice was there for an anti-realist, between some kind of "intersubjective" world for sharing, and a slippery slide into solipsism? Few philosophers were brave enough to espouse solipsism in public (though one person supposedly did, writing, according to philosophical legend, a letter to Bertrand Russell saying "I'm a solipsist, and frankly I'm surprised there aren't more of us.") So the upshot seemed to be that the world, reality, knowledge, facts, and truth, all these things just *had* to become "intersubjective." Even if nobody could explain what the devil *that* meant, or how it was even thinkable.

Nevertheless, philosophy bravely soldiered on, unafraid to assure a naive public that there could be for us no external world of things as they really are, but only a world we create, a world consisting entirely of our own thoughts.

Worse, these are thoughts which cannot be justifiably considered to *resemble* or otherwise *correspond* to anything beyond themselves. Why not? Because, for one thing, if we can't access anything outside our minds, then we can have no way of knowing, nor even a reason for thinking, that there is any such "resemblance" or "correspondence." As Michel de Montaigne had argued:

> The uncertainty of the senses makes everything they produce uncertain...the conception and semblance we form is not of the object, but only of the impression and effect made on the sense; which impression and the object are two different things...And as for saying that the impressions of the senses convey to the soul the quality of the foreign objects by resemblance, how can the soul make sure of the resemblance, having itself no communication with foreign objects? Just as a man who does not know Socrates, seeing his portrait, cannot say that it resembles him."[32]

Hume agreed:

> The mind has never anything present to it but the perceptions, and cannot possibly reach any experience of their connection with

objects. The supposition of such a connection is, therefore, without any foundation in reasoning. [33]

> That our senses offer not their impressions as the images of something *distinct*, or *independent*, and *external*, is evident; because they convey to us nothing but a single perception, and never give us the least intimation of anything beyond. A single perception can never produce the idea of a double existence, but by some inference either of the reason or imagination. When the mind looks farther than what immediately appears to it, its conclusions can never be put to the account of the senses; and it certainly looks farther, when from a single perception it infers a double existence, and supposes the relations of resemblance and causation betwixt them.
>
> If our senses, therefore, suggest any idea of distinct existences, they must convey the impressions as those very existences, by a kind of fallacy and illusion. [34]

It's one of philosophy's big conundrums, as Kant's critic G. E. Schulze remarked in 1792:

> Where do the representations that we possess originate, and how do they come to be in us? This has been for a long time one of the most important questions in philosophy. Common opinion has rightly held that, since the representations in us are not the objects themselves being represented, the connection between our representations and the things outside us must be established above all by a careful and sound answer to this question. It is in this way that certitude must be sought regarding the reality of the different components of our knowledge. [35]

As Hilary Putnam put it:

> The mind never compares an image or word with an object, but only with other images, words, beliefs, judgments, etc. The idea of a comparison of words or mental representations with an object is a senseless one. So how can a determinate correspondence between words or mental representations and external objects ever be singled out? How is the correspondence supposed to be fixed? [36]

We cannot view our perceptions "sideways-on"[37] to see whether or not they conform to reality. "We can't get outside our skins," said Donald

Davidson, "to find out what is causing the internal happenings of which we are aware."[38]

Farewell to Truth

So, what does all this do to the notion of *truth*? If our thoughts and ideas can't be known to resemble or *correspond* to anything beyond themselves, then how do we know if our beliefs are *true or false*? Isn't *truth* a correspondence between our thoughts, beliefs, claims, perceptions, and ideas and an actual external world existing independently of us, i.e., a reality that largely just is what it is in spite of what anybody thinks or says?

No. As Rorty explained it, we must now see "truth, as in James's phrase, as 'what it is better for us to believe' rather than as 'the accurate representation of reality.'"[39]

> The notion of 'accurate representation' is simply an automatic and empty compliment which we pay to those beliefs which are successful in helping us to do what we want to do.[40]

As Davidson put it:

> The approach to the problem of justification we have been tracing must be wrong. We have been trying to see it this way: a person has all his beliefs about the world---that is, all his beliefs. How can he tell if they are true, or apt to be true? This is possible, we have been assuming, only by connecting his beliefs to the world, confronting certain of his beliefs with the deliverances of the senses one by one, or perhaps confronting the totality of his beliefs with the tribunal of experience. No such confrontation makes sense, for of course we can't get outside our skins to find out what is causing the internal happenings of which we are aware.[41]

"Justification is not a matter of a special relation between ideas (or words) and objects, but of conversation, of social practice,"[42] Rorty explained. "We understand knowledge when we understand the social justification of belief, and thus have no need to view it as accuracy of representation."[43]

> The claim that we are responsible to reality is as hopeless as the idea that true sentences correspond to reality....we have no responsibilities except to fellow-players of what Sellars and Brandom call 'the game of giving and asking for reasons.'[44]

Madhouse Philosophy

It gets worse. Indeed, if this were all, it might just be funny. But now comes the creepy part. Here's where the comedy goes tragedy, and we find out philosophy has more than a few skeletons in the closet.

Rewind to Germany in the period just after the French Revolution. After decanting *The Critique of Pure Reason*:

> Everyone saw at once that the conception of a thing-in-itself is a self-contradictory and impossible abstraction. It is a flat self-contradiction. Its existence is assumed because Kant thought there must be an external *cause* of our sensations. On the one hand, therefore, the thing-in-itself is alleged to be the cause of appearances. On the other hand, however, it cannot be a cause, because cause is a category of our minds, and the categories do not apply to the thing-in-itself. ...Moreover, even if we say that the thing-in-itself is not a cause, but that it nevertheless exists, this position is, firstly, still self-contradictory, and secondly, quite gratuitous. ...It is gratuitous because, if the thing-in-itself is not the cause of our sensations, there is no ground for assuming its existence. Why assume that there is a thing-in-itself at all? Why not suppose that things as they appear to us, appearances, are all that exist? Only because, according to Kant, our sensations must have an external cause. This is the only ground for assuming the existence of the thing-in-itself. Hence, since it now appears that the thing-in-itself cannot be such a cause, there is, consequently, no ground for assuming its existence. [45]

Anybody hoping here this might have led everyone to a rejection of idealism is in for a sore disappointment:

> Thus the whole conception of the thing-in-itself collapses. And we must carefully note the effect of this collapse on the Kantian philosophy. The forms of knowledge, space, time, and the categories, are the product of our minds and issue from nothing external. Kant assumed that the *given* factor of knowledge,

sensation, the matter or filling of the forms of space, time, and category, are due to an external source. This leads to the self-contradictory thing-in-itself. Therefore, the only conclusion is that this given factor does not arise from any external source. And in that case must be, just as the *a priori* forms are, the product of mind. But if both matter and form are the product of mind, this means that the whole object of knowledge, and every object, and so the entire universe, is a product of mind. This leads to an absolute idealism.[46]

Hegel's "absolute idealism" drew upon the pantheism of Spinoza and the General Will of Rousseau. Hegel not only dispensed with the external world, but he also got rid of the problematic *other minds*, and even his own mind too. Or, rather, he rolled them all up into one, and said there was one Mind only, one World-Spirit. Something like "thought thinking itself." As Rorty put it, "Spirit never confronts anything other than itself."[47]

The Hegelian World-Spirit seemed to serve something like the same function as God had served for Berkeley, which was to confer existence upon things by having them in mind. Knox's limerick put Berkeley's doctrine in memorable form:

> There was a young man who said "God
> Must think it exceedingly odd
> If he finds that this tree
> Continues to be
> When there's no one about in the Quad."

> "Dear Sir, your astonishment's odd;
> I am always about in the Quad
> And that's why this tree
> Will continue to be
> Since observed by Yours faithfully, God."

Hegel's World-Spirit sort of played an analogous role. But, since it was not so much the God of Moses as the Divine Universe of Spinoza combined with the General Will of Rousseau, the World-Spirit therefore became "the Divine State, this actual god." Politically, this gave a fateful new twist to *l'etat c'est moi:*

> Only in the State does man have a rational existence...Man owes his entire existence to the State, and has his being within it alone.

Whatever worth and spiritual reality he possesses are his only through the State.[48]

> Truth is the unity of the universal and subjective will; and the universal is to be found in the State, in its laws, its universal and rational arrangements. The State is the Divine Idea as it exists on earth. [49]

As with several other bad ideas, a careful paternity suit might focus attention on Kant's baleful follower J. G. Fichte:

> The individual life has no real existence... since it has no value of itself, it must and should sink to nothing, while on the contrary the Race alone exists, since it alone ought to be looked upon as really living.[50]

The State, said Hegel, is the general substance, while individuals are mere accidents. The State "has the supreme right against the individual, whose supreme duty is to be a member of the State."[51] Accordingly, "freedom is nothing but the recognition and adoption of such universal objects as right and law, and the production of a reality that is accordant with the State."[52] Indeed,

> The definition of the freedom of the press as freedom to say and write what one pleases, is parallel to the one of freedom in general, viz., as freedom to do what one pleases. Such a view belongs to the uneducated crudity and superficiality of naive thinking.[53]

Hegel's World-Spirit was even identified with Napoleon the dictator. If 'spirit' refers to the force which animates---moves---bodies, then he who moves the world must be the World-Spirit, just as Hobbes and Rousseau had suggested that the sovereign of the state functions as its head or will.

Before Hegel, Kant's work had received a lot of attention, and, of course, you always get more of the behavior you reward. Like other followers of Kant, Hegel enveloped his claims in a snowstorm of mumbo-jumbo thick enough to deter all but the most susceptible:

> Self-consciousness thinks of itself as being self-consciousness; in being self-conscious it is independent, but still in this independence it has a negative relation to what is outside self-consciousness. This is infinite subjectivity, which appears at one time as the critique of

thought in the case of Kant, and at another time, in the case of Fichte, as the tendency or impulse towards the concrete. Absolute, pure, infinite form is expressed as self-consciousness, the Ego.

This is a light that breaks forth on spiritual substance, and shows absolute content and absolute form to be identical; ---substance is in itself identical with knowledge. Self-consciousness thus, in the third place, recognizes its positive relation as its negative, and its negative as its positive, or, in other words, recognizes these opposite activities as the same, *i.e.* it recognizes pure Thought or Being as self-identity, and this again as separation. This is intellectual perception; but it is requisite in order that it should be in truth intellectual, that it should not be that merely immediate perception of the eternal and the divine which we hear of, but should be absolute knowledge.[54]

"Only one man understands me," said Hegel, "and even he does not." Lucky for Hegel, more found him convincing than understood him. Hegelian ravings provoked even a fellow German idealist, Schopenhauer, to complain that with Kant's style serving as the original *"exemplar vitiis imitabile"*

> The height of audacity, in serving up pure nonsense, in stringing together senseless and extravagant mazes of words, such as had previously only been heard in madhouses, was finally reached in Hegel, and became the instrument of the most barefaced general mystification that has ever taken place, with a result which will appear fabulous to posterity and remain henceforth as a monument to German stupidity.[55]

Unfortunately, that sunny prediction didn't pan out, since German idealism took the world by storm. Even Americans took to calling themselves "transcendentalists." Heidegger, still living in the life-world of Hegel, seems to have done little more than update German Idealism, explaining---now that Napoleon was gone---that "the *Fuehrer* himself and he alone is the German reality."[56] In the same century that Heidegger, Habermas, and DeMan imbibed totalitarian collectivism as National Socialists, Althusser, Gramsci, Sartre, Camus, Putnam and Rorty imbibed it as international socialists. As early as 1843, Friedrich Engels had almost predicted it:

> Either all the philosophical efforts of the German nation from Kant to Hegel have been useless---worse than useless---or that they must end in communism...the Germans must either reject their great

Solipsism – self can be aware of nothing but its own experiences... nothing is real or exists or is real but the self.

philosophers whose name they hold up as the glory of their nation, or they must adopt communism.[57]

Finally, in 1949, surrounded by the wreckage of a world inspired by German Idealism, George Orwell was provoked to caricature collectivist epistemology in his novel *1984*. The book's totalitarian spokesman O'Brien says of his philosophy:

> "This is not solipsism. Collective solipsism, if you like. But that is a different thing; in fact, the opposite thing."[58]

Postmodernists read Orwell, but, of course, a mere parody of a philosophy doesn't refute it. Rarely is it enough to cure somebody merely to show him that he's not doing well. "Orwell has," Rorty admitted, "been read as a realist philosopher, a defender of common sense against its cultured, ironist despisers." The trouble is, as Rorty complained, "Orwell has no *answer* to O'Brien." That's why Orwell couldn't help Rorty. As Rorty explained:

> I do not think there are any plain moral facts out there in the world, nor any truths independent of language, nor any neutral ground on which to stand and argue that either torture or kindness are preferable to the other. So I want offer a different reading of Orwell. ...In the view of *1984* that I am offering, Orwell has no *answer* to O'Brien, and is not interested in giving one. Like Nietzsche, O'Brien regards the whole idea of being "answered," of exchanging ideas, of reasoning together, as a symptom of weakness...[Orwell] does not view O'Brien as crazy, misguided, seduced by a mistaken theory, or blind to the moral facts....I take Orwell's claim that there is no such thing as inner freedom, no such thing as an "autonomous individual," to be the one made by historicist, including Marxist, critics of "liberal individualism." This is that there is nothing deep inside each of us, no common human nature, no built-in human solidarity, to use as a moral reference point. There is nothing to people except what has been socialized into them.[59]

what?

Undaunted by the coming and going of *1984*, postmodernists to this day continue to profess a "communitarian epistemology," arguing for "knowledge by agreement." They point out that "we take our peers' agreement as a sign that we've got things right," and so "all knowledge is essentially political." [60] In fact, "knowledge is a social status," they say, "knowledge and its cognates, like *know* and *knower*

31

mark a social status---like 'head of department'"[61] Or, perhaps, like Minister of Information.

> The Party told you to reject the evidence of your eyes and ears. It was their final, most essential, command.[62]

Like a man who's made a wrong turn, but stubbornly refuses to admit it and go back, postmodern philosophy blunders on without remorse. Scientific claims to "truth" must yield to political interests. Why? Because "science is best seen as a socially constructed discourse that legitimates its power by presenting itself as truth,"[63] and "the true, to put it very briefly, is only the expedient in the way of our thinking."[64] Truth is "interest-relative," says Martin Kusch. Perhaps some "want objectivity to be more than, and independent of, consensus." [65]   But "that is a mistake. What objectivity there is exists only as, and is dependent upon, agreement."

As postmodern philosopher Jean Baudrillard put it, "Intellectuals must stop legitimizing the notion that there is some 'ultimate truth' behind appearances." The world is our construction, and what we have to answer to, in our collectivist world-making, is never things as they really are in themselves (a "hopeless" notion), but, on the contrary, the "purposes" of the community which "may be served."[66]   Indeed, "there is no right and wrong outside social institutions."[67]

Farewell to Reason, says the title of Paul Feyerabend's "deeply learned"[68] philosophy of science sequel to *Against Method.* Besides "vindicating the Church's battle with Galileo,"[69] Feyerabend also explains that "the sciences should be subjected to a democratic control."[70] As the blurb on the back cover sums it up:

> *Farewell to Reason* offers a vigorous challenge to the scientific rationalism that underlies Western ideals of 'progress' and 'development,' whose damaging social and ecological consequences are now widely recognized. ...The appeal to reason, he insists, is empty, and must be replaced by a notion of science that subordinates it to the needs of citizens and communities.

In Feyerabend's brave new world, "drastic interventions are not excluded," but "objective judgments are out."[71]

We have now arrived at what's been called, since about 1980, "the postmodern condition."[72] As Rorty recently said (though he meant it in a different way) "philosophy as we understand it was something invented by the German Idealists."[73]

The Postmodern Prison-House

Paddling around above the dam, philosophers now toy with various puzzles left over from what is usually called "linguistic idealism." According to linguistic idealism, the socially constructed world of non-corresponding representations in which we are trapped might be identified with our *language*. "The world is the totality of facts, not of things," said Wittgenstein, "the facts in logical space are the world." So, "the limits of my language mean the limits of my world."[74] Language is our "prison-house," said Heidegger, "language speaks Man." As Harvard philosopher Nelson Goodman puts it, "We can have words without a world, but no world without words or other symbols."[75] In Jacques Derrida's formulation, "There is nothing outside the text."[76]

Linguistic idealism almost seems to suggest that only another Frenchman can share the same bus with a Frenchman. It also seems to suggest that goats cannot ride buses because they don't use language. Indeed, for "mere animals," John McDowell suggests, "the world cannot be in view."

> The objective world is present only to a self-conscious subject…it is only in the context of a subject's ability to ascribe experiences to herself that experiences can constitute awareness of the world. …Creatures without conceptual capacities lack self-consciousness and---this is part of the same package---experience of objective reality. …It follows that mere animals cannot enjoy "outer experience," on the conception of "outer experience" I have recommended. …[Gareth] Evan's conclusion will not fit into a Kantian framework…the framework precludes supposing that sensibility by itself yields content that is less than conceptual but already world-involving. In the absence of spontaneity, no self can be in view, and by the same token, the world cannot be in view either.[77]

Wilfrid Sellars said "all awareness of sorts, resemblances, facts, etc., in short all awareness of abstract entities---indeed, all awareness even of particulars---is a linguistic affair."[78]   As Rorty put it, "mastery of language is prerequisite for conscious experience."[79]

> Thought is impossible without language. Revulsion against this claim has caused philosophers to become obsessed by the need to achieve an access to reality that is unmediated by, and prior to, the use of language. ...we are going to have to get rid of the hope for such non-linguistic access.[80]

"On the Lockean account, the pre-linguistic child already knows the difference," notes Rorty, "between red and blue, before having learned any words." But this will not do, because "pre-linguistic infants do not find anything obvious." In fact, he says, before language was invented, "Nothing at all was obvious."[81]

> There is no difference between the thermostat, the dog, and the pre-linguistic infant except the differing degrees of complexity of their reactions to environmental stimuli. The brutes and the infants are capable of discriminative responses, but not of acquiring information. For there is no such thing as the acquisition of information until there is language in which to formulate that information."[82]

The doctrines of linguistic idealism trace their ancestry back to the same eighteenth century German neighborhood, so, here, again, some mention is due Kant's uncanny friend J. G. Hamann, a.k.a. "the Magus of the North."

> He is a solitary figure in his century, hostile to its spirit, contemptuous of its triumphs, and forms a link between German mystical visionaries like Eckhart and Boehme on the one hand, and anti-rationalist romantic thinkers Herder, Schelling, Kierkegaard and Bergson and their existentialist followers in the two hundred years that followed. As with Giambattista Vico half a century before, whom (as Goethe noted) he much resembles, Hamann's darkly oracular writings are often penetrated by flashes of insight of a very arresting order. His greatest discovery is that language and thought are not two processes but one: that language (or other forms of expressive symbolism---religious worship, social habits and so on) conveys directly the innermost soul of individuals and societies...[83]

"The eloquence of the flesh...takes us to the cradle of our race and religion," said Hamann, and "every court, every school, every profession, every closed corporation, every sect---each has its own vocabulary."[84] This is important because "all idle talk about reason is mere wind; language is its organon and criterion." In a letter to Herder in 1784 Hamann explained:

> If I were as eloquent as Demosthenes, I would do no more than repeat one sentence three times: Reason is language, Logos. On this marrow-bone I gnaw, and will gnaw myself to death on it. There still remains darkness on the face of this deep for me; I still wait for an apocalyptic angel with a key to this abyss.[85]

So, if, as Kant says, "the objects with which we have to do in experience are by no means things in themselves"[86] because "all bodies together with the space in which they are...exist nowhere but in our thoughts,"[87] and thought is made of language, then maybe everything in the world with which we have to do in experience is made of language.

Sometimes linguistic idealism's mental prison-house seems more "lingo" than language: where instead of being trapped in our "language," we're supposed to be trapped in our "theories." The claim is that with our theories we make the world and everything in it. Again, this is intended to be more than mere poetic metaphor. Such worlds as exist are "created by us" and "when I say worlds are made," Goodman explained, "I mean it literally."[88]

This seems to suggest that a Copernican can't share the same planet with a Ptolemaist, or even look at the same Sun. As Goodman explains, "we cannot find any world-feature independent of all versions," and "there are no absolute elements, no space-time or other stuff common to all, no entity that is under all guises or under none."[89]

A familiarity with this tradition helps explain why some people today can, with a straight face, deny that the New World Amerindians could *see* the ships of Columbus. That is, until their shamans told them to. Not that they couldn't see them as "ships," but that they just plain couldn't see them. In the 2004 postmodern film with the appropriately skeptical title "What the Bleep Do We Know?" an indigenous shaman in full regalia taps a clueless woman on the forehead, causing three wooden ships suddenly to materialize, nearby, out of thin air. Says the narrator:

He tells everybody else that ships exist out there. Because everybody trusted and believed in him, they saw them also.[90]

Hopefully, this brief flyover of a problematic tradition has helped to explain how things came to such a pass. Step off the ship of Reason, and it's all one sea. As Kant wisely observed, "we would say of a man who undermined the foundations of his house, that he might have known *a priori* that it would collapse."[91] What we now call postmodernism was already there in Fichte, writing more than two centuries ago:

> In all seriousness, and not only in a manner of speaking, the object shall be posited and determined by the cognitive faculty and not the cognitive faculty by the object.[92]

A person who has rejected realism, observes Fichte, "becomes conscious of his self-sufficiency and independence of everything that is outside himself." He

> does not need things for the support of himself, and cannot use them, because they destroy that self-sufficiency... the self which he possesses, and which is the subject of his interest, annuls this belief in things; he believes in his independence out of inclination; he embraces it with feeling.[93]

If it seems that a noisy freight train is bearing down upon you, just remember that "in all perception, you perceive only your own condition," and therefore,

> You will no longer tremble at a necessity which exists only in your own thought; no longer fear to be crushed by things which are the product of your own mind; no longer place yourself, the thinking being, in the same class with the thoughts which proceed from you. As long as you could believe that a system of things, such as you have described, really existed outside of, and independently from, yourself, and that you yourself might be only a link in this chain, such a fear was well grounded. Now, when you have seen that all this exists only in and through yourself, you will doubtless no longer fear that which you now recognize as your own creation.[94]

Now that we've enjoyed some sobering peeps into the black forest where philosophy for centuries has groped about, signs of exhaustion are beginning to show. Of course, choosing the wrong path and getting lost can often be exhausting, especially for stubborn men, who hate to backtrack, but instead prefer to grasp at the faintest trail, just so long as it's further ahead. Eventually, the temptation is to declare that there never really was any other way to go in the first place. There is only this darkening wood, and these tortured paths, and it's simply our destiny to wander here forever.

Many have remarked on the "somber" or "melancholy" tone of Rorty's voice, but it seems entirely appropriate for the leading postmodern philosopher:

> The difference between myself and Conant is that he thinks that someone like [Orwell's] Winston, trapped in such a society, can turn to the light of the facts. I think that there is nowhere for Winston to turn.[95]

Hume has had his way with philosophy, and convinced the race that "the observation of human blindness and weakness is the result of all philosophy, and meets us at every turn, in spite of our endeavors to elude or avoid it."[96] And everybody knows what tends to follow after that.

Blind Submission

Hume's *Dialogues Concerning Natural Religion* took great pains to demonstrate that religion cannot be proved true by an appeal to reason or to the empirical evidence of the senses. Because of this fact, Hume's radical skepticism is sometimes imagined by secularists to be friendly to scientific rationalism. Nothing could be more sadly mistaken.

Humean skepticism renders the same judgment upon scientific beliefs as it does upon religious ones. As a matter of fact, even our most ordinary beliefs, such as the belief that the Sun will rise tomorrow, and even the belief that trees and houses really exist, suffer the same fate at the hands of Humean skepticism. According to Hume, *none* of these beliefs can be supported by reason or empirical evidence; *all* these beliefs are both empirically groundless and irrational.

Quine said, "the Humean predicament is the human predicament."[97] But it would be truer to say that the postmodern condition is the Humean predicament. The origins of postmodernism lie in Hume's skeptical idealism, destined in due time to sweep all before in a compelling Romantic reaction against the confident, scientific spirit of the Age of Reason. In the place of scientific rationalism was preached, instead, a sort of helpless fideism, in which all our beliefs are ultimately based upon nothing better than a "blind submission" to the irrational prejudices of habit. [98]

"To be a philosophical skeptic," said Hume, "is, in a man of letters, the first and most essential step towards being a sound, believing Christian."[99] When it came time for him to close the *Dialogues Concerning Natural Religion*, Hume chose to end the work with these words:

> Believe me, Cleanthes, the most natural sentiment, which a well-disposed mind will feel on this occasion, is a longing desire and expectation, that Heaven would be pleased to dissipate, at least alleviate, this profound ignorance, by affording some more particular revelation to mankind... A person seasoned with a just sense of the imperfections of natural reason will fly to revealed truth with the greatest avidity. [100]

Far from being any friend to science, skepticism had long served, even for centuries before Hume, as the main prop to fideism, which is, after all, the most proudly irrational and dogmatic of all creeds. The idea is that, if philosophical skepticism cannot be refuted, that proves that human reason and empirical evidence are powerless to obtain any objective truth or real knowledge, and the only option left for mankind is to prefer the promptings of the heart to those of the head.

Francis Bacon, founder of modern science, had argued that "knowledge is power." Skepticism took an opposite tack. The medieval philosopher Hamid al-Ghazali had argued for submission to Islam on skeptical grounds. Though he lived in the eleventh century, al-Ghazali's skepticism bears a startling resemblance to Hume's:

> I then set myself earnestly to examine the notions we derive from the evidence of the senses and from sight in order to see if they could be

  fideism

called in question. The result of a careful examination was that my confidence in them was shaken...

To this the notions I derived from my senses made the following objections: "Who can guarantee you that you can trust to the evidence of reason more than to that of the senses? You believed in our testimony till it was contradicted by the verdict of reason, otherwise you would have continued to believe it to this day. Well, perhaps, there is above reason another judge who, if he appeared, would convict reason of falsehood, just as reason has confuted us. And if such a third arbiter is not yet apparent, it does not follow that he does not exist."...

"Do you not see," I reflected, "that while asleep you assume your dreams to be indisputably real? Once awake, you recognize them for what they are---baseless chimeras. Who can assure you, then, of the reliability of notions which, when awake, you derive from the senses and from reason? In relation to your present state they may be real; but it is possible also that you may enter upon another state of being which will bear the same relation to your present state as this does to your condition when asleep. In that new sphere you will recognize that the conclusions of reason are only chimeras." ...Our present life in relation to the future is perhaps only a dream, and man, once dead, will see things in direct opposition to those now before his eyes; he will then understand that word of the *Quran*, "To-day we have removed the veil from thine eyes and thy sight is keen."

Such thoughts as these threatened to shake my reason, and I sought to find an escape from them. But how? In order to disentangle the knot of this difficulty, a proof was necessary. Now a proof must be based on primary assumptions, and it was precisely these of which I was in doubt. This unhappy state lasted about two months, during which I was, not, it is true, explicitly or by profession, but morally and essentially, a thorough-going skeptic. ...God at last deigned to heal me...I owed my deliverance, not to a concatenation of proofs and arguments, but to the light which God caused to penetrate into my heart---the light which illuminates the threshold of all knowledge.... It is by the help of this light that the search for truth must be carried on....

My object in this account is to make others understand with what earnestness we should search for truth, since it leads to results we never dreamed of. Primary assumptions have not got to be sought for, since they are always present to our minds; if we engage in such a search, we only find them persistently elude our grasp.

Likewise inspired by ancient Greek skepticism, "Christian Pyrrhonists" inevitably came to argue similarly. One was none other than Savonarola, the book-burning Prophet of Florence who denounced the flowering of wealth that ended the long dark poverty of the Middle Ages. Savonarola led his zealous followers in 1497 to destroy irreplaceable Renaissance art and books by throwing them onto a great public "Bonfire of the Vanities."[101]

Savonarola's Christian Pyrrhonism seems echoed shortly thereafter by Erasmus in 1509:

> The notion that happiness comes from a knowledge of things as they really are is wrong....Human affairs are so obscure and various that nothing can be clearly known...anyway, man's mind is much more taken with appearances than with reality.[102]

A tradition continued by Agrippa von Nettesheim in 1527:

> Nothing can chance unto men more pestilent than knowledge...

> It is better therefore and more profitable to be idiots, and know nothing, to believe by faith and charity.[103]

By 1554, a whiff of postmodernism can almost be detected in the philosophy of Jesuit founder Ignatius Loyola:

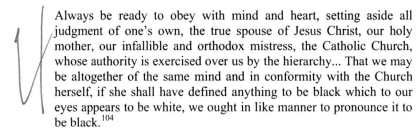

> Always be ready to obey with mind and heart, setting aside all judgment of one's own, the true spouse of Jesus Christ, our holy mother, our infallible and orthodox mistress, the Catholic Church, whose authority is exercised over us by the hierarchy... That we may be altogether of the same mind and in conformity with the Church herself, if she shall have defined anything to be black which to our eyes appears to be white, we ought in like manner to pronounce it to be black.[104]

Not long after, in 1576, comes Michel de Montaigne, who observed that skepticism "presents Man naked and empty, acknowledging his natural weakness, fit to receive from above some outside power; stripped of human knowledge, and all the more apt to lodge divine knowledge in himself, annihilating his judgment to make more room for faith; neither disbelieving nor setting up any doctrine against the common observances; humble, obedient, teachable, zealous; a sworn enemy of heresy...a blank tablet prepared to take from the finger of God such forms as He shall be pleased to engrave on it."[105]

> Let us bring to it nothing of our own but obedience and submission. For, as it is written, *I will destroy the wisdom of the wise, and bring to nothing the understanding of the prudent.* [1 Corinthians 1:19] [106]

> Things do not lodge in us in their own form and essence...external objects surrender to our mercy; they dwell in us as we please. [107]

> We no longer know what things are in truth; for nothing comes to us except falsified and altered by our senses....The uncertainty of the senses makes everything they produce uncertain... The senses do not comprehend the foreign object, but only their own impressions. ...The conception and semblance we form is not of the object, but only of the impression and effect made on the sense; which impression and the object are two different things. Wherefore whoever judges by appearances judges by something other than the object. And as for saying that the impressions of the senses convey to the soul the quality of the foreign objects by resemblance, how can the soul make sure of the resemblance, having itself no communication with foreign objects? Just as a man who does not know Socrates, seeing his portrait, cannot say that it resembles him. [108]

> I must see at last whether it is in the power of Man to find what he seeks, and whether that quest that he has been making for so many centuries has enriched him with any new power and any solid truth. I think he will confess to me...that all the profit he has gained from so long a pursuit is to have learned to acknowledge his weakness. The ignorance that was naturally in us we have by long study confirmed and verified. [109]

"The heart has its reasons, of which reason knows not," insisted the famous fideist, Blaise Pascal. This was about a century before Hume.

About the time Hume was born, the Calvinist Pierre Bayle was a best-selling author. True to tradition, it was Bayle's radical skepticism that was supposed to provide the rationale for an irrational leap of faith:

41

If a person is first convinced that he can expect no satisfaction from his philosophical studies, he will be more inclined to pray to God; he will ask God for the conviction of the truths which he ought to believe, rather than flattering himself with the success of his reasoning and disputing. It is therefore a welcome inclination to faith to know the defects of reason.[110]

The point of all this history is to recall that in the centuries just before Hume published his works, various philosophies had been swept up in a prolonged struggle, during which time skepticism had served to *oppose* the new scientific rationalism. There was a saying attributed to Martin Luther that "whoever wants to be a Christian must tear the eyes out of his Reason." If so, the most effective instrument for tearing out Reason's eyes had been, for hundreds of years, radical skepticism.

Far from rejecting this irrational, anti-scientific tradition, David Hume was ultimately its greatest champion. While the Rationalists and the Empiricists tried to adjudicate the rival claims of Reason versus the Evidence of the Senses, Hume called down a plague on both.[111] Human understanding, he said, "entirely subverts itself, and leaves not the lowest degree of evidence in any proposition, either in philosophy or common life."[112] "We have," Hume argued, "no choice left, but betwixt a false reason and none at all."[113] "Blind submission," he insisted, is the only answer, and "in this blind submission I shew most perfectly my sceptical disposition and principles."[114]

In other words, Hume's reputation among casual readers of his *Dialogues* as an opponent of blind faith, or friend to reason and science, has it exactly backwards. On the contrary, nobody should be surprised to learn that Hamann used to say "Hume is always my man."[115] As Hamann's friend Kant said of his own work, "I had to deny knowledge in order to make room for faith."[116]

With this reactionary turn began the dark, Romantic period of *sturm und drang*. The confident sun of Reason had passed its zenith and began to go down in the west, ushering in a long twilight in which we still wander. Neither the American Pragmatists nor the French postmodernists are really the originators of our "postmodern condition," but, like an honest mirror, they've embarrassed us by providing for the canonical tradition its necessary *reductio ad absurdum*.

42

> "That there is nothing whatever but my presentations is, to the natural sense of mankind, a silly and ridiculous conceit which no man can seriously entertain and which requires no refutation. To the well-informed judge, who knows the deeper grounds for this opinion, grounds which cannot be removed by mere reasoning, this thought is one of despair and annihilation."[1]
>
> ---J. G. Fichte

CHAPTER 3

Seeing Things

Philosophers may be crazy, but they're not stupid. So why do so many of them continue on this wrecked train of thought? What *is* it that has driven so many into the collectivist prison-house of postmodernism? Is it possible for future generations to resist the urge to follow in their footsteps? This is really what needs to be figured out. It does no good to ridicule postmodernism, while at the same time continuing to accept and promote claims which entail it. As Richard Fumerton admitted, just before himself taking the fatal plunge:

> It is by abandoning certain versions of naive realism that we force upon ourselves the myriad epistemological and metaphysical questions that have so beset philosophers. When rejecting a view gives rise to so much trouble, one should do so only after the most careful consideration.[2]

Good advice. Postmodern despair draws its sustenance from serious philosophical arguments---including various canonical arguments supposed to prove the naive realism of the vulgar untenable. Philosophers who take the postmodern plunge do so because they have swallowed at least one of these various arguments. It is therefore these arguments which need to be scrutinized and refuted.

Perhaps the easiest way to show how that can happen, is to present the usual arguments in a dialogue form. The dialogue might as well begin where we find ourselves, with a question about two people being able to perceive the same things. So, let's suppose two people, who have never met, and speak different languages, both watch for a certain ship on the horizon. One is a red/green colorblind Christian male from Ethiopia using a dirty old telescope, and the other is an Inuit woman born in Siberia using a pair of cockeyed binoculars with red lenses that see everything double.

Finally, a ship appears over the horizon, and is spotted by them both. Now, ordinary people with common sense will agree that both of these people perceive the same ship, and that what they both see is a ready-made, independent thing, i.e., a thing which would not be harmed if---for example---the two ship-watchers were to be suddenly eaten up by a giant shark. Yet sometimes philosophers seem to disagree.

So, let's imagine a dispute on the dock, between an imaginary philosophy professor and his student.

STUDENT: "Of course the man and woman there see the same thing: they see the same horizon, the same object, the same ship."

PROFESSOR: "Well, not really. I mean, I think, ultimately, we have to say that what they see isn't the same."

STUDENT: "I'm not sure what you mean. Are you denying that they live in the same world, or that they can see the same objects, and the same world?"

PROFESSOR: "Let's just say you have to get beyond your initial, unsophisticated way of understanding these issues."

STUDENT: "I wonder if you're just talking metaphorically."

PROFESSOR: "No, I'm not, I sympathize with your feelings, but trust me, my boy, you are simply young and naive. If you really study philosophy, you'll see that I'm right. First of all, you must admit that these people do not see the ship directly, but only by means of a medium, that much is clear."

STUDENT: "Clear as mud."

PROFESSOR: "Are you saying they see the ship directly?"

STUDENT: "Isn't directness relative? Relative to seeing it on TV, they see it 'directly,' yes."

PROFESSOR: "What about relative to you, who see the ship without any dirty telescope or red binoculars?"

STUDENT: "Relative to me, they see it less directly. So?"

PROFESSOR: "Well let me just put it the way Hume did, and point out to you that

> The mind has never anything present to it but the perceptions,' so that, 'properly speaking, it is not our body that we perceive, when we regard our limbs and members, but certain perceptions of the mind.[3]

STUDENT: "Properly speaking?"

PROFESSOR: "Well that's how we like to speak in the philosophy department."

STUDENT: "So I gather."

PROFESSOR: "You don't buy it?"

STUDENT: "I don't think so. Should I?"

PROFESSOR: "Well, yes, I mean, here, let me read a little more Hume to you…"

STUDENT: "Is this how you got to where you are? By reading this stuff?"

PROFESSOR: "Patience, boy. You might learn something. I'm going to wake you from your dogmatic slumber. Here, try this one. In Hume's book the example speaks of a white table, but we can just as well apply the same argument to this little blue rowboat, here, that's sailing away from our dock."

STUDENT: "What little blue rowboat?"

PROFESSOR: "That one."

STUDENT: "What one?"

PROFESSOR: "*That one.*"

STUDENT: "I see it."

PROFESSOR: "Ha ha. Okay, Hume says:

> Men are carried, by a natural instinct or prepossession, to repose faith in their senses; and that, without any reasoning, or even almost before the use of reason, we always suppose an external universe, which depends not on our perception, but would exist, though we and every sensible creature were absent or annihilated.
>
> It seems also evident, that, when men follow this blind and powerful instinct of nature, they always suppose the very images, presented by the senses, to be the external objects, and never entertain any suspicion, that the one are nothing but representations of the other. This very [boat], which we see blue, and which we feel hard, is believed to exist, independent of our perception, and to be something external to our mind, which perceives it. Our presence bestows not being on it: our absence does not annihilate it. It preserves its existence uniform and entire, independent of the situation of intelligent beings, who perceive or contemplate it.
>
> But this universal and primary opinion of all men is soon destroyed by the slightest philosophy, which teaches us, that nothing can ever be present to the mind but an image or perception, and that the senses are only the inlets, through which these images are conveyed, without being able to produce any immediate intercourse between the mind and the object. The boat which we see, seems to diminish as it sails away farther from us: but the real boat, which exists independent of us, suffers no such alteration. It was therefore, nothing but its image, which was present to our minds. These are the obvious dictates of reason, and no man, who reflects, ever doubted, that the existences, which we consider, when we say, *this boat* and *that tree,* are nothing but perceptions in the mind, and fleeting copies or representations of other existences, which remain uniform and independent. Therefore the mind has never anything present to it but the perceptions, and cannot possibly reach any experience of their connection with objects. The supposition of such a connection is, therefore, without any foundation in reasoning.[4]

STUDENT: "Wow."

PROFESSOR: "You like that?"

STUDENT: "No, I don't think so."

PROFESSOR: "What's the matter?"

STUDENT: "I feel like I'm being bamboozled by a fast talking car salesman. Let's take it slowly. First of all, he says, there are two boats, one which I see, and seems to diminish, and another boat which suffers no such alteration."

PROFESSOR: "Well..."

STUDENT: "If the first one is, Hume says, 'the boat we see,' then I take it that we don't see the other boat, which Hume calls 'the real boat,' and 'independent' and which he says 'suffers no alteration'."

PROFESSOR: "Well, if we take it literally..."

STUDENT: "It says we don't see the real boat. I mean, that's the logical conclusion."

PROFESSOR: "We see an image we perceive in the mind."

STUDENT: "But we know there are these two different kinds of boats?"

PROFESSOR: "Well, no, actually---"

STUDENT: "Let me put it this way. Do you see two boats?"

PROFESSOR: "No, of course not."

STUDENT: "Well, how many boats are we dealing with here?"

PROFESSOR: "Of course, there's only one that we perceive..."

STUDENT: "I see one little blue rowboat sailing away. I mean, I see one boat that I believe to be a real little blue rowboat which exists outside of my mind, and we can both see it."

PROFESSOR: "Well, such are the beliefs of the naive. Now see here, can you notice that the boat appears to you to be getting gradually smaller and smaller."

STUDENT: "It doesn't look like it's shrinking. It just looks like it's sailing away."

PROFESSOR: "Oh, come on, don't be so stubborn, you know what Hume means. He means that it takes up a smaller amount of your total visual field, in that sense, it looks like it's shrinking."

STUDENT: "It doesn't look like it's shrinking."

PROFESSOR: "Don't play dumb. Didn't you ever take perspective, in art class?"

STUDENT: "Yes."

PROFESSOR: "So, you'd draw a farther boat smaller."

STUDENT: "Right."

PROFESSOR: "So that proves that what you're seeing is a mental impression."

STUDENT: "How does it prove that?"

PROFESSOR: "Look, something is in some sense shrinking, and it isn't the real boat in itself that's shrinking, (because we know the real boat in itself isn't shrinking), which proves that what you are seeing is not the same thing, as a real boat in itself. One of these two things is, in some sense, seeming to diminish, and the other one isn't."

STUDENT: "Are you saying that what I see, is a shrinking boat, and that the real boat (that isn't shrinking), is a real boat that I'm not seeing?"

PROFESSOR: "Well, isn't that true?"

STUDENT: "No it isn't. I see one boat. What I see is, it seems to me, one real boat, a boat in itself, that's sailing away, a real, independent, boat which exists independently of me. And it doesn't really, literally, 'seem to diminish,' instead, it seems to recede."

PROFESSOR: "Sheesh. Okay, look, is the boat taking up a smaller and smaller percentage of your total visual field?"

STUDENT: "I guess so..."

PROFESSOR: "Well then, in that sense, it---so to speak---'seems to diminish'."

STUDENT: "So to speak?"

PROFESSOR: "Yeah."

STUDENT: "Why should I speak like that? It seems dishonest."

PROFESSOR: "You're just being peevish."

STUDENT: "I'm being careful, you're not. You tolerate loose talk. That's risky; look where it got you. I save my metaphors for poetry."

PROFESSOR: "I'm not speaking metaphorically."

STUDENT: "Are you sure? It seems to me that you are."

PROFESSOR: "How so?"

STUDENT: "Surely, you don't mean for me to take it completely literally when you say 'the boat which we see seems to diminish as it sails farther away from us.' If you want me to take it literally, then I can only say 'no' to it. If you want me to agree with it, then I have to take it as some kind of misleading metaphor."

Cross Your Eyes

PROFESSOR: "Alright, look, forget that one. I've got plenty more where that came from. Here, cross your eyes and look at the blue rowboat again."

STUDENT: "Okay."

PROFESSOR: "You see two blue rowboats."

STUDENT: "No, I see the one boat with crossed eyes."

PROFESSOR: "You see two boats."

STUDENT: "Are we speaking metaphorically again?"

PROFESSOR: "No. I say you see two boats---this time, you literally see two boats."

STUDENT: "Well, I'm seeing double."

PROFESSOR: "And you're seeing two boats."

STUDENT: "I am?"

PROFESSOR: "Yes."

STUDENT: "I'm really, literally, *seeing...two...boats*? How is it possible for me to be really, literally, seeing two boats if there's no two boats for me to be seeing? Is this the kind of 'seeing' as in 'he was so drunk he was seeing things'? Isn't that a metaphorical use of the word, or at least, a secondary sense of the word *seeing*? Is there more than one meaning listed in the dictionary under 'seeing'?"

PROFESSOR: "So what? Who cares? Is it a crime to get metaphorical? Maybe it will help you learn something. Maybe it will help to wake you from this stubborn, dogmatic slumber."

STUDENT: "Look, when we first talked about this, you told me that that man and woman on the dock were not seeing the same ship on the horizon. You said they did not see the same thing. I said you were just being facile, too clever, and merely speaking metaphorically. You said you were serious, and meant what you said literally. You said it was more than just a metaphor. If you told me that the man was a sturdy oak, and the woman was a faded bloom, I would know that you didn't mean it literally, and I would just nod and smile. Is that the way you meant it when you said 'they don't see the same thing,' and 'they live in different worlds'? Was that just supposed to be lousy poetry?"

PROFESSOR: "No."

STUDENT: "I didn't think so."

PROFESSOR: "Okay, never mind that, look, let's just agree for the sake of the argument to use the word 'perception' in a certain way, for one minute, so that I can have a word to use to refer to what it is you're seeing two of, when you see double."

STUDENT: "Is this going to obligate me to concede that's the right way to use the word perception, tomorrow?"

PROFESSOR: "No, no, no obligation. Just humor me for one minute, okay? Let's just agree for the sake of argument to say that, when you cross your eyes, the thing you see two of, the thing that gets doubled, we'll call a 'perception,' okay?"

STUDENT: "Umm, I'm not sure I get it...what is it exactly that we're calling a perception?"

PROFESSOR: "The two boats."

STUDENT: "There's only one boat."

PROFESSOR: "Are you crossing your eyes? Cross your eyes!"

STUDENT: "I am."

PROFESSOR: "The two boats you see now!"

STUDENT: "I see one boat, albeit with double vision."

PROFESSOR: "I mean, you're seeing two 'perceptions'. You're seeing two boat-perceptions."

STUDENT: "So, now, I'm 'perceiving' two boats?"

PROFESSOR: "That's not what I said."

STUDENT: "Good, because I'd have the same problem with it."

PROFESSOR: "Fine. I won't say you're 'perceiving two boats.' But I will insist, and continue to insist, that you are perceiving two *somethings*, and I don't care what you call them!"

STUDENT: "Two worlds?"

PROFESSOR: "I didn't say that."

STUDENT: "Are you going to start saying it later?"

PROFESSOR: "Don't change the subject. When you cross your eyes, you see two of something."

STUDENT: "Which dictionary definition of 'see' is this?"

PROFESSOR: "Does it matter?"

STUDENT: "Yes. What would you say if I said to you that the only thing you *see* when you look at that rowboat is your own retina?"

PROFESSOR: "Well, I might be inclined to agree."

STUDENT: "That's just what's the matter with you."

PROFESSOR: "It's true, isn't it?"

STUDENT: "The problem is, that if you're going to start using the word 'see' like that, you're going metaphorical again. What if I tried to argue that, since my father is a sturdy oak, that, therefore, my father is made of wood?"

PROFESSOR: "You're accusing me of committing the fallacy of equivocation."

STUDENT: "I'm glad it has a name."

PROFESSOR: "So, if I say 'the only thing anyone can see is his own retina, therefore nobody's ever seen a rowboat', I'm trading on a false equivalence between two different senses of the word 'see'?"

STUDENT: "Yes. Exactly. Because if the relationship between your brain and your retina is called 'seeing,' then we're going to need a new word to use to refer to the relationship between your eyeball and a boat on the horizon. And maybe even a third word to refer to the relation between your brain and the boat on the horizon. Look, when I say I think somebody 'sees' something, I'm talking about the whole trip, from the boat, to the eyeball, to the mind. The *whole* nine yards."

PROFESSOR: "But how do you know the whole nine yards is even possible? Maybe you're just like that guy in a pod in *The Matrix*, or a deluded, dreaming brain in a vat of fluid, hooked up to the electrodes of super-computer."

STUDENT: "Well, in that case, I still need a word to talk about the whole nine yards of seeing, from mind to horizon, that I *falsely* believe I'm enjoying, whether I really am enjoying any such nine yards or not. And the only word I feel entitled to use for that, is 'seeing.' Now if you're going to highjack that word, use it metaphorically, and say you '*see*' your retina, then I'm going to insist that you're committing a fallacy of equivocation. I mean, I think maybe that kind of liberty-taking with the word 'seeing' is enough to make your argument look valid, when it really isn't. If there's more than one kind of 'seeing', then the deluxe, extended kind, from horizon to mind, is the kind that should be in dispute, not the truncated kind of so-called 'seeing', from brain to retina."

PROFESSOR: "Well, okay, but just remember one thing. If I agree to give up my previous use of words like 'see' and 'perceive' then you have to promise not to try to pull a fast one when it comes to the question of skepticism."

STUDENT: "What's that?"

PROFESSOR: "Well, when it comes to the question of whether or not you might be just a brain in a vat, and not really seeing a real boat on the horizon, don't try to pull a fast one by appealing to nothing more than a bare definition of a word to prove, by definition alone, that you've got the whole nine yards."

STUDENT: "Agreed. Anyway, you don't need to worry, you can just frame your skepticism by questioning whether or not I'm really, in my nine-yard sense, 'seeing' any real external thing at all."

PROFESSOR: "Fine. Now let's get back to your double vision. What word will you let me use to refer to what you see two of when you cross your eyes?"

STUDENT: "You just did it again. You said 'see'."

PROFESSOR: "How about 'experience'?"

STUDENT: "Um, okay. Maybe that's alright."

PROFESSOR: "How about: 'you experience two scene-images'?"

STUDENT: "Okay, when I'm looking at one boat with crossed eyes, I temporarily experience two scene-images."

PROFESSOR: "Is that your final offer?"

STUDENT: "That's top dollar."

PROFESSOR: "Fine. I've got all I need."

STUDENT: "We'll see about that."

PROFESSOR: "Yes we will. Okay, so, now, looking at one boat with your eyes crossed, you experience two scene-images. Now, suppose another identical rowboat was conveniently to happen along just now, just at the moment you uncrossed your eyes. Now, when you really do see two real blue rowboats with eyes uncrossed, you, likewise, are experiencing two blue rowboat scene-images. Right?"

STUDENT: "Wrong."

PROFESSOR: "What now?"

STUDENT: "First of all, it doesn't seem the same. The double vision doubled everything, not just the boat. I mean, for example, I wouldn't mistake the one experience for the other. In the second case, when two boats are really there, and both my eyes are focused on them properly, then, there aren't two scene-images anymore. Instead, there's two boats, next to one dock, with one sun in the sky, and no headache. It's different."

PROFESSOR: "What if you go home tonight and have a dream in which everything seems the same as it seems here and now. Then you'll be seeing---or, at least *experiencing*---the same *scene-image* as you do right now. Right?"

STUDENT: "Is that the *same* scene-image? Or is that a *different* scene-image? Or are you merely proposing, suggesting, to me that we establish a certain rule of identity for our new concept, which calls these two cases the same? I'm wary of agreeing to that, since these three situations are not the same. I'm wary of extending our freshly-minted word so far as to put such different things into one basket so carelessly. Looking at two boats, versus crossing my eyes while looking at one boat, versus having a dream about boats---those are all different things. They don't even seem or feel alike---at least, not *exactly* alike. But even if they seemed exactly the same, that wouldn't make them the same in reality, since in reality they aren't the same. If we toss them all into the same word-bin and call them by the same name, we could be setting ourselves up to make the same kind of error we make when we commit a fallacy of equivocation. Let's be careful."

PROFESSOR: "You're just foot-dragging."

STUDENT: "Maybe it's good to drag one's feet, when nearby a slippery slope. You're too footloose; I say a little extra carefulness now, may save us a lot of later regrets. Look where you were when I found you, telling me we all live in different worlds. I mean, if you don't drink the Kool-Aid in the first place, then you won't need to waste time later, looking for an antidote."

PROFESSOR: "Okay, how does a dream of a boat *seem* different, as an experience, from seeing a real one?"

STUDENT: "Well, because, for one thing, I wake up afterward."

PROFESSOR: "Afterward."

STUDENT: "Yes."

PROFESSOR: "So, how do you know you're not dreaming right now?"

STUDENT: "Maybe I don't, but if I am dreaming, I guess I'll find out soon enough when I wake up."

PROFESSOR: "And waking you up is just what I'm trying to do. Here's a new case...

The Case of the Bent Oar

PROFESSOR: "Watch, now as I take this oar, here, on the dock and stick it down into the water."

STUDENT: "I'm watching."

PROFESSOR: "Now, with half of it submerged, the oar looks bent."

STUDENT: "It looks like a straight oar half-submerged in water. I wasn't born yesterday."

PROFESSOR: "I don't think you have the right kind of mind for philosophy."

STUDENT: "Okay, okay. It looks somewhat similar, although not identical, to the way a bent oar looks when not submerged. How's that?"

PROFESSOR: "No good. Look, it's very simple. The oar you see is bent. But the real oar in itself is straight. Therefore, the oar you see, is not the same oar, as the real oar in itself."

STUDENT: "Poppycock. 'The oar I see' is the real oar in itself, the straight oar."

PROFESSOR: "No it isn't---you can't see the oar in itself."

STUDENT: "So, besides, being straight, it's also invisible?"

PROFESSOR: "Don't be so literal."

STUDENT: "If you won't speak literally, I won't follow you. I won't agree. I shouldn't agree. I can't agree."

PROFESSOR: "Okay, okay, I'll speak literally. Literally speaking, *what you experience* is the same thing as what we have agreed to call a *scene-image*."

STUDENT: "I never agreed to call a real oar in itself a scene-image."

PROFESSOR: "Remember, I said 'experience,' I didn't say 'see.' I said *what you experience* is what we agreed to call a scene-image."

STUDENT: "Actually, now it's the word 'what' that bothers me more. I'd rather say that '*what* I experience' is the real oar in itself. You sound like you're trying to set up something besides the real oar in itself, as the only *object* an experience could possibly have or be of. And I'm not going along with that, since I'm not yet ready to deny that I can experience the real, straight, oar in itself. Look, gimme that oar."

PROFESSOR: "Here, take it."

STUDENT: "I can feel it with my hands, and it feels very straight. I feel no bend in it. I don't need my eyes to experience this real, straight, oar in itself. A blind man could tell you it's a straight oar. A blind man could tell you it's a real oar, and a straight one. If it were made out of chocolate I could eat it. This oar is more than a mere scene-image."

PROFESSOR: "Look, for all you know you're dreaming right now."

STUDENT: "Yeah, but, if I wake up in five minutes, should I then say 'I just dreamed that I was holding a straight, heavy, wooden *scene-image* in my hands'? No. If you're dreaming now, you'll say you dreamt about a boat, and a dock, and a straight, heavy, wooden oar that looked bent when you stuck it in the water. You won't say you dreamt of a bent oar."

PROFESSOR: "Okay, fine, then, I'll just say that when I stuck it in the water, you *experienced a bent scene-image.*"

STUDENT: "A bent scene-image? No. A bent scene-image would be like if you experienced the world as if it looked like a movie projected upon a folded movie screen."

PROFESSOR: "Okay, then, you experienced a scene-image of a bent oar."

STUDENT: "No, *of* a straight oar."

PROFESSOR: "You want me to say you experienced a scene-image of a straight oar?"

STUDENT: "Well I admit it's horrible, but your other way of saying it is even worse. If you want something better, then you should say that you saw a straight oar look sort of like it was bent, but not exactly. What would be best of all would be to say you saw a straight oar, half submerged in water, and looking just as a straight oar in itself should look in such a situation. And if you wake up five minutes later, just tack 'I dreamt' on to the front of that statement. The only thing on this dock that's bent is the crooked way you want me to agree to talk. I mean, to say that yesterday you saw a scene-image, is like saying that last night at dinnertime you ate a chewing. I'm starting to regret ever agreeing to the proposition that crossing my eyes doubles something."

PROFESSOR: "Are you going back on our agreement to use the term scene-image?"

STUDENT: "I'm thinking about it. Maybe it would be less misleading to simply say that crossing your eyes does not double the number of whatever things it is that you happen to be perceiving."

PROFESSOR: "Yes it does! Crossing your eyes *does* double the number of what you perceive."

STUDENT: "No it doesn't. Not really. That's metaphorical talk."

PROFESSOR: "No it isn't."

STUDENT: "Yes it is."

PROFESSOR: "Well crossing your eyes doubles the number of perceptions, or perceptible objects, or perceived objects."

STUDENT: "No it doesn't. How can you possibly say that you are perceiving an object if it doesn't exist? You can't tell me I'm 'perceiving two boats' if there's no two boats really out there for me to be perceiving. I'm just not going along with that bogus way of talking."

PROFESSOR: "You're just stonewalling. I mean, there is *something* that doubles, whatever you want to call it. Admit it."

STUDENT: "Well, it's called your vision. It's not called doubling the world, it's called giving yourself 'double vision.' And for good reason. I mean, you're not going to tell me you can double the number of dollars you possess merely by looking at them with crossed eyes?"

PROFESSOR: "Well, in a certain sense, you can."

STUDENT: "How's this for an argument: I doubled the number of dollars I had by looking at them with crossed eyes, and therefore, I have to pay tax on the gain."

PROFESSOR: "That's silly."

STUDENT: "I'm glad to hear you say so. I was worried."

PROFESSOR: "Look, let's try to hold on to our new noun, 'scene-image', for yet a little while longer. Maybe you can feel better about it if I stop saying you 'see' or even 'experience' scene-images. I'll agree, temporarily, hypothetically, for the sake of argument, that you don't even 'experience' scene-images. I'll agree, for a minute, that what you see and what you experience are, at least when you're awake and sober, real boats and oars in themselves. So, instead of saying you 'see' or even 'experience' mere scene-images, I'll use some other word, some new word, which we can coin for the purpose of referring only to the relationship between you and a scene-image. I'll say, okay, you don't experience, or see, scene-images, you *inviddy* scene-images. Okay?"

STUDENT: "Yes. Much better."

PROFESSOR: "Okay. So, let's plug our new items into the basic form of Hume's "table" argument again, and see how it works out:

> The oar of the scene-image we inviddy is bent: but the *real* oar, which exists independent of us, suffers no such bend. The bent oar was, therefore, nothing but a scene-image, which was inviddied by

our minds. These are the obvious dictates of reason, and no man, who reflects, ever doubted, that the existences, which we consider, when we say, *this oar* and *that boat,* are nothing but scene-images in the mind, and fleeting copies or representations of other existences, which remain unbent, uniform and independent. Therefore, the mind has never anything present to it but scene-images, and cannot possibly reach any experience of their connection with real objects. The supposition of such a connection is, therefore, without any foundation in reasoning.

STUDENT: "That's an improvement, but it's still a terrible mess. For example, right away, I have a complaint about the first proposition. It says 'the oar of the scene-image we inviddy is bent.' I say there's only one oar, and that oar is straight. There is no bent oar. So I think it better, less misleading, if you want to use this new vocabulary, to say: 'the oar of the scene-image we inviddy is straight'."

PROFESSOR: "No, no---false. The oar you *inviddy* is bent. The object you inviddy, is, by definition, a scene-image, remember? It's true by our agreed definition of 'inviddy', that the oar you *inviddy* is bent. Come on."

STUDENT: "Wrong, because you can't inviddy an *oar.* If you're holding a real oar in itself, and you're not asleep, and you're not crazy, and you're not mistaken, then you're not *inviddying* an oar. In that case, you're *seeing* it---in the full nine-yard sense of the word seeing."

PROFESSOR: "Well, in that case you're doing both. You're both seeing and inviddying it at the same time."

STUDENT: "So sometimes inviddying is seeing, and sometimes it isn't seeing? I never agreed to that. Is this another suggestion, another proposal, about how you think we should agree to use our new word? Because that's how it sounds to me. I thought the whole purpose of the word *inviddy* was to have a word that meant something a lot less than the whole nine yards. I mean, maybe we can agree that inviddying refers to the relationship between a person's retina and his brain. Or, instead, perhaps, between his visual cortex and his frontal lobe. Or between the retina and the frontal lobe. We could agree, for example, that the frontal lobe inviddies the retina, by means of the interposing medium composed of the optic nerves and the visual cortex. If you like that one. But whichever it is, let's be clear about it."

PROFESSOR: "Do we really need to get that precise? I don't even know what a frontal lobe is."

STUDENT: "Well, I'm no neurologist either. But if we don't pin down this new concept, then we'll be sure to run into some trouble--- some fallacy of equivocation. It's a fallacy of equivocation waiting to happen. I think maybe we're going to need a half dozen new words to get out of these woods."

PROFESSOR: "This is a fine snarl. Look, can't I just say that we're talking about a scene-image of an oar?"

STUDENT: "*Of* an oar. And the oar it's 'of,' is the real one. The straight one. The real oar in itself. If you stood here on the dock and painted the scene from life, it would be a painting *of* a real straight oar in itself."

PROFESSOR: "But you'd make your brush turn a corner as you painted it."

STUDENT: "So what?"

PROFESSOR: "So the oar in the painting would be, in some sense, crooked. My point in a nutshell."

STUDENT: "What's the point?"

PROFESSOR: "It would be a painting of a crooked oar."

STUDENT: "No, it would be a painting *of* a straight oar."

PROFESSOR: "How about if I say we're seeing a bent oar, *as* a straight oar."

STUDENT: "It seems like you've got it backwards."

PROFESSOR: "What if we mailed the painting to my cousin. Notice that, not being here on the dock with us, all he would have to go by would be the painting."

STUDENT: "Yeah."

PROFESSOR: "So, then he'd think the oar really had been crooked."

STUDENT: "No he wouldn't. That's like saying he'd think the ship you painted on the horizon was a tiny toy, if you used perspective."

PROFESSOR: "Well I'm a lousy painter."

STUDENT: "Well if Rembrandt did it, your cousin would get a pretty good idea of our view here, and he'd know the oar was really straight, and the ship on the horizon big."

PROFESSOR: "Then it would be a trustworthy painting. But how would my cousin really know? How would he know if the painting was a trustworthy one or not? Come to think of it, how do you know if your own scene-images of this place are trustworthy? How can you tell the difference between seeing a real oar, and just inviddying a scene-image? How do you know you've *ever* seen a real oar, rather than just inviddied a lot of oarish scene-imagery? How do you know your whole life isn't a dream?"

STUDENT: "Is this skepticism again?"

PROFESSOR: "Yes."

STUDENT: "You keep harping on that. You seem like you're worried about skepticism."

PROFESSOR: "Well, it's an issue."

STUDENT: "Is that what all this stuff is about? Is this why you want me to talk about seeing things the way you do? Is it because of this worry, about skepticism?"

PROFESSOR: "Well, let's just say that I think you may have more cause to worry than I do."

Are Observations Theory-Laden?

PROFESSOR: "Look, think about Johannes Kepler and Tycho Brahe. At sunrise, when they looked to the East, one of them saw the sun coming up, while the other saw the Earth rotating forward, or down. Thus, they saw the same thing so differently, that, really, we can't even say they were seeing the same thing."

STUDENT: "Are you even listening to yourself? I mean, if Kepler and Tycho Brahe didn't see the same thing, then they couldn't have been seeing the same thing differently. You can only be seeing the same thing differently, if you're seeing the same thing. *If you aren't seeing the same thing, then you can't be seeing the same thing differently.* It strikes me as almost perverse that you would pick out the case of Kepler here, since it's one of the salient features of that event, that Kepler was able to achieve what he did, because he had Tycho Brahe's wonderful wealth of astronomical observations to draw upon. Here, as usual, there were two competing theories (Heliocentrism vs. Aristotelianism) competing to explain *the same observations.* I mean, isn't that what made them *competing* theories?"

PROFESSOR: "You are the most plodding, literal-minded person I have ever met."

STUDENT: "I thought I was naive and vulgar."

PROFESSOR: "That too."

STUDENT: "Maybe that's been your trouble. Maybe what you really need more than anything else is to be held to account by a really naive, vulgar, plodding, and literal person."

PROFESSOR: "Well, let's keep going, and see how long you can keep up your naiveté. The trouble with *naiveté* is, it's a hard thing to hang on to."

STUDENT: "Well, I seem to be doing okay, so far. Let's also keep in mind that we don't want to rush over a cliff with a mob in pursuit of sophistication."

Direct vs. Indirect

PROFESSOR: "But what about that woman with the cockeyed double-vision binoculars with the red lenses? Isn't there some sense in which we can say that, when she scanned the horizon, what she saw--- *immediately* or *directly*---was two red ships?"

STUDENT: "She saw one ship, the real ship, in itself. I mean, maybe we can say 'she saw two red ships' in some kind of metaphorical sense, or in the sense in which 'saw' means 'inviddied' and 'ship' means 'scene-image.' But unless you're trying to write poetry or fiction, that's a dishonest or misleading way to talk. It's humbug. It's bogus talk. I say that what she saw was the one real ship in itself on the horizon, the same ship in itself as the guy with the dirty telescope saw."

PROFESSOR: "Okay, then, when did they see it? I mean, it took the light rays a certain amount of time to get to them, right? So did they see the ship immediately, or a little time later? What if they saw a supernova? Would you still say they saw the real supernova in itself? Even if it took years for them to see it?"

STUDENT: "Why not? Yes, I'd be inclined to say they saw the real supernova in itself."

PROFESSOR: "Well how much delay, mediation and indirectness can your realism stand? I mean, if you see Bob Hope in a movie, through cockeyed binoculars, and I see him standing next to me at baggage claim, are you still going to say that you saw the real Bob Hope in himself?"

STUDENT: "Yes. I mean, you saw him *more directly* than I did. But so what? That doesn't mean we saw two different people. We saw the same person. I saw, more indirectly, in a movie, the same man you saw more directly, standing at the baggage claim. Directness is a more or less kind of thing, not an all or nothing kind of thing, isn't it?"

PROFESSOR: "What do you mean? Aren't you a *direct* realist?"

STUDENT: "I don't know---what's that?"

PROFESSOR: "Don't you claim you can experience the world *directly, immediately?*"

STUDENT: "Well, I guess it's tough for me to think of a more 'direct' or 'immediate' way to experience an apple than to grab hold of one and take a bite out of it. Then I'd see it, feel it, smell it, taste it, and even hear it crunch, all at the same time. That's relatively direct, isn't it?"

PROFESSOR: "But then your senses would be functioning as a medium between you and the apple, so therefore you wouldn't be experiencing the apple directly or immediately, but mediately or indirectly. Right?"

STUDENT: "The way you talk it sounds like you think your senses make you blind, like they come between you and the world, as if you can't see the world because your retinas are in the way. That just doesn't make sense."

PROFESSOR: "Doesn't it?"

STUDENT: "No. It's like you're saying that you're not tasting the apple directly when you're actually biting the darned thing, or that you aren't touching it directly when you squeeze it with a bare hand, or that if an apple smacks a man in the forehead, then that isn't a case of direct contact between an apple and a person. That's a silly way to talk."

PROFESSOR: "Well, I guess I still don't see how you can escape what seems to be a kind unavoidable logic that just flows logically from the scientific facts upon which we agree. Let me put it like this. If you accept the modern scientific account of how vision works, then you must admit that *what* your eyes are built to see is *light*. But a *chair* is not the same thing as *light*. Nor is a chair composed of light. A chair is made of wood, and wood isn't light. Therefore, you must admit that *what* you are really seeing is *not* a wooden chair. You are really seeing light, while the wooden chair must be something that your mind has created, inferred or composed out of the data of sensation. If you accept the science, this conclusion just follows logically."

STUDENT: [Sigh.] "I wonder if *blind* people find anti-realism less beguiling. You know, you can't bark your shin on a mere bundle of light rays."

PROFESSOR: "Come on. I just proved anti-realism to be a logical necessity for you. How are going to wiggle out of it this time?"

STUDENT: "Why don't you prefer to say that the science just as well proves that eyes are built to detect *chairs*, by capturing their reflected light?"

PROFESSOR: "Look, think about how seeing works. When you go outside and look at the stars, you're only seeing a visual image of them as they were *years* ago. You know this perfectly well. So how can you deny it when I say this proves there's some disconnect, some distinction, some *difference*, between *what you see*, and the world as it is, so to speak, in itself? How can you deny that there is some kind of *gap* there, something that's less than simply or perfectly *direct* and *immediate*? You're denying the scientific facts here. The fact is, you don't see *external objects*. *What you see* is *light* rays. You don't hear a drum, you hear sound waves."

STUDENT: "And you don't taste apples, you taste...?"

PROFESSOR: "Molecules."

STUDENT: "I thought you were going to say 'flavors.' So, I guess, when I run smack into a flagpole, what I really encounter, in that case, is not a external, mind-independent flagpole in itself, but a mere..."

PROFESSOR: "Sense-datum."

STUDENT: "A mere sense-datum."

PROFESSOR: "Yes."

STUDENT: "Well, heck, why stop there? Why don't you keep going, and point out that *what we really see* isn't even *light waves*, but only our own retinas? Or that we don't even see our own *retinas*, really, since *what* we really experience are mere data streams from the optic nerves. Except that what we *really* see isn't even signals from the *optic nerves*, but mere patterns of neuron-firings from the *visual cortex,* after it has finished processing the raw data from the optic nerves. We could play this game all day. You might as well say that what you see is merely your own eyeballs. It's silliness. It's like saying you can never really play tennis with another tennis player, because the only thing you contact directly is the ball, and that therefore what you really play tennis against is in truth never a person, but always and only a mere tennis ball. Therefore, no two people can play tennis with each other."

PROFESSOR: "Look, you admit the whole thing requires a complex causal chain. So much for your *immediate* perception of objects or *direct* realism. As Bertrand Russell said, 'Naive realism leads to physics, and physics, if true, shows that naive realism is false.' You only perceive physical objects *by means of* sense data, whereas those sense data are what you directly perceive."

STUDENT: "Actually, I don't remember ever claiming that sense-perception was 'direct' or 'immediate.' When did I say that?"

PROFESSOR: "Well, then, maybe we agree."

STUDENT: "No, we definitely don't."

PROFESSOR: "You don't agree that we perceive external objects only by means of sense-data, or sensory qualities, like colors and so on?"

STUDENT: "I wonder why you don't switch it the other way around, and say that you can only perceive sense data like colors *by means of* physical objects? Why does the 'redness' get the place of pride, at the front of the line, in your scheme, instead of the apple? Why don't you put things the other way around, and say that 'redness' is merely derivative, since it is obtained by a secondary process of intellectual abstraction from the apple, which is epistemologically more primary? Isn't thinking about 'redness,' in the abstract, a more sophisticated thought or concept than just noticing an apple? Even a dog can notice an apple. But can a dog think about an abstraction like 'redness'? Let's go talk to some toddlers, and see which of the two they find easier to grasp. I'll wager I can teach a two year old what an *apple* is, before you can get him to understand what you mean by *redness*. I'm not sure even I understand what *you* mean by redness."

PROFESSOR: "Are you proposing to switch it the other way around, and have an apple be considered something known more easily and directly than redness?"

STUDENT: "No, not really. I mean, why do we need a single-file line? I'm just trying to point out how unjustified or arbitrary your scheme seems to be. It's like you imagine you're trying to lay down the order of precedence for a bunch of courtiers, and you have to get them all in line and decide who's at the front of the line, and who sits at the head of the table. It's a one-dimensional scheme. I just don't know why I should buy into it. You've got two eyes, and a whole tangle of brain connections all over the place, so right away you've got something that doesn't look like a nice single-file line there. I mean, you've got two retinas, so if what you're really seeing is merely a retinal image, then you can never see less than two apples, so you can never see one apple."

PROFESSOR: "Well, you're going to have a hard time if you want to deny that you perceive apples by means of sense-perception."

STUDENT: "I'm not denying that---*you* are!   Look, you say I've never directly felt an apple, but only a mere sensation. Gee, I wonder what it would be like to reach out and feel a real *external object*, rather than to reach out and feel a *mere sensation*. I mean, it really hurts to run smack into a mere *sensation* of a tree. Just think what it would be like, instead, to encounter a real, independent, external tree in itself. That would *really* hurt."

PROFESSOR: "As Kant was the first to teach us, that's an unintelligible thought."

STUDENT: "It certainly is."

PROFESSOR: "You're being sarcastic."

STUDENT: "Yes I am."

PROFESSOR: "A sneer is not an argument."

STUDENT: "Good heavens, man---give me your hand!   Take this oar! Hold it. Feel its weight, its solidity, its roughness. It's cold and heavy. It's a real thing in itself, independent and external to your mind, and you're actually feeling it!   You're feeling an external object, existing independently of you, outside your mind."

PROFESSOR: "Of course, you silly child, I feel the weight, the solidity, the *roughness*, the *chill*. Yet, what are these---'roughness,' 'chill'---but *sensations*?   And how can *sensations* possibly exist independently of the mind?"

STUDENT: "An *oar* is more than a mere bundle of sensations locked up in your head. This oar doesn't need you to exist, and if you never notice it, it won't be harmed!   Your mind is in you, and this oar is not in you. I can see this same oar just as well as you can. And I can see you, and can see that the oar isn't in you. It's in front of you; not inside you. It's seven feet long, it's too big to fit inside you. Besides, if it existed *merely* as an appearance in you, I wouldn't be able to see it at all. I'm no mind-reader.

70

When you play tennis, you play against another person, not just a ball. Likewise, when you eat a real apple, you're not 'merely' seeing light rays, you're *also* seeing something else: an honest to goodness external object. Namely, an *apple*."

PROFESSOR: "Look, it's really simply a matter of scientific knowledge here, that sense data exist and therefore you just can't see apples *immediately*, or *directly*, because seeing things involves a complex causal chain. The light bounces off the apple and enters your eyeball, after being bent by the lens, it strikes the retina and triggers a chain reaction which travels down the optic nerve to the visual cortex, which processes the data, etc., etc. If you accept these facts, then it obviously proves that what you're most directly perceiving just has to be a mental representation, or a phenomenal item, or a mental object. You seem to be in scientific denial."

STUDENT: "No I'm not! Seeing comprises a complex causal chain, and no doubt if you wanted to you could break that chain up into a half dozen steps, at least. As you yourself pointed out, there's more than one way to chop up the world into pieces. But what you keep trying to do is to chop up the stream of events and then arbitrarily point to step number four or five and then say: 'Ah---here it is, *this* is the item I'm really perceiving, and, therefore, *what* I'm perceiving must be some item in my mind, and therefore, the apple I think I see *out there,* is actually a mental item in me, and it cannot exist independently of me.' Wrong!"

PROFESSOR: "What's the problem?"

STUDENT: "Look, we both accept the same physical story about how seeing works. Now, given that agreement, think about a hypothetical case in which you're really eating a real, actual apple, and you aren't deceived or dreaming. In that lucky, happy, *hypothetical* case, do you not agree, *can* you not agree, that *what you're seeing*, i.e., the *object*, i.e., the *apple*, in that particular hypothetical case, isn't anything nearer than the far end of that chain?

If you want to chop up the process into two pieces, or three pieces, or twenty pieces, that's fine with me. You go right ahead. All I'm saying is that *really seeing* a real apple *includes all of those pieces,* and any kind of 'seeing' things that doesn't stretch all the way from one end to the other isn't really *seeing*. It's just quote-unquote 'seeing things,' as in, 'he was so drunk he was seeing things.' The way you talk it sounds like you want to disown even your own corneas. Did it ever occur to you that your corneas are a part of your self?"

PROFESSOR: "Are you going to claim that my eyeballs are a part of my *mind*?"

STUDENT: "I don't know. I don't want to quibble over the definition of the word mind. But I will take a stand against Hume, who says your eyeballs and arms and legs are no part of your *self*. That's just loony. My eyeballs are a part of me, and when I use my eyeballs to capture some of the light being reflected off my chair, then I see the chair itself. And when I *bark my shin* on the chair, then I bark my shin on something a lot more substantial than a *mere appearance* or *mental representation*."

PROFESSOR: "You know, you don't like it when I call you a 'direct' realist, but then I notice you seem to be at war with the idea of letting anybody talk about anything in any way operating between you and the apple you see. I don't mean just the old dubious items: Locke's 'qualities,' Hume's 'perceptions,' Kant's 'appearances,' or Russell's 'sense-data.' But even when it comes to less ambiguous items, like light rays, retinas, and the electrical impulses of the nervous system, you seem to shy away. You don't deny these things are real and important, and yet you get upset when I talk about them. I can't imagine there's anything I could say about these items that you wouldn't disparage. I'd just like to hear you admit they exist."

STUDENT: "Okay, they exist. At least the latter set---the less ambiguous items. I'll say that much."

PROFESSOR: "Okay, then, why are you trying to take these things away from me?"

STUDENT: "Well, let's just say that whiskey also exists, but when I see a philosopher handling sense-data or representations, it gives the same sort of feeling I'd get if I saw a baby with a bottle of whiskey."

PROFESSOR: "Well, you can't take these things away from me. I need these items."

STUDENT: "What do you need them for? You'll just get hurt. I don't trust you not to misuse them. I don't think you can get a hold of a representational reification for five minutes before I'm going to catch you up to your old tricks."

PROFESSOR: "What old tricks?"

STUDENT: "Your old trick of saying it's the only thing we really *know about*."

PROFESSOR: "Well, that's true."

STUDENT: "Stop that! You're incurable! You see? You just need to stay away from that stuff. You can't stop yourself."

PROFESSOR: "Well, it's no good. We can't get rid of light rays and retinas. They exist. Besides, we need them."

STUDENT: "Well I don't think you need anything like a 'sense-datum,' or anything I'd agree to call a mental representation."

PROFESSOR: "Yes we do. We need those kind of things too."

STUDENT: "What? Aren't retinas, light rays, and nerve impulses *enough* for you? What do you need to start talking about 'mental representations' for? You'll only get into trouble."

PROFESSOR: "I need them for cases like the Wittgenstein's duck-rabbit, and the Necker cube. I need to be able to talk about the fact that one person perceives a duck while another perceives a rabbit."

STUDENT: "No, you don't. Why don't you just be honest and say they both perceive the same drawing? If they didn't see the same drawing, then they couldn't be interpreting the same drawing differently."

Arguments from Illusion

PROFESSOR: "Okay, look. When Descartes sat before the fire, he felt the heat of it, and saw its light. But if you want to claim that he just *saw* the fire directly, immediately, incorrigibly, or unproblematically---"

STUDENT: "I *don't* say that!"

PROFESSOR: "---Okay, well, let me just say my question is, how is it possible that sometimes we make mistakes? Sometimes people might hallucinate a fire, when there isn't really any fire there to be seen. In that case, you'll have to admit that *what* they're seeing is, as you like to put it, inside their own head. Or, as I would put it, they're perceiving something that is merely mental. If you want to do it your way, then you need to find some new way to explain how and why the person mistakes one for the other.

The way I explain the mistake is to say that there's an objective resemblance between the hallucinatory scene-image (though I prefer the word representation, or sense-datum) and a veridical scene-image (or representation, or sense-datum). That's plausible, because you can imagine that one mental entity can resemble another. One mental image, or representation, or sense-datum, can resemble another. But the way you've got it, you're going to have to explain how it's even *conceivable* that a purely material real-world physical object can be so much like a purely mental representation that one can be mistaken for the other!

On your account, how or why should anybody ever mistake the one for the other? How can anybody confuse a purely mental entity with a purely material object? You need that other, veridical, mental entity as a go-between, to explain how or why mistakes are made. My account can explain the mistakes, but your naive realism cannot."

STUDENT: "I disagree. The hallucination mistake is due simply to the fact that one external physical object objectively resembles another external physical object."

PROFESSOR: "What do you mean? In the case of an hallucination, there *isn't* any external physical object there!"

STUDENT: "I can tell you've never hallucinated."

PROFESSOR: "Have *you*?"

STUDENT: "Well, you know students like to party, so, let's just say I've been there when other people were hallucinating, and it isn't like Macbeth's dagger. It's like the duck-rabbit. What happens is that they take one thing for another, like they momentarily mistake a gnarled stump for a sleeping dog. It's basically like an optical illusion, and not entirely different from cloud-gazing, or from the child's mistake of his striped pajamas hanging over a chair in the dark, for a tiger, until somebody turns on the light. And in all these cases I can't help noticing that the illusion isn't very persistent or convincing. For example, the pajamas don't growl and the stump doesn't bark."

PROFESSOR: "Are you claiming the other senses always give the game away?"

STUDENT: "I'm saying I think philosophers' accounts of the magnificent power of optical illusions and hallucinations to deceive people are often quite exaggerated, and don't seem to me to hold up well under scrutiny, so that you can lead yourself astray if you're not careful---as I think you just did, when you assumed that hallucinations don't involve perceiving real, external objects.

You demand to know *what* did he see, when a person hallucinated a sleeping dog. You want me to say *what* he saw was something in the mind, like a mere appearance or mental representation, and not an external object. You want me to say he saw a dog, but nothing was there. But *what* he saw was a gnarled stump, just as *what* the child sees is his own striped pajamas. These aren't cases of seeing things that exist only in the mind. These are cases of seeing *real, external things*, and yet misinterpreting them. You say these people aren't seeing things as they really are, and yet it seems to me to be an objective matter of fact that the gnarled stump, from one angle, really does look an awful lot like a sleeping dog, as even the soberest observer might agree. So why should we analyze hallucinations the way you do? It doesn't seem right."

PROFESSOR: "Well what about cases in which people hallucinate daggers the way Macbeth did?"

STUDENT: "Are you sure they ever do? Macbeth is a fictional character."

PROFESSOR: "What about crazy people who hear voices?"

STUDENT: "Maybe they're hearing the rustling of the leaves, or the gurgling of the pipes. I don't know, I've never closely observed anybody like that, have you?"

PROFESSOR: "Well, no, but I assume such cases exist."

STUDENT: "Let's be careful what we assume."

PROFESSOR: "What about dreams? Ha! I've got you there. In dreams you see things which exist only in your mind."

STUDENT: "Well, I'm a person who seems to dream every night, and all night long, and to remember my dreams, at least for a short time, every time I wake up. And yet, for all that, I can't say I remember ever having a dream in which objects could be seen, touched, smelled, and heard, all at the same time. I even remember having dreams about eating food, and yet I don't recall that the food seemed to really exist for all *five* senses, or even for more than one sense at a time.

Dreams don't really seem exactly the same as waking life. When I try to read something in a dream, it never works right. The words keep changing, like they can't make up their minds. And if I fall off a cliff it doesn't hurt. In dreams I can breathe when I swim underwater, and fly by swimming through the air. Dreaming of a house seems more like *thinking about* a house, than like *seeing* one. Dreams seem more like thoughts than like sensations. When dreaming and waking are experienced side by side, when the alarm clock rings, then it becomes obvious how much dreams really pale in comparison to sensation. And waking up isn't like falling asleep."

PROFESSOR: "So what? My point is this: *there are no external objects* corresponding to the objects in our dreams."

STUDENT: "And therefore…"

PROFESSOR: "Therefore you'll have to admit that *what* you perceive or experience, when you dream of a lake, is a purely *mental* entity. There it is. That's my scene-image, my 'mental representation,' my phenomena, my mere perception of the mind, or whatever you want to call it. Here we have a case where you'll have to admit we're dealing with just such a beast, the kind of beast you keep trying to deny and exterminate: a purely mental object of perception which corresponds to *nothing* in reality."

STUDENT: "Can't I just say I'm not *seeing* anything, and that this lake doesn't 'exist' in *any* place, because it's not real, and therefore doesn't *exist* at all? Or, if I dream of Lake Michigan, then you might say I dreamt of the real lake which does exist, externally. I mean, I thought you were a Pragmatist. So, shouldn't you be trying to argue that we're better off if we don't abandon your precious 'mental representations'? I keep waiting for you to show me how they're so darn indispensable, that we ought to keep them around and put up with all their dangerous tendencies, for the sake of their great usefulness. But all I can see is their bad side. What's the cash value of mental representations?"

PROFESSOR: "Well, how can you escape them---at least, in the case of dreams? We need the concept of mental representations in order to explain our experiences."

STUDENT: "Well, I wonder if it's really true that science needs this concept. And anyway, isn't that for scientists to decide? I mean, it seems to me that as philosophers it's not our place to tell neurology or psychology what sort of concepts it supposedly can't do without. In fact, maybe our real duty here is to point out to the scientists how this traditional concept has caused so much confusion for the last few centuries that we'd like them to tell us if we can get rid of it."

PROFESSOR: "I'm afraid you may not find them very helpful. They don't necessarily understand our concerns, and tend to see us as useless hair-splitters."

STUDENT: "Look, a minute ago you accused me of supposing that perceptual judgments are incorrigible, or that we can't make mistakes, or be deceived by appearances. But I never claimed that. I'm just complaining that you want to keep talking as if you imagine you have a tiny little soul-man with tiny little eyes living in your frontal lobe and gazing at your visual cortex through binoculars, and another little man in the visual cortex talking to a retina on the phone."

PROFESSOR: "No I don't! What do you mean?"

STUDENT: "I'm just not comfortable saying that dreams involve the 'perceiving' of mental entities. Even if science someday decided that dreams were caused by the frontal lobe's 'inviddyings' of the visual cortex's idle firing noise, that wouldn't mean that in a dream anything is really seen. Inviddying isn't seeing. We might be blamed for preferring an old, equivocating metaphor, if we say the frontal lobe 'sees,' or even 'perceives,' some idle firing noise. We could be rightly blamed for refusing to draw crucial distinctions enough to give the relation a new, more precise verb like 'inviddying' to prevent those old perennial fallacies of equivocation that have so plagued us.

Sometimes, when we repeatedly fall into troublesome conflations, a few new distinctions may be necessary to clear up all the confusion. So what excuse do we have for stubbornly continuing to throw around all these metaphors so carelessly? Russell once said when a neurologist looks at another person's brain, he really sees a part of his own brain. That was silly and wrong.

Until science figures out how dreams work, anything we say about them is bound to end up as some clumsy metaphor. I don't even want to go there. I'm not a neurologist, and neither are you. When I say I saw a lake, in a dream, I mean I dreamed that I saw a lake. I'm speaking loosely, carelessly, metaphorically, or poetically."

PROFESSOR: "So, basically, your move here is just to say that explaining why having a dream about a lake seems, in some sense, to be somehow 'like' seeing a real one, is a fact of nature that it just isn't our job as philosophers to explain. It's somebody else's job, namely, it's the job of scientists who study the human brain."

STUDENT: "Something like that."

PROFESSOR: "Okay, but you must realize that there's such a thing as the Philosophy of Mind, and the poor fellows in that field need to be able to hash out some kind of ontological scheme that works."

STUDENT: "My heart goes out to them. It reminds me of the ancient Greeks trying to hash out an ontological scheme for physics, without knowing all the things about physics that we know now. At this point in time, it may be asking too much. Maybe before we can settle the ontological issues, we need first to get some more of the brain science accomplished."

PROFESSOR: "Well, you're not going get very far if you need to deny that non-veridical experiences exist."

STUDENT: "It all depends on what you mean by *non-veridical.* Since the word *veridical* means *truth-telling,* then yes, maybe I am trying to stake a claim that there is *some* level on which *all* empirical data is in some sense "veridical." All empirical data is information, and all information is in some sense or in some way informative. But raw data is just data. It isn't judgment or interpretation. That's where the mistakes come in. Yet, even a brain in a vat enjoys a certain level of veridical information telling him *something* about the real software running on the real computer of the evil scientist. Thus, even a vat-brain enjoys experiences which are, at some ultimate level, in some sense, veridical."

PROFESSOR: "You must be joking."

STUDENT: "Not at all. Think about it. The vat-brain knows what the roller-coaster program looks like and feels like from his point of view, and that may be something the evil scientist himself only wishes *he* could know. Imagine a case in which the computer scientist was not quite so evil, and he and the vat-brain were somehow in communication. Maybe the scientist might get his programs mixed up, because he forgot to label them, and so he has to get help from the vat-brain and ask him: is this the roller coaster program or the snowstorm program? Is this the one where the snow seems cold and white, or the one where it tastes like salt and burns?

Even a dreamer knows what kind of dream he's having. Neither the dreamer nor the vat-brain is in a state of being entirely without information. Raw data is information, and all information is in some way informative. Mistakes are the result of wrong judgments, misinterpretation. There's always some ultimate level at which the data itself is just too raw to tell a lie. Don't blame the raw data for your misinterpretation of it.

Besides, it seems to me that you suffer from a need to rule out the very *possibility* of a very ordinary veridical experience. My vulgar realism can easily admit that we make mistakes of judgment and interpretation and that we can hallucinate, etc. But even one ordinary, realistic veridical experience is enough to destroy your anti-realism. You can't allow it. You can't allow one case of a person ever seeing or feeling a rock or an apple that actually exists outside the mind, because if that is possible, then it just isn't true, as Hume said, that it's *never* the case these are *the very things we see and feel*."

Are Objects Objective?

PROFESSOR: "Okay, look, you told me that 'when you eat a real apple, you're not 'merely' seeing light rays, you're *also* seeing something else: an honest to goodness external object---an *apple*.' That's what you said. But try to understand that a young baby might be there next to you and not see what you see, but just a blooming, buzzing mass of sensations. He can't report to you that he's seen 'an apple' until he's begun to chop up the world into such more or less arbitrary sections, and been conditioned by evolution, and socialized by his parents, to individuate and objectify his experiences into handy little medium-sized objects like 'apples.'

That so-called 'apple,' is a mental construct, composed by your mind, out of your own private sensation data. Moreover, some other-sized creature, who doesn't eat apples, might perceive instead a thin mist of particles, or an indistinguishably tiny fraction of a galaxy.

That's why I say that both mind and world are made up of mind and world. Maybe reality is in some sense 'objective', but objects aren't."[5]

STUDENT: "So the apple doesn't really exist."

PROFESSOR: "I didn't say that."

STUDENT: "You didn't?"

PROFESSOR: "No."

STUDENT: "Look, if objects aren't objective, then apples don't exist."

PROFESSOR: "Not so."

STUDENT: "Let me get this straight. Objects do not objectively exist. Apples are objects. Therefore apples do not objectively exist. Where did I go wrong? Isn't it true that things which don't exist objectively are either merely subjective, or fictitious, or imaginary, or else just don't exist at all? I mean, I thought that to *exist* at all was to *be* objective. And how could anything be more 'objective,'---i.e., *object-like*---than an *object*? I'm not trying to lay down a doctrine here, I'm just trying to figure out what you're *saying*. I always supposed that to exist was to *ex-sist*, as in to *sist* (stay, sit) *ex* outside, as in outside us, outside of the mind. Isn't that what the word means?

If to exist is to *ex-sist* outside the mind, then there's no such thing as a thing which, strictly speaking, 'exists' in the mind alone. If a thing doesn't exist independently of thought, or apart from the mind, then, by definition, it does not, strictly speaking, *exist* at all. If it *exists*, then it must be outside of or apart from mere thought, i.e., objective. At least, if you want to say that 'objects aren't objective,' then that is going to sound like a person who says that fur isn't furry, wool isn't wooly, and reality isn't real. It sounds self-contradictory. Isn't it just one of those things that's true by definition, that *objects* are *objective*?"

PROFESSOR: "Not if they don't actually exist."

STUDENT: "Aha! So you *are* saying that objects don't exist!"

PROFESSOR: "I didn't say that."

STUDENT: "Well make up your mind. If objects exist, then they're objective, by definition; just as it's true by definition that if bachelors exist then they're single."

PROFESSOR: "Okay, yeah, objects are objective by definition."

STUDENT: "I don't want to quibble. But I just can't understand you. Why do you talk the way you do, if not merely to obfuscate? Is there some subtle point you want to make poetically, by talking this way? I need you to spell it out."

Is Reality Socially Constructed?

PROFESSOR: "There *is* an important point I'm trying to make. The question of *which objects exist* is a thing subject to linguistic and ontological fashion. It's relative to social convention. Let's take the question of atoms. We say we split atoms. But a Greek would say that's impossible by definition. He would say that if you split it it's not an *atom*, that 'atom' by definition is unsplittable. It's by definition a particle so small and elemental that it cannot be further divided. And he invented the word, so he should know its definition!

So we run into a sort of strange conundrum. At some point, once we started using the word 'atom' to refer to things which, later, turned out to be splittable, then we had a dilemma on our hands. We had to choose whether to stop using that word to refer to them, or, instead, we had to give up the proposition that the word 'atom' by definition must mean something indivisible. The same kind of thing happened with so-called 'black swans.' When they were discovered for the first time, people could have chosen to call them *black swans*, and to give up the proposition that *all swans are white*, or else, they could have stuck to their guns and say 'those can't be swans, because *swans* are white by definition,' and given the new birds a new name They had a choice, to go either way."

STUDENT: "Okay…so what?"

PROFESSOR: "Well, that should make you see that the question of *what objects exist*, depends upon social conventions."

STUDENT: "When you say that, it sounds like you're saying that's *all* it depends on! As if we could turn lead into gold just by agreeing to change our social conventions."

PROFESSOR: "Well, we could! Look, if we all started to call 'gold' the stuff we used to call 'lead,' then we could indeed *turn lead into gold*. Can't you see that?"

STUDENT: "Very funny."

PROFESSOR: "I'm not kidding. It's perfectly true. And, as a matter of fact, we do things like this all the time, especially at the cutting edge of science, as the *atom* case so eloquently shows. First we made *atoms* divisible, and the next thing you know we split them."

STUDENT: "You sound like you think it works like *Harold and the Purple Crayon*. You sound like a medieval con artist trying to convince people they can turn lead into gold, and otherwise alter reality by saying magic words. No wonder you people are constantly insisting we change what we call everything. You've got yourselves convinced that you can change the world just by re-naming everything."

PROFESSOR: "Don't lump me together with those crazy people. I'm just trying to help further the progress of physics."

STUDENT: "Maybe so, but if you ask those people where they get their insanity, they cite you."

PROFESSOR: "Is it my fault they think crazy things?"

STUDENT: "Yes! You told them that we all live in different worlds, that everything they see is 'merely a perception of the mind,' and that objects like freight trains and bullets cannot exist independently, outside our thoughts. And then you're surprised when they take you seriously."

PROFESSOR: "Look, you misunderstand me, and so do they. I'm not saying *anything goes*. I'm not a kook, I'm a scientist. I say quite plainly that it's possible for nature to show us our mistakes, when we get things wrong. Of course, I know that; it happens all the time in science."

STUDENT: "How could nature possibly be *able* to 'show you your mistakes,' if nature, as it really is in itself, is invisible to you? You say that all you have got is, as you put it, the 'phenomena,' and no phenomenon is any more objective than 'a mere representation of the mind.' How can 'nature' show you your mistakes, if things as they really are, are, for you, never possible objects of experience? Does the world show the brain in the vat his mistakes?"

PROFESSOR: "Well, that's just the beauty of it. What isn't a possible object of experience for me, doesn't concern me. Why should it?"

STUDENT: "It should concern you because, in fact, real things in themselves *are* possible objects of experience for you! The world is not in your head! Your head is in the world. And if your head is lying on the railroad tracks, then everybody in the world agreeing, all at once, to call a *train* a *raisin* isn't going to soften the blow. There's a whole lot more to reality than mere perceptions of the mind or linguistic social conventions. Rocks existed long before there were any 'perceptions of the mind' or linguistic social conventions, and they'll probably exist long after. But you say that rocks are dependent on minds, and created by minds. So, according to you, there could not have been any rocks, in the days before evolution created minds."

PROFESSOR: "Well, don't you see what I'm driving at there?"

STUDENT: "You're driving at insanity---you're driving me nuts!"

PROFESSOR: "The point is, that before there were speakers of the

English language, there could not have been any quote-unquote 'rocks,' i.e., 'rocks' as opposed to 'boulders,' which are bigger, or 'pebbles,' which are smaller. In other words, this whole ordinary ontology we have now, of 'rocks' versus 'boulders' versus 'pebbles,' is just an arbitrary classification scheme we've imposed upon the geological world. There's nothing about the world, *per se*---as it is in itself---that determined or *dictated to us* a 3-tiered English ontology of stone size. We could have made fewer distinctions between stones on the basis of size, or we could have made a lot more. Right? Look, Eskimos have a half dozen words for different kinds of snow. It's a matter of what we feel happens to be most convenient to us at the moment. It's a thing relative to our purposes, and subject even to fashion. It's a social construction. Different cultures can wield different cookie cutters on the same dough."

STUDENT: "Okay, but, good God man, it isn't *just* that! If there were nothing more to rocks than linguistic fashion, then we could create diamonds just by saying certain words."

PROFESSOR: "Well, yeah, that's right, we can. We can make diamonds out of pig's ears, just by changing our speech habits."

STUDENT: "Stop that! Can't you see that the craziness of those people you disavow is in fact your own doctrine, come home to roost? There's a huge difference between saying there were no pebbles, rocks, or boulders before there were English-speakers, and saying there were no *quote-unquote* 'pebbles,' 'rocks,' or 'boulders' before there were English-speakers. I don't mean to say that, before minds and English-speakers, there were *so-called, quote-unquote* 'rocks.' I mean *there were rocks*. And there were planets, and stars, and water, even if there weren't any *minds* around to notice them. And those planets and stars would have had more or less the same nature or properties, even if no minds had ever evolved to notice them, and if we all died tomorrow, and there were no longer any *minds* around, the Sun would not be harmed. Remember Lincoln's philosophy joke: how many legs does a dog have, if you call a tail a leg?"

PROFESSOR: "Five."

STUDENT: "Four! Calling a tail a leg doesn't make it one! And don't give me that stuff about how you can wield your own cookie cutters on the 'dough' any old way you please, the world as it is in itself is far more uneven than *dough*. The world is not like cookie dough or homogenized milk. It's more like chunky soup. It's lumpy. It's highly uneven. It already has independent, objective, pre-existing non-homogeneities in it, before you and your cookie cutter get there.

Reality is not *merely* a social construct. Even a dog or a newborn baby can see an objective difference between a tiger and a mouse, or between a black swan and a white swan, and this without ever having adopted any language, or conceptual scheme, or words, or names, like 'black' or 'white.' I just don't think an animal even has to have anything we'd call 'concepts,' in order for it to be able to perceive the difference between red hot coal and an ice cube, or a rock and a feather. The non-homogeneity of the world is a brute given, which forces itself upon us, without first getting permission from us to do so. But you always make it sound like that isn't true. You can call tails 'legs' if you want to, but even if the whole human race goes along with this new usage, merely doing that won't decrease the real, objective dissimilarity, between those things previously known as tails, and those previously known as legs. The real, objective things as they are in themselves remain unchanged."

One Truth, or Many?

PROFESSOR: "You need to understand my motives. You said the world is like chunky soup, that it's not like homogenized milk. So, how many objects are there in a bowl of chunky soup? And how many object types? Don't you see that you could ontologically divide up chunky soup many different ways, and more than one might be equally valid?"

STUDENT: "When did I ever deny that? What you *can't* do is decide that there's no natural, pre-existing distinction or difference between, say, a feather and a boulder. There are objective differences which really exist in themselves, and which force themselves upon us, whether we choose to acknowledge them or not. You can't erase those objective differences just by ignoring them, or refusing to acknowledge them. You could be deaf, dumb, blind, insensible, and in a deep sleep, and it would still make a *difference* to you whether or not it was a feather or a boulder that fell on you, and everybody in the world agreeing to call them both 'feathoulders' wouldn't change that fact, or eliminate that difference. The real, actual, objective, physical existence of that difference doesn't depend upon anybody's mind or language game. The fact that feathers are not the same as boulders wouldn't be any less true, nor any less a fact, even if there were not a single mind in the universe to notice it."

PROFESSOR: "Look, I already told you I'm not saying that *anything goes*. I said *nature shows us our mistakes*."

STUDENT: "Nature? I can only wonder what that word could possibly mean, on your lips! I wonder what more *you* could mean, when you say 'nature,' than a world of mere inviddied scene-imagery, where oars are really bent by water, tables shrink when you walk away, and stars are socially constructed or made out of words. Is your 'nature' just another of your 'mere appearances,' which exist only in you? Kant says 'the mind is the lawgiver of nature; save for it, nature would not exist at all.' In that case, how can this so-called 'nature,' a mere creature of your mind, also be *showing you your mistakes*? I don't get it."

PROFESSOR: "Your problem is that you think there's only one Truth. You think there's only one valid point of view, and only one true and complete description of the world."

STUDENT: "When did I ever say that? I said there's one *world*, one *reality*, not one *description* of reality. You're the one who can't tell the difference between words and the world---not me. The world isn't made out of words, any more than it's made out of thoughts, or mere perceptions of the mind. If I say 'there's only one truth,' I simply mean there's only one *world*, one *reality*, not that it can only be *described* in one way. Yes there's only one truth, but that doesn't mean there's only one way to express it. Where did you get the idea that I must believe otherwise?

And anyway, how is it supposed to be possible, for there to be more than one true way to describe the world, and more than one point of view from which to see it, if there isn't one real world out there for them all to be looking at from more than one point of view? If you want to say that two different descriptions of reality can both be true, then first of all you need one reality, one truth, for them to be two different versions *of*. You can't be seeing the same thing from a different point of view, if you aren't seeing the same thing in the first place."

PROFESSOR: "Wrong, because 'truth' cannot be a synonym for reality or the world, because 'truth' is a mere property of *statements*. Therefore, there can be no truth without language, and truth is merely a property or feature of linguistic entities. No language, no truth."

STUDENT: "Well, that's one way the word is used. But that's not the only way. People also use the word *truth* to mean *the* truth, as in reality, the world, the facts. The world outside your head."

PROFESSOR: "Well, *facts* are also purely linguistic."

STUDENT: "What?"

PROFESSOR: "*Facts* are linguistic things, *facts* are logical entities, like *sentences* and *propositions* are."

STUDENT: "What planet are you from?"

PROFESSOR: "Look, I'm not wedded to any particular doctrine. I'm really very flexible. I'm a pragmatist. I just believe in going with what works. I'm just trying to be practical, and not doctrinaire."

STUDENT: "Well, then I don't think your philosophy, as it is now, is working. Look how it's causing all this confusion, error and misunderstanding. Can't you see that something is deeply wrong with it?"

PROFESSOR: "Well, I've been around too long to return to your kind of *naiveté*. I know too much about the history of science to really suppose that today's version of physics is going to last. Our little quarks, forces, strings, electrons, and whatnot are eventually destined to go the way of yesterday's geometric corpuscles, effluvium, and *élan vital*..."

STUDENT: "Okay, I'm not denying that. I'm not putting my money on the reality of *quarks*. I'm going for rocks and apples. Do 'quarks' really exist? Who knows? I don't even know what a quark is. On the other hand, I would like to point out that rocks and apples have never gone out of style."

PROFESSOR: "Well, maybe that's just because we always need to eat."

STUDENT: "Or, *maybe* it's because they really exist, and would go *on* existing, even if there were no minds, or even if we stopped believing in them, or if we all dropped dead!   Look, why can't you admit that even as a *possibility*?"

PROFESSOR: "You're not taking seriously enough my point that, while we have our atoms and molecules, five thousand years ago it was all spirits, gods, and demons doing all the work. They just had a different ontology. We think of 'photons' as little 'particles,' as if they were teeny tiny grains of sand. Or 'waves,' as if light is ripples in a pond. You disparage metaphors, but can't you see that *these* are just metaphors? They're just mental tools we have fashioned for ourselves, in order that we might assimilate these tiny things to the medium-sized things with which we're acquainted in our everyday sense experience. Should we think that one of these ontologies is 'true,' and the other 'false,' ---or, rather, should we simply realize that they are both instruments, fashioned for our use?"

STUDENT: "You make it sound like the ancients' notion of mindful, soulful, animated little atomic demons filling the air, having wills, desires, thoughts, and intentions, was a physics no more false, or less true, than ours. I mean, ours is *better*."

PROFESSOR: "Sure it is. Because ours *works* better. We can do stuff with our physics that they couldn't do with theirs."

STUDENT: "Yeah but maybe it *works* better because it better corresponds to reality. Theirs was more false. They believed in demonic possession and disembodied minds. No doubt we're still getting it wrong, partly, but surely they got it even wronger. Hopefully, the scientists of the future will look down on us, just as we look down on the ancients. But won't they also admit that we weren't quite as bad as the ancients? Aren't our current scientific theories of, say, bacteria, *any* less false, than those of people who believed, or still believe, that what we call bacterial diseases, are caused by demonic possession? Today, we believe that what happened in Salem, Massachusetts was caused by a toxic mold that grew on their rye crop. But they followed their own textbooks, and instead called it witchcraft. Can't you admit that our belief, in this case, is probably more true and/or less false, than their belief?"

PROFESSOR: "I prefer to speak in terms of what works or doesn't work. If it works, then call it true. What more is there in being 'true,' practically speaking? I'm looking for the cash value."

STUDENT: "Well, I guess I see at least three problems with that. First is that I don't see why it's supposed to be somehow *easier* for us to know that anything *works*, than it is to know that anything is *true*. I mean, how could you possibly know that anything really does---as a matter of fact and existence---*work*, if you couldn't know that it's *true*---as a realistic matter of fact and existence---to think it does?

Secondly, saying 'if it works then its true,' leaves the hanging question of *why* some theories work better than others. Isn't the most likely *reason* they *work* better because they are somehow, in some way, more in conformity or correspondence with reality? I mean, I guess it *could* just be pure luck, and sometimes maybe that's all it is, but do you suppose that's all it *ever* can be? That just seems hard to believe.

Thirdly, if we should call whatever works 'true' then there's no such thing as a useful lie. If it's useful, if it works, then it's true. That's not right. And it isn't true. It's Orwellian to say 'whatever works is true.' The Party didn't *really* invent the airplane, even if it 'works,' for the Party, to say so. I mean, picture a prosecutor saying to his assistant, who objects to using illegally planted evidence: 'don't worry, if it works, then its true.' That's grotesque. Again, it seems like you've got it backwards. Better you should say 'if it's true then it works.' I like it that way."

PROFESSOR: "Well you're the one who suggested that theories that work must be working on account of their truth-value. So doesn't that drive you to believe that if it works, then it's true?"

STUDENT: "Yes, a little, but the two things aren't the same thing. It sometimes happens that a lie gets lucky and works for a while. That doesn't make it true for a while."

PROFESSOR: "So then 'it's true' just means 'it *keeps on* working'."

STUDENT: "No it doesn't. Something might be true that's never been tried. Maybe it would work if tried."

PROFESSOR: "Okay so 'true' just means '*if tried*, it keeps on working'."

STUDENT: "No, then a steel hammer would be 'true' if it never broke."

PROFESSOR: "I mean it 'works' to predict the future---it accords with the data of future experience."

STUDENT: "What about theories about the past?"

PROFESSOR: "Okay, it 'works' in the sense that it fits the data of experience, whether that data be experienced in the past, present, or future."

STUDENT: "Perfect. 'True' means it conforms to reality. In other words, it corresponds to the real world of things in themselves, the one real visible, palpable, pungent, audible, flavorful world of real, perceptible, empirical things in themselves. A world in which we all live together!"

PROFESSOR: "Unless you're just a mad, diseased brain hallucinating while asleep in a vat of chemicals in an otherwise lifeless universe made up almost entirely of empty sardine cans."

STUDENT: "Right."

Reference & the Oval Coin

PROFESSOR: "Okay. But, since, I'm not out of ammunition yet, please permit me to run by you one more of these old cases from the classics. It's the coin case. Look, here, in my hand I have a coin laying flat on my palm. Now, please notice that the coin as you see it, from your perspective over there, looks oval or elliptical, while the real coin as it is in itself is round like a circle. I mean, the appearance, the representation, or, shall we say, the coin as it is in terms of your scene-image of it, is in the shape of an ellipse, while the real coin in itself is round like a circle, and not shaped like an oval or ellipse. Do you understand?"

STUDENT: "Sheesh. Is this one supposed to be better? It's just the same. The coin I see is the real coin in itself, the round one. I believe the coin is round, and even looking at it sidelong, from over here, I can only say it looks like I'm right about that. It looks, it seems, it appears, like it's a normal, round coin lying on your hand, seen from the side."

PROFESSOR: "But you could be wrong?"

STUDENT: "Yes, I could be mistaken, I guess."

PROFESSOR: "You could be wrong."

STUDENT: "I suppose I could be wrong."

PROFESSOR: "Exactly. You see the problem?"

STUDENT: "What problem?"

PROFESSOR: "Skepticism! The skeptics are going to get you!"

STUDENT: "Well, we'll see about that. You haven't got me yet, so why should I be afraid of them? Are they tougher than you?"

PROFESSOR: "Yes, they *are*."

STUDENT: "Well let's worry about you first."

PROFESSOR: "Good, because I'm going to prepare you---to arm you---to disabuse you of your naiveté, so that you won't have to be afraid of the skeptics."

STUDENT: "Well, somebody around here is afraid of them."

PROFESSOR: "Ah, foolish lad..."

STUDENT: "Back to the coin."

PROFESSOR: "Yes, back to the coin. Okay, will you, at least, admit that, in terms of the scene-image at stake here, we can speak of an appearance with an oval or elliptical shape?"

STUDENT: "No."

PROFESSOR: "Why not?"

STUDENT: "Well first of all, I'm really not comfortable with this scene-image concept any more. It's just too misleading. It's a confused, ambiguous idea, and I don't really know what the term 'scene-image' does and doesn't refer to. I mean, we started out by trying to define the term with one example. Can one example a clear concept define? Trying to give birth to new concept like that, and then to proceed to use the term as if it really had some kind of meaning, a meaning that we both understand, and agree about---no.

But, on the other hand, I don't want to say I have no idea what you're thinking. That wouldn't be honest. Let's try a new way to say what you seem to me to be trying to say. Let's agree that we can say that if we're talking about the rods and cones on my retina, then maybe there's an elliptical area there, which is being stimulated by light that has bounced off the coin. I can agree to that. Just don't start with the "two coins" talk again, because that's a crock."

PROFESSOR: "Well it was nicer when you called it metaphor."

STUDENT: "Okay, metaphor. Whatever."

PROFESSOR: "Okay. So you think we need to replace this ambiguous talk of a 'scene-image,' with talk about a retina?"

STUDENT: "Yes I do."

PROFESSOR: "What's the point? What's the difference?"

STUDENT: "Well, at least I know what we're talking about. A retina is real. And it's something I can understand. I know what the word retina *means*. There's nothing murky or metaphorical about a retina."

PROFESSOR: "Suit yourself."

STUDENT: "Good. Okay, proceed with the coin argument."

PROFESSOR: "Okay, um, so, I'll just rephrase the argument using retina. No problem. Look, here, in my hand I have a coin laying flat on my palm. Now, please notice that the coin on your retina is elliptical, while the real coin in itself, as you know, is round."

STUDENT: "I have a coin in my eye?"

PROFESSOR: "Did I say that?"

STUDENT: "Well it sounded like you did."

PROFESSOR: "I didn't."

STUDENT: "Just so we're clear."

PROFESSOR: "I never said you had a coin inside your eyeball!"

STUDENT: "Are you sure about that?"

PROFESSOR: "Where did I say you had a coin in your eye?"

STUDENT: "Just checking."

PROFESSOR: "Sheesh."

STUDENT: "Are you going to tell me I have a coin inside my brain?"

PROFESSOR: "Did I *say* you have a coin inside your brain?"

STUDENT: "Not yet, but I'm starting to worry."

PROFESSOR: "Now who's worried?"

STUDENT: "I am. I don't want you to start saying people have coins in their heads."

PROFESSOR: "You're getting ahead of the story. Try to listen. Try to open your mind. Look, the appearance, or, shall we say, the coin as it is in terms of your retina, is in the shape of an ellipse, while the real coin in itself is round, like a circle, and not shaped like an oval or ellipse. The coin as it is to you, is oval, elliptical. The coin as it is in itself, is round, like a circle."

STUDENT: "There's one coin. The coin is real. The coin as it is to me is round like a circle. It looks round to me. I think it's round. It seems round. It appears to be round. It feels round. And, it really is round."

PROFESSOR: "Well, the coin as it is to your retina is not round. It's elliptical. The area of your retina struck by the light that bounced off the coin is an area that's shaped like an ellipse, not shaped like a circle!"

STUDENT: "Maybe."

PROFESSOR: "You know it's true!"

STUDENT: "Okay, okay, the retinal surface area in that case is, I suppose, not round like a circle, but oval like an ellipse. I guess."

PROFESSOR: "Bingo!"

STUDENT: "That's it?"

PROFESSOR: "That's it."

STUDENT: "I thought you were going to relieve me of my *naiveté*."

PROFESSOR: "I just did. You admitted you had an ellipse of some kind on your retina. Case closed. I win."

STUDENT: "I don't understand."

PROFESSOR: "What, do you want me to lay out the whole argument again?"

STUDENT: "Please."

PROFESSOR: "Well, okay, I'll lay out the whole thing, as before. Though I think you might have it memorized by now. With apologies to Hume:

> The image of the coin on your retina is oval, elliptical. But the real coin, which exists independent of us, is round like a circle. It is therefore, nothing but a retinal patch which is present to your mind. These are the obvious dictates of reason, and no man, who reflects, ever doubted, that the existences which we consider when we say "this coin" and "that ship," are nothing but retinal patches, and fleeting copies or representations of other existences, which remain uniform and independent. Therefore we must admit that the mind has never anything present to it but retinal images, and cannot possibly reach any experience of their connection with real objects in themselves. The supposition of such a connection is, therefore, without any foundation in reasoning."

STUDENT: "So, when we say *this coin,* really, we're simply referring to the elliptical patches on our retinas?"

PROFESSOR: "Now do you see why I said that we're looking at two different things?"

STUDENT: "Yes."

PROFESSOR: "So, now, you, too, agree that we're perceiving two different things?"

STUDENT: "No."

PROFESSOR: "Why not?"

STUDENT: "Well, first of all, because I object to this use of 'present to' for exactly the same reason I objected to your equivocal and fallacious use of the word 'seeing' to obfuscate the distinction between really seeing a real ship on the horizon and, so to speak, 'inviddying' a retinal patch caused by a real ship on the horizon. This phrase 'present to' in the argument is a kind of mask that serves to cover the distinction between something really being 'present to' you, in the way a real freight train is present to you when it's bearing down on you, and some other, very different sense in which a freight train is 'present to' your mind in a dream. They're not the same thing. I also object to the claim that when you say 'this coin,' you're referring to a patch on your retina---or on my retina either. That's just not true. If it were, you'd be saying that we've got at least two cents between us here. We'd have at least two 'coins' here. Nor does it follow, logically.

You're *referring to* the real coin, the one, single, real coin in itself. The round one. Not some elliptical-shaped patch of rods and cones on your retina, or my retina, or anybody else's retina. I don't have a coin in my eye, and neither do you. And I don't have a coin in my brain."

PROFESSOR: "Well, I'm not so sure I don't have a coin in my mind."

STUDENT: "Well I'm not so sure you don't either."

PROFESSOR: "Look---you keep insisting that you don't want me to talk as if there are two coins here. Okay. But can't you see that there are, so to speak, two different coins, in a certain sense? The first one, which Hume would call the 'real coin in itself,' is the one you say is round like a circle. The second one, which Kant would call 'the coin as it is for us,' is the elliptical one, with an oval shape. The first one is what a philosopher might call the noumenal coin, i.e., the real coin as it exists in itself. The second one is what philosophers call the phenomenal coin, i.e., the coin as phenomena, the coin as it appears to us, the coin as we perceive it."

STUDENT: "And this is not supposed to be mere poetry, mere metaphorical talk, right?"

PROFESSOR: "Right."

STUDENT: "So, since that coin in your hand is a penny, you're basically trying to convince me that between us we've got at least three cents here. I mean, we've got one circular, noumenal penny and two (or is it four?) oval, phenomenal ones between the two of us, so that's at least three cents, and maybe five cents, since we have two retinas each."

PROFESSOR: "No, no. The retinal or phenomenal coins exist only in the phenomenal realm, while the one noumenal coin as it is in itself exists in the noumenal realm."

STUDENT: "So there are two worlds now, one in which there's at least two cents, phenomenal, and another world in which we have 1 cent, noumenal. But in neither world do we have three cents. Unless we phone a friend, and get him to come over, in which case we can wind up phenomenally with at least three cents. Or should we call that six cents, since we each have two retinas? Hey, let's try this with a hundred dollar bill!"

PROFESSOR: "No. Wrong again. Your phenomenal world and mine are separate. There's no more than one cent in any one world."

STUDENT: "So, there's six billion worlds?"

PROFESSOR: "Okay, look, maybe I am speaking metaphorically. But, you know, maybe all talk is to some degree metaphorical. Is there really any such thing as a perfectly literal truth?"

STUDENT: "I don't know---why not? I'm holding an oar in my hand. That's pretty darn literal. Anyway, you're not going to deny that some ways of talking are a whole lot more literal than others?"

PROFESSOR: "Maybe."

STUDENT: "Okay then. Again, to me you simply seem addicted to loose talk. Instead of saying you have a 'coin' on your retina, you could have chosen to say you have a 'patch' or an 'area' on your retina. Your retina is in your eye. You don't have a coin in your eye. If you want to talk about an elliptical region on your retina, fine. Just don't start calling it a coin. And don't try to tell me that a retinal patch is all that a sober, wakeful person can possibly be seeing, when he looks at a real ship on the horizon, nor that a retinal region is the only thing that is present to him, in that case. If he's dreaming, then there's not a real ship present to him. But if it's a real ship, then it's really there, in itself, and really present to him. I mean, look, if that that ship over there on the horizon is real, then it doesn't just exist on your retina, and it's a whole lot farther away from you than your retina is."

PROFESSOR: "If."

STUDENT: "Yes, 'if.'"

PROFESSOR: "*If* I'm awake, *if* I'm sober, and not crazy, or mistaken."

STUDENT: "Yes."

PROFESSOR: "That's a big if."

STUDENT: "It's not too big."

PROFESSOR: "It looks like a very big if, to me: how can I ever know for certain that I'm awake, sober, sane, and not mistaken?"

STUDENT: "Why do you think you have to be 'certain'? Look, I can vouch for you being *awake*, but I don't know about *sane*. And I see a ship there too, so we'd *both* have to be mistaken, if it isn't really there."

PROFESSOR: "How do I know you're not a random brain-wave in my sleeping head, telling me all this?"

STUDENT: "Is this skepticism again?"

PROFESSOR: "Yes."

STUDENT: "I thought you said you were going to save me---that you were going to protect me from the skeptic."

PROFESSOR: "Exactly."

STUDENT: "Well, I don't quite know how to say this, but it seems to me, in my *naiveté*, that *you are him*."

PROFESSOR: "No, no, I'm not the skeptic."

STUDENT: "You're not?"

PROFESSOR: "No."

STUDENT: "Is Hume?"

PROFESSOR: "Is Hume a skeptic?"

STUDENT: "Yeah."

PROFESSOR: "Um, well, he certainly presents the skeptical case, yes."

STUDENT: "And then he shows where the holes are, in it? The fallacies?"

PROFESSOR: "Well, not exactly. I mean, the skeptical case doesn't really have, necessarily, any holes in it."

STUDENT: "It doesn't?"

PROFESSOR: "Not that I'm aware of."

STUDENT: "Are you saying that, in your opinion, the case for skepticism is fallacy-free, iron-clad, and water-tight, but *you're not a skeptic*? If I told you I thought the arguments for atheism were iron-clad, water-tight, and fallacy-free, but that I myself was a Christian, would you believe me?"

PROFESSOR: "Yeah. I mean, maybe you just have faith."

STUDENT: "A groundless faith, contrary to reason and evidence?"

PROFESSOR: "Sure, why not?"

STUDENT: "But why so---I mean, why choose one particular groundless and irrational dogma over a rival faith? I can only say I hope I may never be forced to such a dishonorable choice! Nobody would settle for that, if they didn't suppose they had to."

PROFESSOR: "Okay, if you're so darn clever, you show me a fallacy in the case for skepticism."

STUDENT: "Alright, then, bring it on. I'm ready. Let's take the bull by the horns."

PROFESSOR: "Indeed I will, but before I do, let me just offer to you one last time the weapons I think you're going to need to survive. I can't bear to see another kid bite the dust."

Losing the World

PROFESSOR: "So, for the last time, here's my advice. I think you'll find it a clever move. You chuck the noumenal world. Just get rid---altogether---of this crazy, unintelligible notion of a *ding an sich* existing independently of any perceiver. Call it *a world well lost.*"

STUDENT: "You mean chuck the *phenomenal* world."

PROFESSOR: "No, no---the noumenal world."

STUDENT: "Chuck the *noumenal* world? The one real world of objective things as they really are in themselves independently of our minds? That world? Get rid of it?"

PROFESSOR: "Yes."

STUDENT: "You're joking."

PROFESSOR: "Absolutely not."

STUDENT: "How do I do that?"

PROFESSOR: "You just say that the very idea of such a world is unintelligible. Then you're left with just one world, the world of phenomena."

STUDENT: "But doesn't that leave us with a radically different world for each mind?"

PROFESSOR: "Well, you only need to deal with the one world of things as they seem to you. Right? What cannot be a possible object of experience for you, need not concern you. I mean, let's be pragmatic."

STUDENT: "So I guess it would be crazy for me to buy life insurance."

PROFESSOR: "Well, no---er, I mean, it might make you feel better to have some."

STUDENT: "Make *me* feel better?"

PROFESSOR: "Yes."

STUDENT: "Not my *children*."

PROFESSOR: "Well, it might make a difference to their future experience, certainly."

STUDENT: "But I thought that what cannot be a possible experience for me, should not concern me."

PROFESSOR: "Well, I didn't mean it that way. Look, the point is, there's no way for us to step out from behind our own way of experiencing the world and see things as they really are in themselves, apart from our own subjective viewpoint. You can't view things from a God's eye point of view. You can only see things from some one particular human point of view."

STUDENT: "I don't understand. You seem completely hung up on an irrational false dilemma.[6] Why can't I see things as they really are in themselves, *while* viewing them from my own humble position? Why can't I get an imperfect peek, at a real, objective, independent world of things in themselves, while using my own imperfect eyeballs? Why do you insist that knowing what an apple tastes like *can't possibly* be a way of knowing *anything at all about* things as they really are in themselves?"

PROFESSOR: "Because that's impossible by definition."

STUDENT: "Really? How do you figure that?"

PROFESSOR: "Well, you need to understand that this idea of a *ding an sich,* or *thing in itself,* is really a bit of sophisticated academic Philosophy Department shoptalk. This is an expression coined by

Immanuel Kant, who wrote a lot of things like 'the objects with which we have to do in experience are by no means things in themselves but only appearances.' You see, Kant explains that 'the senses never and in no single instance enable us to know things in themselves.' And again, according to Kant's conceptual scheme, 'phenomena are not things in themselves, and are yet the only thing that can be given to us to know.' This is why he says 'how things may be in themselves is completely beyond the sphere of our knowledge.' I mean, Kant invented the idea of the thing in itself, and he himself said that 'things in themselves cannot be objects of experience.' That's why he says 'the understanding itself is the lawgiver of Nature; save through it, Nature would not exist at all.'"

STUDENT: "You are a lunatic."

PROFESSOR: "Well, you're an ignorant rube."

STUDENT: "Well, I guess I am, because I assumed that when Kant said that things in themselves are invisible, I figured he ripped that off from Hume's slightest philosophy. I mean, did Kant read Hume?"

PROFESSOR: "Well, yes, as a matter of fact, Kant really appreciated Hume. He said that Hume awakened him from his dogmatic slumber---something you'd be advised to consider."

STUDENT: "You're all crazy---you, Kant, and Hume."

PROFESSOR: "Well, I'm honored to be tossed in with the two greatest philosophers since the Middle Ages, thanks."

STUDENT: "Those two lunatics are supposed to be the greatest?"

PROFESSOR: "That's the general consensus, yes. Certainly they've been the most influential."

STUDENT: "Well, I guess that explains a lot. But, see here, I don't care how darn famous Kant is, still, I don't see why any amount of fame should give him the authority to declare to the whole human race that, *by definition,* 'the senses never and in no instance enable us to know things in themselves,' because 'the things with which we have to do in experience are never things in themselves' but 'appearances only,' and 'mere representations in us.' I mean, how is this claim supposed to differ from Hume's claim that 'nothing can ever be present to the mind but an image or perception'? Are those claims supposed to be true *by definition* too? No. Look, if Kant wants to make the same claim, fine, let him *argue* for it---like Hume and Berkeley did. Don't try to pull a fast one by telling me it's just 'true by definition.' Gimme a break!"

PROFESSOR: "Well, if Kant coined the phrase, then I guess he's entitled to define its meaning."

STUDENT: "Baloney. He's not coining any new words. He didn't invent the words, or the idea. Did he claim to be introducing a brand new concept, of his own invention?"

PROFESSOR: "Well, I'm not sure, but, look, you really are misunderstanding me again. I'm no fan of this notion of a 'thing in itself,' and, for that matter, neither was Kant! You need to understand that if you find this notion of a 'thing in itself' to be nonsense---so do we. As a matter of fact, *that's our whole point.* The very idea of a 'thing in itself' is misguided, it's a completely unintelligible concept. That's why I'm telling you that the answer is to just get rid of it. Now do you understand?"

STUDENT: "Are you nuts? The 'thing in itself' is the straight oar, the round coin, the one ship on the horizon, the single blue rowboat, and the non-shrinking table. You want me to get rid of the round coin and the straight oar? Forget that. I'm going to chuck something all right, but it's not going to be the round coin and the straight oar; it's going to be the oval coin and the crooked oar, and the two blue boats, the shrinking table, and the six different ships on the horizon, and the inviddied scene-images. You keep your phenomenal world, I prefer the real world of things able to exist apart from subjective mental perceptions of them. I prefer the world with prehistoric rocks, reasons for buying life insurance, and objective apples which are sometimes more than 'mere perceptions in the mind,' and aren't 'the same waking that dreaming.'"

PROFESSOR: "I don't think you understand. Hume didn't draw this distinction between the phenomenal world versus the noumenal world. That's Kant."

STUDENT: "I thought you told me it was Hume who drew that distinction between '*the table which we see,*' and '*the real table which exists independent of us.*'"

PROFESSOR: "Well, yes, that was from Hume."

STUDENT: "So, I thought 'the table we see' is supposed to be the phenomenal table, and 'the table which exists independent of us' is the noumenal table."

PROFESSOR: "Well, no---you're projecting Kantianism backwards upon Hume, which I'm not sure is proper."

STUDENT: "No, I'm projecting Humeanism forward onto Kant, which seems to me highly plausible. You said Kant read Hume, right?"

PROFESSOR: "Okay, but we should follow the principle of charity and give Kant the benefit of the doubt. I mean, at least let Kant speak for himself. When Kant speaks of the thing in itself, *perhaps* he's referring to something other than Hume's 'real table which exists independent of us'."

STUDENT: "I don't understand. What else could Kant possibly have had in mind?"

PROFESSOR: "Maybe he meant, you know, what I said he meant, before when you said you didn't think I should be treating it as if Kant had coined a new word."

STUDENT: "You mean maybe, instead of Hume's 'real table which exists independent of us,' perhaps I should rather suppose that Kant had in mind some other idea of a 'thing in itself'---namely, that notion which you insisted was completely unintelligible?"

PROFESSOR: "Basically."

STUDENT: "I thought you said we should be charitable."

PROFESSOR: "Well, look, obviously, you cannot disagree with Kant until you first understand what the man was saying. And you'll certainly not be able to understand what he was saying, until you first understand what he meant by a *ding an sich*, or *things as they are in themselves*. Nobody can possibly understand Kant if they don't understand this."

STUDENT: "But according to you, nobody can! You said it was a completely unintelligible notion."

PROFESSOR: "Well, I think I understand it."

STUDENT: "Please---let me in on the secret."

PROFESSOR: "You see, um, when Kant refers to *things as they are in themselves*, what he means is external objects as they are conceived by the *realist*. You know, such as yourself."

STUDENT: "I couldn't agree more."

PROFESSOR: "Okay, so that's the problem."

STUDENT: "Problem? I don't see any problem. If he says that objects as I, the realist, understand them are things as they actually are in themselves, then he seems to be saying I've got it right---practically by definition. Great! I should consider this a problem?"

PROFESSOR: "No, no, I didn't mean it like that. Heh. I mean, ah, he says, for example, that

> All objects of an experience possible for us are nothing but appearances, i.e., mere representations, which have outside our thoughts no existence grounded in itself. But the *realist* makes these modifications of our sensibility into things subsisting in themselves, and hence makes mere representations into things in themselves.[7]

Now do you see?"

STUDENT: "Yes, sure I do. He seems to understand me quite well! I'm saying just what he says I'm saying. I'm saying that the very things you feel and see are things in themselves, which, as he so nicely puts it, 'subsist in themselves,' and 'have an existence outside our thoughts.' Really, I could hardly have said it better."

PROFESSOR: "Well, here, remember that I'm just trying to explain to you what *Kant* meant by that famous, tricky phrase: '*things as they are in themselves.*' Do you have some understanding now of its meaning?"

STUDENT: "Absolutely. He just means, you know, tables and chairs, as I, the realist, understand them. Surely, nothing could be easier than that, for me to understand. He means rocks and trees and freight trains."

PROFESSOR: "No, no! Aren't you paying attention? Rocks and trees and freight trains are *phenomena*---mere representations--- nothing but appearances which have outside our thoughts no existence."

STUDENT: "The *heck* they are!"

PROFESSOR: "I mean, that's what they are *for Kant.* I'm just trying to get you to understand, just a little bit, one of the greatest thinkers who ever lived. I'm just explaining the meaning of certain crucial *expressions* he used, and their place in the overall scheme of his philosophy. Okay?"

STUDENT: "No you're not. You're trying to *convert* me to it. If realism is true, and Kant is wrong, then tables and chairs and rocks and trees *are* independent things in themselves able to subsist outside our thoughts. Phenomena are noumena; if I'm right, and he's wrong, then these two are one and the same, whether Immanuel Kant thinks they are the same or not. You shamelessly beg the question."

PROFESSOR: "Okay, so, I guess you're saying you want to amend Kant, to reverse his doctrine, and instead say that 'the things with which we have to do in experience' *are* real, objective, independent things in themselves."

STUDENT: "Sort of. Except, rather than saying I'm *amending* Kant, I'd prefer to say I'm completely rejecting Kant---and Hume with him. As I said, if you don't drink the Kool-Aid in the first place, you don't need to run around for the next couple hundred years looking for an antidote."

PROFESSOR: "Well, I find that incredibly presumptuous, on the part of a complete novice, a newcomer to the practice of philosophy, to presume to toss into the garbage the greatest works of the two greatest practitioners in the field. Ya think?"

STUDENT: "What other choice do I have? I mean, it's them or the world. How can I possibly accept a doctrine that first of all, leads to absurdity, and secondly, isn't compelling? I can't go along with it. The only reasonable response to an argument that is less than compelling and leads to absurdities is just to reject it. Especially if you seem to have a perfectly good alternative, which also happens to accord with common sense. And if I'm going to avoid ending up like you, then the only way to do that, is to reject Hume and Kant from the start. It seems to me that if you had done the same, when you were a beginner, you would have avoided all sorts of later problems."

PROFESSOR: "Well, if you're going to cling so tenaciously to your naive, vulgar realism, then you're talking about rejecting so much of the philosophy canon that I'm not sure I can even see you as a person who is a part of the community of people who are practicing Philosophy."

STUDENT: "Well, if people can't be allowed to reject this doctrine and still be considered philosophers, then philosophy would be just another moribund religion. I don't think that's the case. Are these books of the philosophy canon supposed to be treated like Holy Scriptures?"

PROFESSOR: "No, of course not."

STUDENT: "Okay. So, the thing is, maybe philosophy should do a little soul-searching, when you think about the fact that they don't start out the freshmen in *medical* schools by telling them to read Galen, Pasteur, and Harvey---you know, as truly great and necessary as those guys undoubtedly were, in their day. Nor does the physics department still cling to the doctrine of phlogiston. A field has to progress."

PROFESSOR: "The problem is, the way you see things, you're proposing to do more than just prune the tree a little. You're proposing to saw through some of the fattest limbs."

STUDENT: "If a limb is dead, then so are its twigs. I'm sure the roots are strong enough that the tree will survive. Besides, the bad old branches are starving potentially better, new branches of the nutrition they need to grow."

Peirce and Turkey Ham

PROFESSOR: "Well, I'm not ready to toss my canonical books into the garbage can quite so fast. You know, I think I should point out, in defense of Kant, that you need to realize that, unlike me, he never doubted or denied the actual existence of an objective, external world of mind-independent things in themselves. I mean, I don't want you to go away with a misunderstanding of his views, on account of me. Kant thought that things in themselves certainly do exist independently of the mind, but the problem is simply that, as he says, 'we can have no knowledge of them at all.' His point is that the only knowledge we can ever have is knowledge about appearances and not about things as they are in themselves. What we know is things as they seem to us, not things as they are. That's why he says the things with which we have to do in experience are not things in themselves, but appearances only."

STUDENT: "Well, I guess the nicest thing I can say about that doctrine, is that I'm sympathetic to your charge that there's something in Kant that's radically unintelligible. And also that perhaps this does prove that you at least tried, to move away, a little, from Kant. But if you're trying to say that this Kantian doctrine is somehow opposed to Hume's doctrine on the same subject, I really don't see any interesting difference."

PROFESSOR: "Well, never mind that, what about the validity of Kant's doctrine, in itself?"

STUDENT: "Well, for a guy who claims to be looking for the cash value, I wonder what you suppose the cash value of Kant's doctrine to be."

PROFESSOR: "Well, for one thing, it's good for refuting superstitions and settling meaningless disputes."

STUDENT: "Really?"

PROFESSOR: "Yeah."

STUDENT: "Like what?"

PROFESSOR: "Well, take the old Christian dispute over transubstantiation, for example. The claim is that during the ritual of communion, the wine is magically turned into blood, *really,* turned into blood, even though it retains all the sensible effects of wine. So, they said, it still looks like wine, tastes like wine, smells like wine, etc., but is actually blood."

STUDENT: "That's a hoot."

PROFESSOR: "Well Charles Peirce analyzed the doctrine of transubstantiation by pointing out that 'we can mean nothing by wine but what has certain effects, direct or indirect, upon our senses; and to talk of something as having all the sensible characters of wine, yet being in reality blood, is senseless jargon.'[8]"

STUDENT: "Well, I could think of better ways to deal with the question of transubstantiation. Like by asking for some reason to think this stuff that tastes like wine and just came out of a wine bottle isn't just *wine*. That seems to be the more obvious, more plausible, and simpler explanation for the taste and color---so why reject it?

Besides, I've eaten margarine that seems just like butter, and I've had turkey you'd *swear* was ham, so obviously Peirce is barking up the wrong tree. According to Peirce, kosher turkey ham can't exist. To our five senses it appears to be ham---it looks like ham, tastes like ham, smells like ham, feels like ham---but in its substance as it is in itself---in its deeper, hidden nature---it's actually turkey.

Peirce says, 'we can mean nothing by wine but what has certain effects, direct or indirect, upon our senses.' But is that supposed to mean that, when I talk about you, I can mean nothing more than what has certain effects, direct or indirect, upon *my* senses? Don't you think there's something more to you than just that? Something like how you are, in yourself, apart from my perception of you? I mean, would it merely be *senseless jargon,* for me to talk about how you might feel after my death?"

PROFESSOR: "Well, maybe a Kantian would say that I'm something like the sum of all perceptions of me, including my own perceptions of myself, and other people's perceptions of me, that will continue on after your demise."

STUDENT: "How could two different people both have perceptions of you, if you're nothing more to me than a bundle of my perceptions? Where's the string that bundles the various perceptions, making them all perceptions of the same person? The only string that bundles up all the various perceptions of a thing, into one bundle, is the thing itself you keep trying to deny. The only string that ties together your oarish scene-imagery and my oarish scene-imagery, and makes them perceptions of the same oar, is the oar itself, out there, between us. Is it 'senseless jargon' for me to speak of the existence of some asteroid that might appear in the future which nobody yet has perceived?"

PROFESSOR: "Maybe it exists as a potential future set of perceptions."

STUDENT: "What about prehistoric rocks or other objects that nobody ever did, or ever will, or ever can, perceive? Is it senseless jargon for us to talk about them? I wonder how they can even be believed to have existed, according to your philosophy. And how do you avoid solipsism? The way anti-realists talk, they sound like convinced solipsists themselves.

I mean, if all the anti-realist means to say is that we need to remember that the only way a human being can form his ideas about objects in the outside world is by using the materials afforded to his mind by his actual experiences, then that doesn't sound bad. If all they mean to say is that your conception of things in themselves are not the things in themselves but only conceptions of and ideas about those things, conceptions that you've constructed in your mind by building them out of notions you derived originally from the data of experience, that would be fine. If all Kant wanted to prove was that there's more to know about the world than you can gather by one glance---that would be fine too. He could have merely pointed out that the way the world looks to you is not necessarily exactly the same as the way it looks from the point of view of other people or other animals. He might have suggested that we should wonder if perhaps the only things we can imagine are things we can, literally, *imagine*. He might have observed that we can't *say* anything about anything without using some socially-constructed language. These are all dandy points to make, I guess.

But, if that's all the anti-realists *mean*, then why isn't that what they say? The fact is, that *isn't* what they say. Kant, for example, says *the objects with which we have to do in experience are by no means things in themselves but only appearances,* and that *appearances are not things, but rather nothing but representations, and they cannot exist at all outside our minds.*[9] He says *all bodies together with the space in which they are, must be considered nothing but mere representations in us, and exist nowhere but in our thoughts.*[10] He says *your object is merely in your brain.*[11] He says *the non-sensible cause of these representations is entirely unknown to us.*[12] He says *if I remove the thinking subject, the whole corporeal world must at once vanish."*[13]

PROFESSOR: "Well, what's your objection to that?"

STUDENT: "Look, what I keep trying to say is that it never seems to occur to Kant that maybe to know how things appear to your humble, imperfect sensing apparatus *is* to know something (not everything, but something) *about* things as they are in themselves. For example, *you know what they look like. You know what they feel like.*

Just suppose, *hypothetically*, for a *moment*, that my naive, vulgar, godless realism is true. Now, if you've ever once been awake and aware and not insane, if you're not, after all, a brain in vat but a material human animal with a conscious brain, and your brain is in your head, and your mind is in your brain, and you have really eaten a mind-independent apple, or seen a mind-independent ship on the horizon, *then* you've done something besides 'merely' seeing a patch on your own retina. In that, shall we say, *hypothetical* case, can you not at least *agree*, that an independent, external apple really eaten by a materialistic human animal *would be, in that lucky, happy, hypothetical case*, something a little more substantial than a 'mere appearance,' or 'mere perception in the mind'?

When you eat an apple, you don't insert it into your mind. It goes down into your stomach. Can you not see, that if there were mosses before there were minds, then those mosses must have been able to be something a little more substantial than *mere* perceptions in the mind? Your mind is in you, and those long-gone mosses never could be."

PROFESSOR: "Okay, look, maybe you just need to stop taking Kant so literally when he says things like '*your object is merely in your brain.*'[14] Okay? Maybe the point we need to take away from Kant is simply that to know merely what things look like from my own humble, limited perspective is not to perceive things from some omniscient God's eye view, independently of my own type of senses and mental ways of understanding. Maybe that's the point. And if so, then maybe that's the point you're missing."

STUDENT: "Missing? Missing how? When? Where? I'm not missing *that* point. I never have. Who would? Who ever claimed to be omniscient, or to see things from a God's eye point of view? If that's Kant's point, then it's an incredibly trivial point, and an insulting straw man. Everybody knows things look different from different angles. Everybody knows we don't all find lobster equally delicious. Everybody knows some people are blind, and some are deaf. Nobody pretends they see the world from a God's eye view!"

PROFESSOR: "Okay, then---fine. Good. We're in agreement then.

I don't know what all the fuss has been about. So, as you see, you have now come to admit that you can't, after all, see things as they really are in themselves."

STUDENT: "Wrong! I can see, for example, that you have mustard on your chin! You don't even know that about yourself. It isn't just that *from my perspective* you have mustard on your chin, and from some other perspective you don't have mustard on your chin. It's an objectively true fact, about you as you really are in yourself, that you actually have mustard on your chin, and you would have it still, even if nobody ever noticed it!"

PROFESSOR: "But what does that statement really *mean*? It simply means that, if a human with good eyesight looks closely, he will experience a sensation of yellowness, etc. As Kant said:

> That there may be inhabitants in the moon although no one has perceived them must surely be admitted. This, however, only *means* that in the possible advance of experience we may encounter them.[15]

As Berkeley explained:

> The table I write on I say exists, that is, I see it and feel it; and if I were out of my study I should say it existed---*meaning* thereby that if I were in my study I might perceive it.

Or, as Hume put it,

> These are the obvious dictates of reason; and no man, who reflects, ever doubted, that the existences, which we consider, when we *say*, this house and that tree, are nothing but perceptions in the mind[16]

STUDENT: "Well that's sure not what I mean to say, when I say 'that tree!' When I say 'that tree', I *mean* that actually existing thing in itself which would still perfectly happily subsist and exist and grow and flower, even if we'd never been born. And when I say I slammed my forehead on a branch, I don't mean I hit my head on a mere perception of the mind, or conked my noggin on a mental representation, or got a bruise from an angry mob of sense data."

PROFESSOR: "Okay but you're not going to deny that you think you probably ran into a swarm of atoms, are you?"

STUDENT: "Of course not. I have no reason to deny that."

PROFESSOR: "Okay. But, can't you see that your realism is vulnerable to skepticism? The problem is, how do you know you've ever *really* seen a *ding an sich*, or slammed your forehead against one, as you say you have?"

STUDENT: "How do you know I *haven't*?"

PROFESSOR: "I never said I knew you haven't."

STUDENT: "Well Kant did. According to him, it's impossible! It's like you and Kant have reacted to the worry that you *might* be in the position of a clueless brain in a vat, by deciding that, in fact, you *are*--- and can't be otherwise."

PROFESSOR: "Well, you have to admit it's a gutsy move. As the saying goes: if you're falling, *dive*. In fact, you have to admit that, if he's right, then Kant's truly the greatest philosopher who ever lived."

STUDENT: "I'll admit that, if you admit that if Kant is wrong, then it's the proudest heap of steaming humbug the world has ever seen."

PROFESSOR: "At least we agree on its importance. Okay, look, I think I understand that what you're trying to say is that you can't see why it should be held to be impossible to learn something about how things independently are in themselves by means of our familiarity with their appearances. So what's the cash value of *that* doctrine?"

STUDENT: "I don't know. I'm not just looking for cash value, I'm also looking for truth. I'm taking your doctrine and reversing it: I don't have a *use* in mind for the doctrine, yet. Instead, I'm just going on the assumption that, to the extent that a belief is true, it tends to work. I'd rather take a voyage with the most accurate map I can get."

PROFESSOR: "Truth! Ah, yes, the big enchilada. Good luck with that quest."

STUDENT: "You want cash value? Look, Kant says 'space is in us.' If *your* world is in *your* mind, and *my* world is in *my* mind, then you and I just cannot be in the same world. I'm sorry, but if you're a *mere appearance*, if you 'don't exist at all outside of my thoughts,' and 'are nothing apart from them,' as Kant repeatedly insists, then it would just be insane and irrational for me to make you the beneficiary of my life insurance policy, because when I die, *you'll be gone.*

I'll also need to cancel my membership in the Save the Rainforest Club, since it would be crazy for me to suppose that there will be any so-called, quote-unquote, 'rainforest' existing apart from or independently of my mind after I die. Ditto for the so-called, quote-unquote, ozone layer. As a matter of fact, I have to wonder how it can even be rational for you to care about *other people's feelings* at all, if things which cannot possibly be an experience for you, such as their inner sufferings, are to you nothing?"

PROFESSOR: "Okay, okay, so now you're speaking my language. I'm beginning to see some cash value that might be at stake here. So maybe society does need your vulgar doctrine of realism in order to function more smoothly."

STUDENT: "Do you mean, maybe realism is true?"

PROFESSOR: "I didn't say that."

STUDENT: "So, you take pains to avoid saying maybe realism is *true*, and yet you admit it may be useful, and perhaps even indispensable?"

PROFESSOR: "That's right."

STUDENT: "How now? What happened to your doctrine that if it works, then it's true?"

PROFESSOR: "Well---hey, you tried to talk me out of that."

STUDENT: "So I did. Fair enough. But, then, I wonder what there is left, at this point, to make you think realism might be just a useful lie, instead of true?"

PROFESSOR: "True, false, useful, useless---look, you've got to understand. I've merely been trying to give you the best advice I can. The fact is, I've got far, far more experience in these matters than you do. Young people do well to listen to those with a lot of experience, and should not necessarily reject everything their teachers can't cogently argue for. Just because your parents can't rattle off a water-tight argument proving with certainty everything they tell you, doesn't mean you'd be smart to ignore their advice. Doddering old fools usually possess precious wisdom of which the cleverest teenager has no clue.

If a vulgar *naiveté* is the way you want to play it, be my guest. Have it your way and good luck. I still fear the skeptics are going to get you, so don't say I didn't warn you. Better anti-realism, than radical skepticism."

STUDENT: "Better? I wonder why I should prefer to see the world lost by the one, rather than by the other."

Color and Subjectivity

PROFESSOR: "The question is whether your vulgar realism can survive in a harsh climate. You say the world is not like dough, but instead contains real, objective, pre-existing non-homogeneities. But let's take the case of a person who is completely, totally red-green colorblind. For him, there is no difference between red and green: the two colors look alike. What to you is a gaudy red and green striped shirt may be for him a shirt of one single, solid, dull color not unlike gray. And heaven knows what it looks like to a fly or a bat. Therefore, we *don't* see the same things, after all. What if there was an entire planet of red-green colorblind people? What to you is a sharp and clear objective distinction out there in the world between red and green, is for them, in their world, no difference at all. For them, that difference doesn't exist."

118

STUDENT: "Yes it does!"

PROFESSOR: "No it doesn't."

STUDENT: "*Yes it does*. They still live in the same reality that I do. Just because they have never perceived the distinction between red and green, that doesn't mean the difference doesn't exist. The difference between red and green is just as real and objective for them as it is for us. The only difference is they're ignorant about it and we aren't. As a matter of fact, we could show them the difference between red and green if we met them, and prove to them that it's real."

PROFESSOR: "No we couldn't."

STUDENT: "Yes we could! Look, suppose you're totally red-green color blind, and I give you two glasses full of oil paint, one red and one green, which look alike to you. Now I tell you I'll pay you a million dollars if you can tell them apart, (but no asking other people, that's cheating). You have to tell me if they're the same color or not, and if not, which one is the red one. Why can't you test them for the presence or absence of cadmium, or use some kind of special instrument that can measure the difference in the wavelengths of the light they reflect in the sunshine? Conversely, if you find out they have the same chemical ingredients, you'll know they must be the same color."

PROFESSOR: "What about poinsettias? Are you sure the red leaves contain different ingredients from the green ones?"

STUDENT: "No, but, there must be some mind-independent difference, they just can't be perfectly identical *in every way* and yet reflect light differently. There must be something in them, some reason why they look different."

PROFESSOR: "What about the fact that two things might seem to you to appear to be the same color, and yet some light-sensing instrument might be able to tell them apart as different colors?"

STUDENT: "Yeah, so what?"

PROFESSOR: "So, your paint story isn't going to prove that the human race hasn't missed a few real differences, no less than those color-blind people had missed one, before you showed it to them. I mean, there's all sorts of electro-magnetic 'colors' or wavelengths that all humans are blind to. Humans are all 'ultraviolet blind' and 'infrared blind,' for example."

STUDENT: "Of course. But ask yourself: did that result in the *non-existence* of the ultraviolet/infrared difference *for* mankind? No. Not only do we have infrared glasses we can wear now, but, more importantly, the difference between infrared and ultraviolet light *always existed in reality*, and therefore always existed "for us," even *before* we were able to perceive that difference. People still got sunburned by ultraviolet rays, and not by infrared ones, even before they knew the difference, or could put on glasses which allowed them to see the difference."

PROFESSOR: "So what?"

STUDENT: "So that should give you pause with regard to your weird Kantian fork of noumena vs. phenomena, or mere appearance versus things in themselves. I don't see how you can analyze this stuff in accord with Kant."

PROFESSOR: "Well, what if I just say that when you put on infrared glasses you obtain a different phenomenal world than you used to have?"

STUDENT: "You mean when I put on infrared glasses, I'm literally (not just metaphorically) transported into a different world? I can just imagine somebody using that as an alibi in court. *Your honor, I couldn't have committed the crime yesterday, because I wasn't even there. I was in a different world all day yesterday: I had my Army-issue infrared glasses on.*"

PROFESSOR: "That's a straw man. I don't think things like that.

You're twisting my words, just like when you try to lump me together with all those crazy postmodernists."

STUDENT: "Well, the trouble for me is that you never seem to show me how your philosophy is in a position to stop the slide down that slippery slope to the lunatic hordes. You remind me of a radical idealist who tries to fend off solipsism by saying you can't tar him with solipsism because *he* doesn't actually happen, *personally*, to believe he's the only conscious person. That's a lame response, because obviously the point is that he's got himself to where he's in no position to say any other minds exist, and that's the problem."

PROFESSOR: "Well people in glass houses shouldn't throw stones."

STUDENT: "I'll quit throwing stones just as soon as you can show me that I'm in a glass house."

PROFESSOR: "Okay, look, let me try it the other way: can't I just say that any difference, that makes a difference, in experience, is *phenomenal*, and that therefore there always was a phenomenal distinction, between ultraviolet and infrared rays?"

STUDENT: "That's better, but still seems wrong. For example, it still seems to me that you can't have anything *phenomenal* existing before the evolution of life."

PROFESSOR: "For Kant."

STUDENT: "Well if you're not a Kantian, why have anything to do with his implausible scheme?"

PROFESSOR: "Well, I'm thinking maybe we can interpret all statements phenomenalistically, as being statements about how things *would* have seemed to us, had we been there, then."

STUDENT: "Wait a minute, now. Something is wrong here. If things like infrared light, atoms, electrons, x-rays, are going to be considered 'phenomena,' then that means they *aren't* going to be 'noumena,' or 'things in themselves.' Right?"

PROFESSOR: "Right."

STUDENT: "And yet, I was just thinking maybe we could try to be charitable and understand Kant as having had something like atoms or light waves in mind, when he talked about a noumenal world of imperceptible, unperceived 'things in themselves' which *cause* our sensations. Yet, here you are, now, saying that Kantian 'things in themselves' cannot be something like atoms or light waves or other scientific-theoretic indiscernibles. Because, you say, you think Kantian things in themselves need to be rejected. So that rules out this possible interpretation of Kant, which I thought might be more charitable to him."

PROFESSOR: "Well that's just the beauty of it! Don't you see? I chuck Kant's world of mind-independent 'things in themselves.' I toss it. Get rid of it. Throw it away. It's *phenomena* all the way down. It's *all* phenomena. That's what's so good about my philosophy. You yourself can see that Kant's noumenal world is an unintelligible notion, so why cling to it? As I said before: it's *a world well lost*. Now do you see?"

STUDENT: "No!"

PROFESSOR: "What's wrong?"

STUDENT: "What I want to reject is the very distinction Kant made between phenomena and mind-independent things in themselves. I don't want to keep one of the two and reject the other. I want to reject them both---I want to reject the whole scheme. I want to keep half of each side, and put those two halves back together as one. I say 'the oar you see' *is* the straight, independent one, 'the table you see' *is* the 'real one that suffers no shrinking.' Don't you understand? If you say let's keep the phenomena and chuck the *ding an sich*, you're saying let's keep the bent oar and the oval coin and reject the straight oar and the round coin. You're saying let's keep the hallucinatory dog and reject the gnarled stump; let's keep the child's imaginary tiger and reject the striped pajamas.

Besides, if you want to make everything phenomenal, then your move puts the whole world inside your mind. There's no longer a far-away ship, just a retinal pattern. There's no longer a world outside you, just irritations in your nerve-endings. Everything is inside you. It's rank idealism!"

PROFESSOR: "Absolute idealism."

STUDENT: "It's loony solipsism. You're moving away from Kant only to fly into the arms of Berkeley!"

PROFESSOR: "Hegel."

STUDENT: "If it's *phenomena* all the way down, then it's your *mind* all the way down, and life insurance is irrational. You need to reject the *whole* picture. You need to see that it was a mistake, from the very beginning---from the first time somebody said that what you perceive exists only in you. That's the fatal premise. If you reject it from day one, none of these crazy paradoxes arise."

PROFESSOR: "Hmmm. Okay, okay, how about this move. I put the world inside my mind, but I take my mind out of my brain. So, now, the world is in my mind, but my mind is out of my head."

STUDENT: "It certainly is."

The Kantian Blind Alley

PROFESSOR: "Okay, smart guy, hold on just a minute. It seems to me you just contradicted yourself. First you told me that Kant's imperceptible things in themselves were things like atoms, x-rays or subatomic particles, and then you said they were things like the straight oar and the round coin. Which is it? Are you saying you think Kant meant it both ways?"

STUDENT: "I don't know. I was trying to do my best to find a way to be charitable to Kant. But it isn't working. Because, either way, I run into a wall. If you want me to go with the latter, then we're stuck in a crazy world where oars are really bent by water, coins truly undulate when you move your head, and tables actually shrink when you walk away. On the other hand, if Kant's 'things in themselves' are things like molecules and atoms, then the sciences of chemistry and subatomic physics are nothing better than senseless jargon and impossible nonsense, since the whole purpose of chemistry and physics is to declare upon the nature of things as they are in themselves, apart from the mere representations of our human sense organs."

PROFESSOR: "No, no. That's not what Kant means! You don't understand. There's nothing wrong with a Kantian doing chemistry and physics!"

STUDENT: "Yes there is. In painting class you study how a table appears to our sensibility. You study color, shading, and perspective. But in chemistry and physics, you try to inquire into how the table may be in itself, rather than merely how it appears to your human sense organs. To say it's brown and shiny, and cold and hard, is to say how it appears to our sensibility. But to say that it is made out of molecules or atoms or subatomic particles or vibrating strings, is to talk about the way it exists in itself, apart from our mere sensibility. Kant rejects chemistry and physics."

PROFESSOR: "No, no! You've got it all wrong. I don't know where you got this ridiculous idea."

STUDENT: "I got it from Kant! He says:

> If then, as this critical argument obviously compels us to do, we hold fast to the rule above established, and do not push our questions beyond the limits within which possible experience can present us with its object, we shall never dream of seeking to inform ourselves about the objects of our senses as they are in themselves.[17]

So it's wrong to try to engage in chemistry or subatomic physics, and scientists ought to prefer painting."

PROFESSOR: "*That* isn't what it means!"

STUDENT: "It isn't?"

PROFESSOR: "No! You don't know what you're talking about. Kant accepted science. He himself was a scientist."

STUDENT: "Well, maybe he was a hypocrite then."

Inferring Things

PROFESSOR: "Okay, look, we don't need to get into a big interpretation dispute about Kant. What really matters is that your kind of realism isn't going to work."

STUDENT: "Why not?"

PROFESSOR: "Because if you want to claim that *the thing you see is outside your mind*, then you're going to have to show how you can logically *infer* the existence of the external object from your inner experiences or mere sensations."

STUDENT: "I don't understand. Why do I have to show that I can logically infer the existence of an oar, if I'm holding the darn thing in my hand? Isn't being able to hold an oar in my hand better than being able to *infer* one? Why should I hanker after inferring apples, if I can eat them? Why do I have to infer the existence of rocks, if I can see them? What makes you prefer the logical inference? Doesn't seeing things beat merely inferring them?"

PROFESSOR: "Inferring them gives you more certainty than seeing them. The trouble with saying that you can *see* them is that you might just be crazy or dreaming, and therefore, you can't tell what's really out there and what isn't."

STUDENT: "You make it sound like everyone must be hopelessly crazy, because nobody can tell reality from delusion."

PROFESSOR: "Well, in a certain sense, they can't."

STUDENT: "What, never? So nobody, ever, has, even once, been able to tell reality from non-reality? Nobody can tell dreams from waking, or figure out that optical illusions are illusory, or tell hallucination from sobriety? Well then, how could we ever have obtained the idea that illusions are even possible? You don't call something an 'illusion,' if you can't tell that it *is* one. I admit I'm fallible, but the only reason I admit I'm fallible is because I believe I've made mistakes. And the only reason I believe I've made mistakes, is because I think I've been able to *detect* them---to *catch* them, later. If you don't think you can tell fantasy from reality, then what reason do you have to suppose that you know that mistakes are even possible?"

PROFESSOR: "Well, I can sense contradictions."

STUDENT: "I guess that's a start."

PROFESSOR: "Look, let's just stick with the brain in the vat story. The point is that the vat-brain represents a logical possibility."

STUDENT: "Logical possibility does not probability make. Besides, if I'm a deranged, diseased, psychotic brain hooked up to electrodes and floating in a vat of fluid, then what good does it do me to suppose I've successfully performed an *inference*? Surely, I could be just as deluded about that. Even if you *thought* that you had never made a wrong inference, you still couldn't be sure it had never happened. Besides, people make errors in pure math and logic problems all the time. If it's absolute certainty you're looking for, then it's no less conceivably possible to wrongly believe you've successfully *inferred* something, than to wrongly believe you've successfully *seen* or *touched* something. Conceivably, I suppose, both are fallible, so why prefer inference to sensation?"

PROFESSOR: "Wait a minute now, you keep saying you can just see things, but you promised not to beg the question like that. Remember that you can't just appeal to the meaning of the word *seeing* to prove you've *got* your whole nine-yard type of seeing that the vat story would deny."

STUDENT: "I know. But I said 'if'---I said 'if' I'm not a brain in a vat. So I didn't beg the question."

PROFESSOR: "Okay, but you haven't shown, yet, that you're out of the vat."

STUDENT: "No I haven't---not yet. But I'm starting to wonder how it is you got the idea that anti-realism can help you defend yourself against skepticism. I mean, if it's *skepticism* that worries you, what's the cash value of anti-realism? Skepticism and anti-realism seem to me to be two sides of the same coin."

PROFESSOR: "I'll let Kant explain. As he says:

> Our doctrine thus removes all difficulty in the way of accepting the existence of matter on the unaided testimony of our mere self-consciousness, or of declaring it to be thereby proved in the same manner as the existence of myself as a thinking being is proved. There can be no question that I am conscious of my representations; these representations and I myself, who have the representations, therefore exist. External objects (bodies), however, are mere appearances, and are therefore nothing but a species of my representations, the objects of which are something only through these representations. Apart from them they are nothing. Thus external things exist as well as I myself, and both indeed, upon the immediate witness of my self-consciousness. The only difference is that the representation of myself, as the thinking subject, belongs to inner sense only, while the representations which mark extended beings belong also to outer sense. In order to arrive at the reality of outer objects I have just as little need to resort to inference as I have in regard to the reality of the object of my inner sense, that is, in regard to the reality of my thoughts. For in both cases alike the objects are nothing but representations, the immediate perception (consciousness) of which is at the same time a sufficient proof of their reality.[18]

STUDENT: "Wow."

PROFESSOR: "That's what you said about Hume."

STUDENT: "Double wow."

PROFESSOR: "You liked it?"

STUDENT: "Not at all."

PROFESSOR: "What's wrong?"

STUDENT: "Where to start?"

PROFESSOR: "At least, can you now begin to understand me a little better?"

STUDENT: "Definitely."

PROFESSOR: "Well, can you feel the attraction of Kant's program now?"

STUDENT: "I'm afraid 'repulsion' might be a better word. I mean, he's selling the program as a way to secure the '*ex*istence,' of '*external*, material objects' like rocks and freight trains, and proposes to achieve this by making them out to be 'nothing more than mere appearances in our minds,' and 'nothing at all apart from thoughts'."

PROFESSOR: "It was a brilliant philosophical move. You see, Kant is not really an idealist. If you spend enough time trying to see things his way, you'll finally come to see that Kant is the true defender of your precious ordinary common sense! In fact, Kant is really a realist! You see, my boy, Kant is what we sophisticated philosophers call an *empirical realist*."

STUDENT: "You must be kidding."

PROFESSOR: "What's wrong?"

STUDENT: "You're joking. You're just funnin' me."

PROFESSOR: "Certainly not."

STUDENT: "You're really serious?"

PROFESSOR: "Yes, of course I'm serious. What's the matter?"

STUDENT: "This is pure flim-flam! It's flat self-contradiction. It's perverse double-talk: slavery is freedom, up is down, square is round, inner is outer, internal is external, idealism is realism. It's all nudge-nudge, wink-wink, quote-unquote talking: 'mere appearances' are quote-unquote 'real,' and they quote-unquote 'exist,' in the quote-unquote 'external' world, but, meanwhile, all of us sophisticated Kantian philosophers know that---actually, and really---freight trains 'exist' nowhere else but in our thoughts, and are nothing apart from us, and therefore can't possibly subsist without us.

Listen, I have news for you: I'm more than a mere appearance in you! I mean, if you really think that I'm a mere appearance and 'nothing apart from' your perception of me, think again, because I intend to go on existing independently of you and your mind a long time after you and your mind get annihilated by that oncoming freight train you think you can turn into a pig's ear by calling it one! This is philosophy? This is the science of critical thinking? I thought you guys were the Humbug Squad, but it turns out you're just another gang of perps! I'm flabbergasted...I'm...I'm...I'm speechless."

PROFESSOR: "I take it this means you're not signed up for the program."

STUDENT: "Well it's been a couple of hundred years. How's it going?"

PROFESSOR: "It's going okay."

STUDENT: "Really?"

PROFESSOR: "Okay, so maybe we've been experiencing some technical difficulties."

STUDENT: "Uh-huh."

PROFESSOR: "Look, I'd be happy to be offered a *viable* alternative."

STUDENT: "How about the ordinary sanity you call *vulgar* and *naive*? How about the wild idea that maybe it's possible that to know how the world appears to you is to know something (not everything, but something) *about* the world as it really is in itself? What is wrong with your plumber's commonplace account of things, that you feel driven to reject it in favor of this strained, heroic insanity? Just what is it about my naive, vulgar view of the world that you consider unworkable?"

Kant in a Vat

PROFESSOR: "Listen, does the brain in the vat know anything about the real world as it is in itself?"

STUDENT: "Well, yeah, as a matter of fact I suppose he would. Wouldn't he? I mean, he knows, for example, that the program the evil scientist calls 'the *snee* program' gives him a cold, white feeling, and that the apple program tastes sour and sweet."

PROFESSOR: "But, he's still vastly ignorant."

STUDENT: "Yeah, but I'm sure we're vastly ignorant too. So? That doesn't prove that *any and all* knowledge of things themselves as they really are is by definition impossible. I mean, there are lots of things the evil scientist knows that the brain in the vat doesn't know, but I wonder if the evil scientist knows what his programs look like from the other side?"

PROFESSOR: "But that's just Kant's point! Kant says, 'the objects with which we have to do in experience are by no means things in themselves but only appearances.' He says, these 'phenomena are not things in themselves, and are yet the only thing that can be given to us to know, and therefore, how things may be in themselves is completely beyond the sphere of our knowledge.' Notice that the things with which the vat-brain has to do in experience are not things in themselves, but appearances only, and the vat-brain's knowledge is therefore not *about* things as they really are in themselves.

I mean, how things are in themselves in the real world of the evil scientist, with his magnificent computer, his white polyester lab coat, his vat of amazing fluid, and those myriads of electrodes is, as Kant would say, completely beyond the sphere of the vat-brain's knowledge. The vat-brain knows nothing of all these things, but knows only his own immediate sense data. His knowledge refers only to mere appearances or representations existing entirely within the mind of the vat-brain, and, as Kant says, 'never and in no single instance,' and 'by no means' could this be knowledge *about* things as they really are."

STUDENT: "I don't agree. There's more than one way to know a little something about pain. One is to be an amazing expert beyond the cutting edge of neuroscience, and the other is to at least once to have been in pain yourself. Not only are both of these ways of knowing, both are ways of *knowing about the same thing*. Not only that, but both of these are ways of knowing something about things as they really are. I mean they're both ways of knowing something about pain as it really is in itself."

PROFESSOR: "No, no. They aren't ways of knowing about pain as it really is in itself. Your ignorance of philosophy is deplorable. You're talking nonsense."

STUDENT: "Look, according to your imagined vat story, the *computer programs* which cause the vat-brain's experiences are, like the evil scientist, and the vat of fluid, among the world of things as they really are in themselves which the envatted brain *knows nothing about*. The deluded, envatted brain's experiences involve only his own mental phenomena, and he can have 'no knowledge at all' about anything besides these phenomena, which are, after all, mere perceptions of his mind, or 'mere appearances.' Right?
But that's not true. The brain in the vat does *know something about* those real, objectively existing, computer programs as they really are in themselves. He knows, for example, what they look like from his angle, something which even the evil scientist himself may or may not know. He knows that the snow simulator program looks white, and feels cold. More importantly, he knows that the part of the program that creates the oarish part of this scene-image is somehow *different*

from the part of the program that creates the handish and the waterish part of the same scene-image. He can tell the one program from the other, and he knows they aren't the same. And that's a real, true, objective fact about the evil scientist's real world of things as they really are in themselves. The evil scientist himself would have to admit that. The brain in the vat is, as a matter of fact, *in touch*, in his own unusual way, with the mad scientist's allegedly unknowable world of things as they really are. The mad scientist is too, but so is the vat brain."

PROFESSOR: "Well, okay, I guess maybe that's so, *indirectly*. So what?"

STUDENT: "Indirect, direct----look, you can break apart any relation into smaller pieces and proclaim to the world to have discovered an arbitrary 'indirectness.' Directness is relative. Forget about your so-called 'directness.' It's a red herring. Look at this oar. The question is *what* are you seeing, what kind of thing is this oar? Is this oar a mind-independent object, or a mere appearance which cannot exist apart from the mind*?* How can you and I perceive the *same* oar?

Or, never mind me, suppose you are a brain in a vat, right now. Now look at my hand holding this oar. Can you not directly perceive the objective fact that this part looks and feels *different* from that part? If experiences are caused by things in themselves---as even Kant supposes---then the variations in the phenomena must be caused by or correlated with some kind of real corresponding variations somehow, somewhere, in things as they really are in themselves, quite apart from us and our perceiving them. For example, doesn't it require non-homogeneity in the world as it is in itself, to make for the palpable non-homogeneity of experience?"

PROFESSOR: "What about dreams? Where's your corresponding real-world distinctions there? You experience empirical distinctions which don't correspond to anything at all in reality."

STUDENT: "How do you know they don't correspond to electromagnetic fluctuations in some area of the brain? Can a dead man dream? Can a brain dream without manifesting any fluctuations on a live, concomitant MRI scan? Can an unborn fetus dream of a blue rowboat with green oars?"

PROFESSOR: "I don't know."

STUDENT: "Okay, I admit that I can't explain exactly how dreams work. But that doesn't mean it can't be done. Let's give science a little more time. It's done very well so far."

PROFESSOR: "Well, how do you know you're not a mad pink elephant, floating all alone in an utter and complete vacuum, suffering delusions and dreaming that you're a man on a dock? In that case, isn't your belief in the existence of non-homogeneity outside yourself a false delusion?"

STUDENT: "Well, in that case, the line, the distinction, between what I madly think of and refer to as 'me' (the man on the dock) versus the 'external world,' has been drawn someplace within the elephant's brain, I guess, so, then, it might still be true that the world outside the part of the elephant brain I call 'me' is still non-homogenous. I mean, like maybe in that case the 'me' (the man) is the elephant's frontal lobe and the non-homogenous 'world' part is the elephant's visual cortex. Or something like that.

Besides, in that case, my belief that I know there really exists at least one elephant is true, and so is my belief that I know elephants can suffer madness. Because if elephants don't exist, or can't go mad, then the story becomes implausible or impossible. (Nor can I consider the story equal in plausibility to the common sense story, since it does not really strike me as plausible or even possible, given my experience, for an elephant to be living in a vacuum without water, food or air.) But, in any case, please notice that even here, Kant would still be wrong."

PROFESSOR: "How's that?"

STUDENT: "He'd be wrong about real objective knowledge of things themselves being completely impossible by definition, since I'd really know that *at least one elephant exists.* I'd also have true, objective knowledge of reality in itself in my belief that *an elephant can go mad,* of course."

PROFESSOR: "Oh, you're just flailing. What's the point? That's so lame. I could just change the scenario so that you were some kind of other sentient being you never imagined before, instead of a mad elephant. I could say you might just as well be a windowless monad floating in space."

STUDENT: "A what?"

PROFESSOR: "A windowless monad."

STUDENT: "What the heck is that?"

PROFESSOR: "Does it matter? Let's just say it's a kind of sentient being that you never thought of before."

STUDENT: "Okay, but notice that the more you frame it like that, the less plausibility your scenario has. Whatever plausibility it has it must borrow that plausibility from our past experiences and reasoning. To the extent that it appears impossible, either physically impossible, or logically impossible, the story is drained of its ability to rival common sense. Unless I have some reason to believe *prima facie* that the story is both logically and physically *possible*, then I have no reason to believe the story *can* rival the competing common-sense theory. These skeptical scenarios are presented as some state of affairs that could *just as well* be true, as any rival, contrary story. I have no reason to suppose a dreaming windowless monad, whatever that means, represents a possible state of affairs, much less an *equally plausible* one."

PROFESSOR: "You're arguing against skepticism now. I'm not sure what this has to do with anti-realism."

STUDENT: "Well, I guess I've been trying to play the game, to show that Kantian conclusions just don't logically follow, even from his own premises, even if you *are* a brain in a vat. It isn't even true for a brain in a vat that knowing how things appear to him is to know nothing whatsoever about things as they are in themselves."

PROFESSOR: "Okay. But you don't seem to have gotten very far in the knowledge department using that method. I mean, even if you're correct, then you've merely claimed that I know that real objective differences must exist in the world as it really exists in itself. So, is that it? Is that all I can know?"

STUDENT: "No. You can know all sorts of things, because you're *not* a mad elephant or brain in a vat. Take my word for it: you're awake right now, and you have arms and legs and no trunk. I can see them. And as for you being a lunatic, you know that was hyperbole. I can vouch for you."

PROFESSOR: "Unless *you*'re a crazy, dreaming brain in a vat."

STUDENT: "Yes, but, *you* know I'm not in a vat."

PROFESSOR: "Yeah, but if *I'm* in the vat, or crazy, or dreaming, then you're a figment of my imagination, and you don't really even *exist,* so, what good does it do me to receive your assurance that you can see me and vouch for my wakefulness, legs, and sanity?"

STUDENT: "Still, I'm sure you'd feel even worse, if I told you that you *are* completely delusional, and that I *can't* see your legs, eh?"

PROFESSOR: "Yes, that would bother me."

You Can't Get There from Here

STUDENT: "I wonder if we could try a completely different approach. I once read a novel by an economist who undertook to demonstrate how all the problems encountered by a socialist economy could easily be fixed one by one, until, and at the end of the story, the result was a pure *laissez faire* economy. In other words, he argued that if you fixed all the problems of socialism one by one, you'd end up back where you started in the first place, at pure capitalism. His point, of course, was that the fastest way to get there, was to skip the whole socialist detour in the first place. Whether you buy that economics argument or not, maybe I could try the same thing with your rejection of vulgar realism."

PROFESSOR: "So you're saying you think I never should've rejected vulgar realism in the first place. Yes, I know. You said that before."

STUDENT: "Okay, but, as you taught me, *if you're falling, dive.* I'd like to try that 'diving' method now. Hear me out. I'm assuming what happened was that Sextus Empiricus, Montaigne, and Locke left philosophy vulnerable to Berkeley, who made people fall for Hume, who drove them into the arms of Kant who gave rise to all this other nonsense you've been trying to teach me and which has been terrorizing the world ever since. So, instead of trying to make you think yourself backwards through a train of errors, let me just try to push you a little bit further ahead, so to speak, and then maybe we can wind up back where we started, before it all began, as a naive plumber's child with common sense. That might be less painful for both of us.

After all, I wonder if you're almost getting there by yourself, without my pushing you. A *second naiveté,* as Putnam calls it. Perhaps it is your inevitable destination anyway; so maybe we can just speed up the natural, inevitable forward progress a little. For example, when you say to me that you want to get rid of the *ding an sich,* maybe what I should say is: good, let's get rid of it. Out with the *ding an sich.* Now all we have left is the supposed 'phenomena.' Fine. You say this oar, this 'phenomenon' is (in the Kantian quote-unquote sense), quote-unquote 'external', and quote-unquote 'public', and quote-unquote 'real,' and quote-unquote 'exists.' So, I guess now we just need to find a way to get rid of the quotation marks. So let's try that.

The remaining problem I suppose is that you want to think of your mind as extending outside of your body and reaching out to include and encompass everything, so that the entire universe, including all the external objects of the past, and even prehistoric rocks, quote-unquote 'exist' nowhere else but in your mind, or in your thoughts. Now, perhaps all that's left is for us to reject the impermissible *universal predication* (not to mention the self-contradiction) involved in the claim that *everything 'exists' only in thought,* or however you like to say it, and we're done. We shave off the noumenal world, and then shave off the transcendental level. We dump them both. Now we've got rid of the claim that everything is mental, gotten your mind out of your neighbor's flower patch and sent it back into your body, where it belongs, and we arrive back where we started, standing shoulder to shoulder with the plumber and his vulgar realism.

Perhaps now we've arrived back where the train left the tracks, at a second *naiveté*. Now you can see, touch, taste and eat an apple as it is in itself, an object existing on its own independently of your thoughts, apart from your mind. Should we explore some program like this?

PROFESSOR: "Of course. This is something very like the path philosophy is in fact traveling. Perhaps now you can begin to understand. It is just as you say: the first thing you must do after reading Hume and Kant is to get rid of the noumenal world. Get rid of it completely, absolutely. That's what Fichte did. That's how we arrive at absolute idealism. That's the first step, and it's a step you need to take. You need to get rid of your vulgar, troublesome notion of an external world constituted by things existing in themselves independently of us."

STUDENT: "Oh dear. Now I think I see why this isn't going to work. The trouble is, you end up as a goofy solipsist living in a phenomenal world full of bent oars and shrinking tables---or a nutty Nazi who thinks the only alternative to solipsism is Orwellian groupthink! Why can't I get you to consider the possibility that the very trees you see and feel can subsist independently of you, and that they're actually existing things in themselves, and not mere perceptions of the mind?"

PROFESSOR: "Because it's simply impossible by definition, to see and feel a *thing in itself*, which is, by definition, a thing that can't be seen or felt."

STUDENT: "Just like it's also impossible by definition to split an *atom*?"

PROFESSOR: "Well, I'm afraid you still don't understand the Kantian scheme. You see, what Kant was driving at…"

STUDENT: "Oh, forget it! Forget the whole forward-to-the-beginning project! It's a bad idea. You can't get there from here. At this point, you've imbibed too much of the canon. There's such a thing as being too far gone. It's just too late for you. Only the young can be saved. If you're falling---*regret jumping*. My plan is to post a big yellow sign at the edge of the cliff. You'll never get over the problems you suffer from, unless you can accept the fact that this weed needs to be pulled up root and branch, and not just pruned. You need to be able to look at Hume and Kant the way an atheist looks at the Bible!"

PROFESSOR: "Good heavens. Didn't your mother teach you any manners? Listen, boy, there's only so much a human being can take. I've spent my entire adult life poring over these texts. I've painstakingly acquired expertise in eighteenth century German, and become an expert on the history of philosophy, just so that I could try to make sense out of Kant. I mastered all his terminology; I internalized his incredible ontology. I suffered through heaps of ponderous Kantian exegesis. After all this, you want me to conclude the whole thing is blunder and madness? You want me to throw it all in the garbage? You want me to write off most of the last three hundred years of philosophy as a pointless wild goose chase?"

STUDENT: "Well, um…yeah. I mean, uh, I know you to be a person of tremendous intellectual integrity. Look at Putnam. Nobody faults him for changing his mind. On the contrary, it's precisely his undeniable integrity that makes everybody admire him so much. Even when he was writing things that drove me crazy, I respected the guy as a great man, simply because it was always obvious that he spoke from the heart, never trying to obfuscate or equivocate, but always in search of truth for its own sake (even, ironically, while sometimes seeming to deny the very possibility of doing so). I see you exactly the same way. I think your love of truth for its own sake makes you forget your concern for your own practical self-interest. I think this is the case even with those philosophers who deny the very existence of truth! I think, in their secret hearts, they desire truth above almost anything. If they didn't, they could have made more money in business, instead of going into philosophy."

PROFESSOR: "Well, thanks, that's nice, but you can save the flattery. Look, put yourself in my shoes. Do you really expect---I mean, would it even be *rational*---for me to let a few facile arguments from an ignorant amateur overturn forty years of careful thinking on my part, and two hundred years of near consensus on the part of men almost universally considered to be the greatest thinkers who ever lived? What kind of epistemology is *that*?

Even if I couldn't immediately answer your challenges, I'd simply be mistaken to let that fact outweigh all the mass I have accumulated on the other side of the scales. It would be not only unjust, but *irrational,* for me to abandon the conclusions of forty years of reasoning in favor of a few minutes of conversation, or to allow a minority of malcontents to override the majority of philosophers. Besides, at my age, it would be folly for another reason, since I'm aware that research shows cognitive skills decline with old age. You may be right that it's too late for me, but that may be because I'm being reasonable. You're asking me to be imprudently and irrationally fickle."

STUDENT: "Don't drive me into the arms of that awful Kuhn, who says the older generation just can't change their minds, but instead must simply pass away!"

PROFESSOR: "Maybe you'd better listen to a wise old head. What are you going to do if you start pulling up the postmodern weed, and suddenly you find its taproot actually runs across your whole front lawn? Let's remember the haunting prophesy of the Church, that freedom of religion would never cure the masses of bad beliefs, but only multiply bad beliefs like rabbits. How many young whippersnappers have come before you, and tried to throw away the ideas of the past? And yet most of these reformers have ended up offering worse doctrines in their stead, and even brought about great tragedies and horrors."

STUDENT: "I'm not sure what you're worried about. Wasn't it your guy Hume, who said 'the errors of Religion are dangerous, but those of Philosophy only ridiculous'?"

PROFESSOR: "Would that Hume had been right about that one. He didn't live long enough to see Auschwitz. What's a mere Spanish

Inquisition---next to a Gulag Archipelago? We went from thousands to millions."

STUDENT: "Okay. I agree with you there. But that's exactly why I draw back from that well-beaten path to which you want to steer me. It keeps taking the gentle sheep to the same destination. Accepting Hume logically leads people to Kant and Rousseau. And those guys lead to irrationalism, totalitarianism and Romanticism, and that way lies a second Dark Age for mankind."

PROFESSOR: "Oh, come now."

STUDENT: "You know, the only reason you let people like Hume, Rousseau, Hegel and Heidegger off the hook for the horrors of the twentieth century is because at bottom you're one of them. You refuse to indict Hume's epistemology, because you like what he wrote about other topics. Besides, somebody who thinks some doctrine is true will never *blame* that doctrine for causing harm, of course. If it's the truth, then it can't be blamed."

PROFESSOR: "You're no different in that regard. You believe Darwinism, and therefore don't blame Darwin for helping to cause the Holocaust."

STUDENT: "Okay. *Touché.* But, look, the problem is that Hume's skeptical idealism contains an almost inexorable logic---a terrible logic---in its historical unfolding. That's why we need to nip it in the bud. And that means attacking our beloved Hume. Not all of Hume, but part of him. Sometimes you have to lose a limb, to save the body."

PROFESSOR: "I know that's what you're saying, but I can't help noticing you haven't refuted my last objection in the slightest. You're just trying to threaten me with an historical fable about dire consequences. You're a Pragmatist in denial! You and your precious 'Truth.'---you lecture me self-righteously about following the evidence wherever it leads, and hewing to logic and reason, no matter whose ox may be gored. But get into a tight spot, and suddenly what really matters is the *practical consequences* of a belief! Why don't you answer my objection? What happened to Truth and Reason?

I said: it isn't *rational* for me to reject two centuries of Kantian philosophy on account of a few sketchy objections from an ignorant amateur. Not only that, I say it isn't rational for *you* either. I say it is irrational, and contrary to epistemological justification, for *you* to reject two hundred years of hard thinking by the greatest minds who ever lived, in favor of your own contrary opinion, no matter how cogent you feel your own reasoning may be. Everybody thinks his own arguments are clever, of course. But it just isn't reasonable---it isn't logical---for you to reject the majority of expert opinion for the last two centuries in favor of yourself. There's a good reason why medical students aren't allowed to perform surgery or write prescriptions. Not even to write prescriptions for themselves. What do you even know about Kantian exegesis? Do you speak German? Can you tell me what's the difference between a sensation and an empirical intuition, in Kant's scheme?"

STUDENT: "No, but I can smell a pile of horse manure when I'm standing right next to it!"

PROFESSOR: "How now? What's this? Some kind of epistemological sixth sense, operating independently of Reason? How about an argument to go with that rhetoric?"

STUDENT: "I'm sorry. You're right. I apologize. Okay. Look…let me be honest. I found the *Critique of Pure Reason* perversely intriguing the first time I read it. I thought it would be fascinating if Kant were truly offering some weird and wildly profound insight or key to the universe somewhere in all that raving lunacy. I'll admit I was attracted. But I was attracted and repelled at the same time. It's almost as bad as Plotinus. The problem with anything that mystical and obscure is that one can get away with committing the grossest blunders, and nobody will have the guts to call them. Or perhaps I should rather say, nobody will be able to discern them in all the fog.

Especially since the only people willing spend the time necessary to decipher the madness are its own devoted acolytes. You seem to feel that I should basically take the same path you have taken, and spend the necessary time to really understand Kant, as you have, before I just throw him in the garbage. But, of course, the only people willing to spend forty years working on Kant, are those congenitally susceptible to humbug and doubletalk!"

PROFESSOR: "Am I supposed to be persuaded by this? You're not arguing, you're just making excuses and hurling spurious insults which aren't even true."

STUDENT: "My argument is this. You keep insisting that if only I really grasped the Kantian ontological and philosophical scheme, as a whole, I would finally see that it is really Kant who is the greatest possible defender of the objective existence of tables and chairs. But what you call an understanding of the Kantian scheme is in reality the unjustified *acceptance* of that scheme. There's a difference between a valid argument and a cogent one. If you start with false premises, then you can follow out the logic of the case as perfectly as you like, and you still won't arrive at a true conclusion.

It seems to me that the only reason you think Kant is the greatest possible defender of common sense, is because you suppose that a less sophisticated defense of common sense is untenable. In other words, it's only because you reject my ordinary, unsophisticated, vulgar, commonplace realism, that you think Kantian lunacy is the best we can do."

PROFESSOR: "But what you want to do *can't be done*. You want to make things in themselves the objects of our experience. But if you understood Kant's insight, you'd realize that's simply impossible by definition."

STUDENT: "You've done something more than just grasp Kant's scheme---you've swallowed it. You've imbibed and internalized it. You've accepted it as right and good. You're always talking to me from inside the Kantian funhouse. But I'm not in there with you.

I'm asking you why I should accept your Kantian "definitions" in the first place. In the meantime, you keep offering me a smorgasbord of various tortuous 'interpretations' and reformations of Kantianism, all of which take for granted precisely what's at issue. It seems like you've stopped wondering whether or not there's a difference between a sensation and an empirical intuition *in reality*, because the only question you think to ask is whether or not such a distinction exists "for Kant." Why doesn't his nutty philosophy have to answer to reality as it is in itself? Because we can't know anything about reality as it is in itself? You beg the question. Listen, if leprechauns don't exist, then they can't exist *for Kant*---okay?"

PROFESSOR: "If you want to disagree with the man, first of all you must understand him, and the principle of charity requires that you put him in the best possible light."

STUDENT: "Well then Kant's place is secure for eternity. Because nobody can possibly make sense out that mass of incredible folderol. What a perfect scam. The only thing his various interpreters seem to agree on is that all the *other* interpreters offer us a self-contradictory system. And therefore the other interpreters must be violating the principle of charity. And therefore we should reject the other interpreters. And by this method each and every writer who treats of Kant thinks himself the only good one, since he is of course *right* that all the others offer us absurdity. But don't think for a moment that this could prove that Kant himself is to blame, or that his system is in reality absurd. Oh, no! How do we know this is not the case? Because the one thing the interpreters of Kant agree upon is that the system can be made to cohere. But only by their own particular method. No doubt this will go on forever. I'd like to buy a share of that business. It's better than a chain letter!"

PROFESSOR: "Do you have some alternative interpretation of Kant to offer?"

STUDENT: "Certainly not! You don't understand---look, suppose, for example, that there turned out to be no distinction anywhere in reality corresponding to some Kantian distinction, say, for example, the distinction between things as they appear to us and things as they really are."

PROFESSOR: "Perhaps that's just the point."

STUDENT: "Sheesh. Okay, forget that. What if there turned out to be something like retinal patches, or atoms, or various wavelengths of light, or particular types of neuron-firings, that roughly, more or less, but not exactly, *did* correspond to various items in the Kantian scheme. Then, wouldn't you be obliged to reject the Kantian items in favor of these real ones? I mean, you might fairly accuse me of not grasping what in the world Kant is talking about. But of course nobody really ever does 'understand' Kant, until they've first been driven off a sensible plumber's realism by all the traditional fallacies. Kant can only be taken seriously in the first place by people who have already imbibed more of the canon than they should have. Unless you come to it with the fallacies of Hume or the others already under your belt, then, of course it makes no sense. I don't agree that things as they are in themselves independently of thought *cannot* be the objects of ordinary sense-experience, and you know I don't share your scheme that wants to make it true by definition. Why can't you understand that?"

PROFESSOR: "Can't you see that you're merely confirming my claim that truth is always relative to a conceptual scheme which we accept for pragmatic reasons?"

STUDENT: "The only 'conceptual scheme' I'm touting is the English language. Besides, *you* don't even accept Kant's scheme! You're always talking about how you need to adjust it. So don't tell me *it's true by definition* that nobody can see a thing in itself. Because even you don't accept Kant's scheme."

PROFESSOR: "Well, I'm allowed to tinker with Kant, because I'm an expert on Kant. You aren't. But, if you admit that, as you said, you don't know what in the world he's talking about, then how can you possibly know that he's wrong?"

STUDENT: "You don't have to walk all the way to the North Pole in order to know that there's no Santa Claus. How do you know you shouldn't become a follower of Plotinus? Isn't it enough for me to notice that it is only the traditional errors that make it attractive; that it entails contradictory doubletalk, and displays a chronic tendency to encourage people to make claims that, even you admit, are preposterous and absurd? Never mind the question of its corresponding to reality, which it doesn't. Kant's scheme doesn't even cohere with itself. He contradicts himself all over the place, and then you tell me that, unlike other people, Kant's *allowed* to contradict himself, because he's talking on two different levels! Where I come from, we call that talking out of two sides of your mouth. For two centuries brilliant men have been devoting whole lifetimes to see if they can make sense out of this German humbug, but it just won't hold water."

PROFESSOR: "We're making progress."

STUDENT: "Only to the extent that you're groping your way back home to the vulgar, commonplace realism your plumber never left. But at this point I doubt whether you can make it back in one piece. Somehow, you have to find it in yourself to be able to go back over the whole history of metaphysics and epistemology and pull up the whole skeptical/idealist weed patch, roots and all. But I'm afraid that means there might not be a whole lot of the metaphysics and epistemology canon left."

PROFESSOR: "All, no doubt, merely on the strength of my plumber's say-so."

STUDENT: "An argument appealing to the authority of the canonical texts can't be decisive. It's hardly as if my attitude towards these issues has been has been unheard of among serious philosophers. What about Reid, Moore, and Austin? They're in the minority, but if you really supposed that the majority should rule, then I'm not sure why the fact that the vast majority of people are, practically by definition, vulgar realists, shouldn't likewise force you to accept vulgar realism? You're the one who likes to make so much of the absolute authority of the almighty Community."

PROFESSOR: "Well, you're the person who keeps insisting that one fool can be right against the whole world."

STUDENT: "Well, yes. So I do. Okay. But, you still haven't explained why I should abandon my vulgar realism. You say the fear of skepticism should motivate me. But, I'm never going to prove I'm not a brain in a vat by ruling it out *a priori* as somehow logically impossible by definition or something like that. That's just not persuasive. If an anti-realist tells the skeptic that quote-unquote 'chairs' quote-unquote 'exist' by definition, then the skeptic can just rephrase his challenge in a different way. There's nothing wrong in asking somebody how do they know they won't wake up tomorrow in a situation so radically different that it would, then, seem that their past experience was all something analogous to, or *like*, so to speak, a kind of illusion, hallucination or dream. If some poor kid watches "The Matrix" too many times, and starts believing he's really in a jelly pod, I don't think you're going to talk him out of it by using some sophisticated anti-realism. Kant doesn't banish the vat, he climbs in and nails the top shut!"

PROFESSOR: "So, I take it this means you're sticking with your vulgar realism?"

STUDENT: "Absolutely. I'm standing by my claim that your chronic disparagement of my ordinary, vulgar realism has always been a gross and unnecessary blunder. Let's just say it would take a truly scary monster to send me anywhere near *The Critique of Pure Reason*."

PROFESSOR: "Well, in that case, prepare yourself, my *naive* friend. Because you're about to meet just such a Beast."

"I will suppose, then…that some malignant demon, who is at once exceedingly potent and deceitful, has employed all his artifice to deceive me; I will suppose that the sky, the air, the earth, colors, figures, sounds, and all external things, are nothing better than the illusions of dreams, by means of which this being has laid snares for my credulity; I will consider myself as without hands, eyes, flesh, blood, or any of the senses, and as falsely believing that I am possessed of these; I will continue resolutely fixed in this belief." [1]

---**Descartes**, *Meditations*

Do not go gentle into that good night;
Fight, fight, against the dying of the light.

---**Dylan Thomas**

CHAPTER 4
Doubting Skepticism

PROFESSOR: "The thing is, if your vulgar realism is going to work, then it will have to pass the hardest test of all, and that test is radical skepticism. Until you beat the skeptics, you're nothing but a hothouse flower."

STUDENT: "I agree."

PROFESSOR: "Okay, then, enough playing around. It's time for me to put on the skeptic's hat, and give you a *real* run for your money!"

STUDENT: "Well, I think you'll be quite good at playing the role. I might even say you just need to be yourself."

PROFESSOR: "You're full of jokes now, but you'll be reeling in a minute, schoolboy. I'm taking the gloves off."

STUDENT: "Go for it."

PROFESSOR: "Okay. First of all, you cannot *know* anything about the world outside your mind, unless you can have some reason to suppose that it is *not* the case that your whole life with all your experiences heretofore has been no more than a very long dream from which you will soon awake, only to discover that you have, in reality, all along been nothing else but an insane green alien with fins instead of arms and legs, high on hallucinogens, in a coma, strapped to a bed, in an asylum on a strange planet in a weird and unfamiliar universe. But there is just no way you can possibly know that this is *not* the case, and therefore, there is no way you can *know* anything about things as they really are outside your mind."

STUDENT: "Ow."

PROFESSOR: "And that's just one. Another possibility is that you're just a disembodied brain floating in a vat of life-preserving fluid attached to myriads of electrodes which feed you all your sense data----data which actually originates not from real rocks and apples, but instead from the elaborate software of a vast super-computer operated by a mad scientist who gets his jollies by making you believe you're a human being with arms and legs on Earth. And, again, since you can't know this *isn't* true, therefore you can't *know* anything at all about the world of things as they are in themselves, apart from mere appearances."

STUDENT: "Mmm."

PROFESSOR: "Well? Come on, boy. Why so quiet?"

STUDENT: "I don't feel well. I think I need a drink."

PROFESSOR: "Ready to fly back into the arms of old Kant?"

STUDENT: "He's looking like a nice old friend, now."

PROFESSOR: "Isn't he though."

STUDENT: "Yeah. Well...I guess I see the attraction now."

PROFESSOR: "Ready to reconsider the anti-realist program?"

STUDENT: "No. No, forget that. It's a dead end. There's got to be another way. Kant's way is no way at all. It's just a way to resign yourself to the vat. You may as well accept Pascal's wager, or join a crazy religious cult on the principles of fideism. I'm not giving up *that* easily."

PROFESSOR: "That's the spirit, boy! But, what now?"

STUDENT: "Well, look---there has to be an answer to this challenge. I mean, what if your best friend comes to you and tells you that he thinks he probably really *is* just a brain in a vat. What are you going to tell him?"

PROFESSOR: "I don't know, what? I guess I'd ask him why he was turning to me for advice, since in that case I'd be nothing more than a mere illusion."

STUDENT: "Yeah. Heh. Well, maybe he'd say he was just using the illusion to help him think out loud. But, I mean, seriously, what would you do?"

PROFESSOR: "Well, I don't see what I *could* say to help him. I can't refute a scenario like that. I can't tell him I see his arms and legs. He can't take *my* word for it. If I'm not real, neither are my assurances!"

STUDENT: "But *you* know you're real."

PROFESSOR: "Yeah, but I can't prove that *to him*."

STUDENT: "And he knows *he's* more than a mere figment of *your* imagination."

PROFESSOR: "Yeah, but he can't prove that to *me*."

STUDENT: "I suppose not. But, I don't think that's what you'd *really* say. I mean, think about it. Think about it *seriously*. What would you say----*really* say----if it was your own child who came to you and said *he really, truly suspected he might be a brain in vat*. I think what you would really say is: *why? You'd say, "Why* do you think that?" I think you'd just disagree that he really had a good reason to reject the mundane, common sense alternative."

PROFESSOR: "But what reason or evidence can I offer him, to show him that he should *prefer* the mundane alternative to the vat alternative? Isn't it a *stalemate?*"

STUDENT: "No, it isn't."

PROFESSOR: "Yes it is! It's a draw! It's a tie. It's a stalemate. What reason is there to *prefer* one theory to the other? They equally predict the same experiences, namely, those you have."

STUDENT: "No. Not true. They are not *equally* plausible."

Chancy *vs.* Chancier

STUDENT: "First of all, the mundane, common sense theory is less dubious, because a chain is only as strong as its weakest link, and to the same old common sense chain, the vat story *adds more links*. It *adds more links*, and the links it adds are relatively *weaker* ones, such as that a brain can survive in a vat, that electrodes can deliver sense data to a brain, that a future super-computer can really perform such an amazing feat. Therefore, we cannot help but consider the vat story to be a weaker chain, overall. If you add a positive amount to a positive amount, the result must be greater than, and not equal to, the amount you started with."

PROFESSOR: "What do you mean?"

STUDENT: "Think about it. When it comes to the question of how likely, or plausible, these competing stories are, *prima facie*, they don't appear to be equal. Not really. Given our experience, the mundane theory looks more plausible. For example, the mundane theory requires only that brains exist, while the vat story requires *more* than that: both that they exist, *and* that they can survive in a vat of fluid, disconnected from a body. Even if we thought that was possible, it's not *equally* plausible.

Likewise, the mundane version requires only that electrodes exist, while the vat story requires not only that they exist, but *also* that they be capable of producing the rich kind of experience we have. The mundane story says computers really exist. The vat story also requires them to exist. But the vat story requires, *in addition*, that *super-*computers exist, and that can do things that you've never seen a regular computer do.

The mundane theory is more plausible, because it possesses the same chance of failure as the vat scenario *minus* the chance of failure associated with the dubious add-ons (that brains can live in vats, that electrodes can do all that the story requires of them, etc.) Therefore, whatever the chance of failure of the mundane scenario, the chance of failure for the vat scenario must be higher. Unless the dubious add-ons are perfectly infallible, the mundane theory wins."

PROFESSOR: "I'm not sure I understand."

STUDENT: "If electrodes cannot actually do what the vat story requires of them, then goodbye to the vat story. If a brain cannot, after all, survive in a vat of fluid, then goodbye to the vat story. The failure of even one these dubious items will collapse the whole vat scenario. Yet these are all things you have to wonder if they are even *possible*---*physically* possible---much less *probable*.

Maybe it *is* physically possible, I'm not sure. But however uncertain we may be of the mundane hypothesis, we can only view this brain-in-the-vat scenario as even less certain. However chancy the first scenario looks to us, the second scenario can only look even chancier.

So we appear to have no choice but to conclude that chances are better for the one than for the other. We can't view the two as equals. The skeptical scenarios seem hopelessly parasitic upon the truth of the anti-skeptical scenario: if I suppose I *am* a brain in a vat, then I have to conclude that, despite appearances, really, I've never even *seen* a vat, or a brain, or an electrode, or a computer, and therefore I no longer seem to have any reason to suppose the brain in the vat story is even *possible,* much less *equally probable*. Unless vats really exist, you can't be floating in one. If, as the skeptic claims, you shouldn't believe vats actually exist, then you shouldn't believe you can be in one. The skeptic says that *it is possible that you're in a vat.* Is that true? Is that right? Is it possible? Should you believe that this *is* possible? So, the vat story is at war with its own plausibility, in a perverse kind of way.

On the other hand, to the extent that a skeptical scenario does *not* avail itself of plausible objects like vats and electrodes, to that extent it lacks *any* plausibility: that I might possibly be a gleebing monop instead of a human being lacks all plausibility because I have no reason to think gleebing monops are possible, nor that I could be one. So, once again, *however uncertain* this mundane world of ours may be, a far-fetched vat-world can only be *less certain.* I mean, the only thing more clueless than a brain in a vat who thinks he's a human being, would be a lunatic green alien in a coma dreaming that he's a human being who thinks he might possibly be a brain in a vat."

PROFESSOR: "Now, I need a drink."

STUDENT: "What's the matter?"

PROFESSOR: "How do you get from there to common sense?"

STUDENT: "Easy. The mundane, common sense theory is the least implausible of the scenarios. That's why it's the story you should believe."

Abducted by Disjunctive Aliens

PROFESSOR: "It sounds like you're going for abduction, or what we call 'appeal to the best explanation.' I'm not sure it's going to work."

STUDENT: "Why not? What's wrong with it? Don't tell me *you honestly believe* that the mundane explanation is no more plausible than those other two far-fetched paranoid fantasies you made up. Don't make me worry about your sanity."

PROFESSOR: "Well, even if common sense is the most plausible, the trouble is that if you frame the contest as an alternative between common sense on the one hand, and a really long disjunction of paranoid fantasies on the other, then you might just tip the scales the other way."

STUDENT: "A long disjunction? What do you mean?"

PROFESSOR: "I mean you take a hundred different paranoid vat-like *Matrix* fantasies on the one hand, and put them all in a string, and join them together with the word 'or' in between each. And then, on the other hand, you put the mundane story all by its lonesome.[2] Then you add up the estimated probabilities and you might find that the mundane side comes out the loser."

STUDENT: "Wait a minute…this contest is rigged. Why do they get to *gang up* together against my side? That's not fair! Why are they allowed to add their probabilities together?"

PROFESSOR: "Well, why can't they? I don't see that it violates any rules of logic."

STUDENT: "You just can't be serious. You can't believe that."

PROFESSOR: "Why not?"

STUDENT: "Because then you'll have to become a mystic, and go around assuming this world is a mere veil of illusion, and everybody else you meet is no more real than a dream, and they exist nowhere but in your own deluded mind. You're saying that esoteric mysticism or paranoid schizophrenia is the worldview to which fair reasoning leads. Empty out the loony bins! You're saying you think that it really, seriously, may be more probable than not, that this world really is a veil of delusion. I just don't think you really believe that. Better you should wonder if there's something wrong with your own procedure. I mean, which is more plausible on its face: that you've made some logical mistake, or that some unspecified paranoid fantasy is more probable than the mundane theory that you're an ordinary human on planet Earth?"

PROFESSOR: "Well, I might still act the way I did before, you know, *just in case* the mundane story is true."

STUDENT: "But you just said it's unlikely to *be* true!"

PROFESSOR: "Well, I may have to pick *one* story, to *live* by, and so pick common sense. Indeed, that might be the *rational* thing to do, since common sense is the *single most plausible one* of the lot."[3]

STUDENT: "Let me get this straight. You're saying that it's rational to pretend, and to act as if, this world I see is real, but it's irrational for me to believe the world I see is real, since *probably it isn't*."

PROFESSOR: "Heh. You're making me hanker after anti-realism again. However bad that was, this is worse."

STUDENT: "Well, you have another choice."

PROFESSOR: "What's that?"

STUDENT: "Go back and re-examine your procedure. Could you ask for a better reason to doubt that you made no mistakes?"

PROFESSOR: "Well, what's wrong with it?"

STUDENT: "What's *right* with it? You yourself said you rationally ought to pick *just one* of the lot to *live* by, and *act* in accordance with. Why should you approach this situation any differently when the question concerns what should be *believed*? Why do you grant to *belief* a kind of disjunctive polygamy that you deny to *practice*?"

PROFESSOR: "Well you can believe the whole disjunction, but can you act in accordance with it?"

STUDENT: "Sure you can. Why not? Mystics do. Cancel your life insurance policy, and don't worry about global warming anymore. The globe is an illusion. Use the life insurance money to buy a big Cadillac, and relax about human rights too, since those people you've never seen, but imagine to be suffering torture in some far away place don't even exist, and even if you could hallucinate a glimpse of them, it's irrational to believe they have any inner experiences like suffering. As a matter of fact, since other people in general probably aren't even real, there's no longer any reason to take their so-called 'feelings' into account. These supposed 'persons,' are but the stuff of dreams. They exist nowhere else but in your imagination. It's all you. So just do whatever pleases you! Shall I go on?"

PROFESSOR: "I get the picture. But you warned me against merely following the Pragmatist dictum. Isn't that what you're doing? It seems like a lot of the time you're arguing that I shouldn't believe something because believing it might have bad practical consequences. I thought you said we ought rather to bite the bullet and follow the evidence wherever it may lead?"

STUDENT: "That's right. But I haven't changed my mind. The reason I keep insisting on pushing some of things you say to their ultimate practical conclusions, isn't really because I think Pragmatism is right. I do it because I want to push these ideas to their logical and practical conclusions for the sake of performing a *reductio ad absurdum* on them. Not because I want to convince you that they are immoral, but because I want to convince you that they're implausible.

If I can show that some doctrine ends up flying in the face of common sense, that cannot by itself prove conclusively that the doctrine is false. After all, Einstein and Newton both gave us doctrines that conflicted with what most people believed. It can happen. But a philosophical doctrine can only be less plausible if it looks crazy on its face, than it would be, other things equal, if it happens to jibe with common sense. Newton and Einstein managed to overcome that disadvantage, but that doesn't make it irrational to give counter-intuitive suggestions a little extra scrutiny. Sometimes they turn out to be right, but more often than not it turns out somebody made a little mistake somewhere along the chain of reasoning."

PROFESSOR: "Well, if that's what you believe, why don't you use that as an argument against skepticism itself? You could just point out that it's less plausible to believe that the skeptic is right in his outlandish, extraordinary claims, than it is to believe that somebody has made a little mistake somewhere in a long chain of tricky philosophical reasonings."

STUDENT: "Okay, consider it a point made. But, to be honest, I don't want to push this point too far. I believe in a level playing field. There are much better arguments I can offer besides that one. For example, I just thought of another one against your disjunction move."

PROFESSOR: "Good, what is it?"

STUDENT: "Well, you said I was using a method you called 'abduction,' and you claimed that means *reasoning to the best explanation*. Yet, according to your reasoning, you can shoot down anything whatsoever, and you can always make any explanation, even the best of all, appear to be a loser. Even if it were far better than the second-best explanation, your disjunction method would call it a loser. I mean, your method of supposedly 'reasoning to the best explanation' looks tailor-made to make the *best* explanation *lose*. In other words, however one truly goes about reasoning *to the best explanation*, the method you proposed can't possibly be it, because what you're advocating is a perfect method for reasoning *away from* the best explanation."

PROFESSOR: "Well, how is it rightly done then, smart guy?"

STUDENT: "I don't know. You're the professional philosopher. You tell me. I've never heard of it before I met you. I'm just trying to use my common sense, as best I can. Somebody must have figured it out. If not, somebody ought to get on it."

PROFESSOR: "I'll put that in the suggestion box."

The Uncertain *Cogito*

PROFESSOR: "Okay, forget that for a minute. I have another move. Look, how do you know that the mundane story is really more plausible than the vat story? Maybe you've made a mistake. Maybe the skeptical scenarios just seem, or merely appear, to you to be more far-fetched, or more implausible, or more unlikely. You could be wrong. You say it's more plausible just to believe that brains exist, than it is to believe *both* that they exist, *and* that that they can survive in fluid-filled vats. You say you know this because you know that 'adding a positive amount to a positive amount makes a greater amount.' But I say you don't know even *that*. Here's why. The simple fact is, you yourself must admit that you are not infallible, and I say it's possible that even when you say that 'one and one equals two,' or 'I think therefore I exist,' that it is possible, it's conceivable, you may have made a mistake. And if you can't know easy things like those, then you're in trouble if you think you're going to be able to know anything tougher."

STUDENT: "So, how do you shoot down those easy ones?"

PROFESSOR: "Suppose right now a deep booming voice were suddenly to come out of the sky and frighten us out of our wits and say: 'You think you know that you exist, but what you meant to say is you *subsist*, not *exist*.'[4]

Or, perhaps, alternatively, you might decide tomorrow, after a good night's sleep and a cup of coffee, that you made a mistake when you thought you knew something like *I think therefore I exist*, since, if you're a dreaming pink elephant floating all alone in a vacuum, and this whole world is locked up in your addled brain, then neither the word 'I' nor the word 'exist' any longer refer to anything like what you used to think they referred to, and therefore your former self, which you used to refer to as 'I,' (before you discovered you were a floating pink elephant), basically goes the way of Stahl's phlogiston. Ditto for the word *exist*. And therefore it isn't really certain, after all, that you exist.

Anyway, how can you of all people say that you know you exist? You told me that to *exist* meant to *ex-sist*, i.e., to stay or sit outside of the mind. And you said your mind is in your head. Therefore you cannot possibly exist, since you aren't completely outside your own head."

STUDENT: "Well I'm outside of yours!"

PROFESSOR: "Stay on point."

STUDENT: "How could I find out one and one aren't two?"

PROFESSOR: "You could wake up a moment from now in a hospital bed, and find out you got hit on the head, and in your delirium you thought you were standing on a dock and 'two' meant what everybody actually calls 'dwoo,' so that the truth is that one and one are dwoo, and you feel quite certain of this obvious fact and laugh with the doctor and the nurse about how delirious you were that you got those dwoo words mixed up.

Besides, everybody knows it's possible to make arithmetical errors, so, obviously   arithmetic isn't necessarily foolproof."

STUDENT: "So, basically, you're arguing that I don't know that one and one are two, nor do I even know that I exist."

PROFESSOR: "Bingo."

STUDENT: "Yes, I see what you mean. I've always suspected that even those things Hume called 'relations of ideas', and the stuff other people call 'analytic' truths, are really just a special category of 'contingent,' empirical truths. I mean, if you say 'no bachelor is married,' you know, that's a truth which depends upon the meaning of its terms, and the meaning of its terms depends upon certain empirical facts about how those words are actually used by people who speak the language, which isn't after all, a thing which could be 'known independently of all experience,' as people sometimes seem to think it is. What I mean is, I don't think there's ever been a newborn baby in history who knew that all cubes have twelve edges, even if you and I, at our age, would be idiots to think we need to examine all the cubes on Earth to know it, now."

PROFESSOR: "Well, there you go. That would be another reason why nothing can be known. You see, some people have argued that we can at least know what they call logical, tautological, analytic, or *a priori* truths. But as you have just pointed out, that's false, since these truths themselves, at bottom, depend upon contingent empirical facts. You can't know that 'all bachelors are single,' if, like a baby, you don't know what those words mean, and you can't know what those words mean, if you have no idea how they're actually used by anybody who uses them, and that is something that cannot be known *a priori*, independently of experience. Therefore, nothing can be known independently of experience, and therefore, nothing is certain, and therefore, nothing can be known."

Infallible Certainty

STUDENT: "Hmmm… I'm starting to detect a pattern here. Your arguments always assume that I have to be perfectly certain in order to *know* something."

PROFESSOR: "Of course! If you're not certain, then you don't *know*."

STUDENT: "Since when?"

PROFESSOR: "Well, that's just an analytic truth. It's just true by definition that knowledge entails certainty."

STUDENT: "I'm not sure what you mean. You mean like absolute, perfect infallibility? As in it cannot possibly, conceivably be false? Or, just some kind of more or less, relative, kind of certainty, such as when people say something is practically as certain as anything can be in this life?"

PROFESSOR: "I mean perfect certainty."

STUDENT: "You mean absolute infallibility?"

PROFESSOR: "Well, yeah."

STUDENT: "Since when is that a requirement?"

PROFESSOR: "Well, isn't it?"

STUDENT: "No. I mean, okay, if a thing must be true to be known, then, yeah, whatever is known must necessarily be true. In one sense.

But that's not the same thing as saying that it must, so to speak, be a necessary truth. You might know something that just happens to be true, even if it isn't, from the point of view of your own information, a thing absolutely, perfectly, and infallibly certain."

PROFESSOR: "Come again?"

STUDENT: "If you believe it, and, luckily, it happens to be true, and you have enough, or more or less sufficient, evidence, reason or justification for believing it, then you *know* it, even if you are fallible and you can't consider it a thing known by you with perfect, absolute certainty.

On the other hand, if it's known, then it certainly must be true, since if it isn't true, then it cannot be 'known.' But, that doesn't mean you have to be certain, in order to know it, just as it may very well be the case that a thing is known by some people and not by others, and it is reasonable for some people, but not for others, to believe it. We don't all share the exact same evidence or information all at the same time. What justifies me in believing it, is that I have sufficient evidence--- that I have reason enough. And the thing needs to happen to be true, so I need a little luck. But I don't need to be infallible."

PROFESSOR: "But if I say *I know* that (for example) lemons cure scurvy, *but I'm not certain*, that makes no sense. To say *I know it but I'm not certain*, sounds like a contradiction. Nobody says that. If you say you *know*, you *mean* you're sure."

STUDENT: "I hear you, but again I think what I just said explains why that sounds contradictory. One reason is because whatever is known must necessarily be true, by definition. But what must certainly be *true*, need not be *certain* in order to be true."

PROFESSOR: "It sounds like you're contradicting yourself."

STUDENT: "Not at all. The world was certainly round before anybody in particular was or could have been certain of it. To say 'I know but I'm not sure' also sounds contradictory because one minute you appear to being assuring your listener that you have sufficient justification or evidence or reason under your belt, for your claim that lemons cure scurvy, and the next minute you seem to be warning him that you're worried that you might not be justified after all. It makes the listener want to say, well, make up your mind.

There's some level that's enough, but different things are variously and unequally sure, or justified, for you. You're more sure that one and one are two, than you are that humans evolved, even if, as I would argue, you do *know* both of these things. You don't know them both, shall we say, *equally*. These things admit of degrees. I say I know lemons cure scurvy, because I feel justified enough to hand you a lemon and recommend that you eat it. It doesn't mean I'm claiming personal infallibility. I'm claiming that I'm justified enough, and that I'm not experiencing any pangs of doubt. I'm also claiming that it happens actually to be *true* that lemons cure scurvy."

PROFESSOR: "Okay, maybe, but if the proposition allegedly known isn't in itself certain, then it isn't something known."

STUDENT: "Can't you see that you're trading on a confusion between the fact that, *what is known cannot be false*, and the fact that *you need to be sufficiently justified* in order to be someone who *knows* it? Can't you see that these are two separate issues that you're conflating? At first glance it might seem as though these two claims entail the idea that in order to be justified, you have to be infallible. But if you take a closer look, you'll see that this just doesn't follow."

PROFESSOR: "Well then, why does it seem like it does follow?"

STUDENT: "You're confusing what's required from the *person* who would be a *knower*, with what's required from the thing to be *known*. It's getting those two mixed up that keeps driving you to think people need to be infallible or else they can't know things. What is known must be true. *It cannot be false.* Because if it's false, then it isn't 'known.' Nobody can know what isn't so. But *you, the knower* don't have to be infinitely justified, or infallible. You just have to be more or less sufficiently justified, and you have to be lucky enough that you just *happen* to actually be right."

PROFESSOR: "Give me some example."

STUDENT: "Okay. You're a child who suspects that there's no real Santa Claus living at the North Pole. In fact, you have come to believe he basically doesn't exist. You don't have absolute proof, but you have various reasons, including the narrowness of chimneys and the familiar handwriting style on your gifts. So your suspicions are justified. In fact, your belief that Santa is a fraud becomes justified, I say, just as soon as the weight of evidence tips the scale to that side. Call it a preponderance of the evidence. A preponderance of the evidence is enough to justify you, and if you're lucky, then you're right, and if you're right and you're justified, then you *know*.

Now, of course, if it is truly something known by you, that no real Santa Claus from the North Pole came down the chimney with your toys last night, then that proposition cannot be false, because if it's false, then it cannot be 'known' by you, or by anybody, but only 'believed.' If, on the other hand, it just so happens to be true, then *you* need not be infallibly certain to be lucky (or unlucky) enough to be one of the kids in your family who knows Santa isn't real."

PROFESSOR: "What is this supposed to show?"

STUDENT: "If it just happens to be true, then something a lot less than absolute certainty may suffice to personally justify you, and therefore, turn you into one of the people in the family who happens to know the truth. This shows that while what is known cannot possibly be false, yet you need not be personally infallible in order to be a person who knows it."

PROFESSOR: "But, can a person be justified in believing something that may possibly be false for all he can tell?"

STUDENT: "Of course. Why not? After all, we can imagine all sorts of cases in which you are temporarily justified in believing something that actually happens to *be* false! Or in which you're justified in doubting or even disbelieving something that actually happens to be true. For each of us, there are many things we don't know, and there is evidence out there of which we are ignorant. The particular evidence we're aware of so far, isn't necessarily all the evidence there is."

PROFESSOR: "So you're admitting that we're never absolutely, perfectly, certain about anything."

STUDENT: "We're not infallible."

PROFESSOR: "So the skeptic wins!"

STUDENT: "Not true. The skeptic loses."

PROFESSOR: "Why?"

STUDENT: "Because, as I've just shown, we can still have knowledge."

PROFESSOR: "You're just trying to redefine the word knowledge."

STUDENT: "No, I'm not."

PROFESSOR: "Yes you are. Look, I agree with you that if we are going to dispute over the meaning of a word, then we must consult the actual facts about how ordinary English speakers use the word. But most ordinary people think that if you 'know' something then you cannot be wrong about it. Therefore, most people must *intend* the word *know* in this way---i.e., the way that makes it an all or nothing kind of thing, and not a more or less kind of thing. Therefore, knowing, or knowledge, by definition entails absolute certainty, and not just more or less probability. If most ordinary people think that if you know something then you cannot be wrong, then that's just something you must accept as true by definition!"

STUDENT: "You're not listening You just said: 'if you know something, then you cannot be wrong about it.' *That's right. I agree.* I just explained why, in one sense, that's true. We just went over this. Because if what you claim to know is actually false, then it cannot be something 'known' by anybody."

PROFESSOR: "Okay, well, let me rephrase that. I mean, most people think that if you claim you know something, then you're claiming that *you, the person,* cannot be wrong, at least, that you cannot be wrong about that particular thing."

STUDENT: "Right!   If you claim you know something, then you're claiming that you cannot be wrong about it. But only in the sense that you're saying: this claim *is true*. And that which is true *cannot* be false. So you're saying this particular claim isn't false. Right."

PROFESSOR: "But, then you're claiming *personal* infallibility!"

STUDENT: "No you aren't. You're merely claiming to believe you're probably right in one case. You're claiming to be justified in thinking this claimed thing is true, and if it is true in reality, then of course (in one sense) you, so to speak, *cannot be* wrong. But that's only because *if* the thing happens to *be* true, then it cannot be false. That is not the same thing as claiming that you, as a person, *can never err.* Can't you see that? Again, you keep mentally confusing the truth issue with the justification issue. These are not exactly the same. The fact that people are sometimes justified in doubting the truth, or justified in believing a falsehood, proves that truth and justification aren't the same thing."[5]

How Much is Enough Justification?

PROFESSOR: "Okay, look, you say that we don't need to achieve complete, perfect, absolutely infallible certainty. You say that there is some sufficient amount of assurance, justification, reason, evidence or warrant for our beliefs, short of my impossible standard of infallibility, that is for us enough. Some amount, some degree, is *enough*. But how much? Where exactly is the threshold?"

STUDENT: "I don't know. How hot is hot? How warm is warm? Some things in life lack bright lines. Maybe it depends upon the number and strength of competing theories. I suppose it's the point at which the balance scale seems to tip. The preponderance of the evidence. Maybe knowing, or even being certain, are not all-or-nothing kinds of things, but more-or-less kinds of things. I think we need to get away from the all-or-nothing mentality. It doesn't strike me as a difficult problem. Maybe we should check out some books on probability and multi-value logic"

PROFESSOR: "So, basically, you don't know."

STUDENT: "No, I don't. I'd have to think about it. Maybe some philosopher has figured it out already. We might go look it up in the library."

PROFESSOR: "Maybe it isn't possible to solve this problem."

STUDENT: "I suspect it probably is."

PROFESSOR: "But, you might be wrong here."

STUDENT: "Yes, I might be wrong. But you need to argue that I probably am wrong, not just that I might be."

Iterative Skepticism

PROFESSOR: "So, it looks like you have a problem. Do you really know that you have knowledge? I mean, do you know that you know?"

STUDENT: "Do I know that I know?"

PROFESSOR: "Yes. And do you know that you know that you know? Do you know that you know that you know that you know?"

STUDENT: "Why do I *need* to? I don't see that I need to know that I know that I know, for example, that lemons cure scurvy. It seems like it's enough just to know. Then I eat one. Why do I need to know that I know? You're being unreasonably demanding. I'm committed to rationality, and to the ideal of proportioning my beliefs to the evidence. But that involves weighing and comparing, not pretending to infallibility. Can't we be rational, reasonable and justified in our beliefs, without being absolutely infallibly certain?

Can't a person, indeed, be quite justified and rational and believe something that happens to be, unbeknownst to him, actually false? I could think of many such cases. Remember that frightened immigrant who shot at a trick or treater who was dressed up like a thug and mimicking the behavior of an attacker? The immigrant didn't know about Halloween, and the trick or treater was on his way to a party but accidentally approached the wrong front door. Wasn't that homeowner, ignorant as he was of Halloween, *justified* in his *belief* that he was probably in danger from this apparently crazy man in a ski mask threatening him at his front door?"

PROFESSOR: "Well, the proposition that the trick or treater was a real criminal would not have been justified for you. You know about Halloween."

STUDENT: "Yes, but the immigrant didn't know about Halloween. So his beliefs, however false, were nonetheless quite justified and reasonable, in the circumstances."

PROFESSOR: "Okay, maybe. But even if you're right that infallibility isn't required for justification, it's a philosopher's job, not just to know that lemons cure scurvy, but to know that we know it. That's epistemology, and that's what we're doing right now."

STUDENT: "Well, if it's the sailor's business to know that lemons cure scurvy, then maybe it's the philosopher's business to show that the sailor *probably can know* that lemons cure scurvy. Okay. But it's nobody's obligation to prove that we know that we know that we know. That's simply unnecessary, just as a perfect, absolute, infallible certainty is also unnecessary: since we always deal in probabilities, not in certainties. You're just trying to sneak your same old unreasonable demand for infallible certainty back in, by another door."

PROFESSOR: "Why isn't it the job of philosophy to prove that we know that we know that we know that we know?"

STUDENT: "What's the purpose of philosophy? To learn how to reason more carefully, to identify and guard against common fallacies. To check ourselves for consistency. To find implausible beliefs and correct, or at least improve on, them. To combat false and harmful doctrines that people are suffering from. False beliefs are a hazard. Knowledge, on the other hand, is power. If you're dying of scurvy on Magellan's ship, you need to know that eating lemons will save your life. You're even better off if you know that what you need isn't lemons, per se, but only a little supply of one vitamin they happen to contain, and that certain other fruits also happen to contain it. Knowledge is useful."

PROFESSOR: "Okay, but, the skeptic says we don't have any knowledge. He says you don't know anything unless you know you're not just dreaming you're eating lemons on Magellan's ship, when in reality you're an accountant named Walter Mitty asleep at his desk in Ohio."

STUDENT: "Well, of course, in that case, it doesn't make any difference, because then you're only dreaming you've got scurvy. I mean, you don't necessarily need to know whether or not you're awake, just as long as you know lemons cure scurvy----just in case you're awake. The ultimate object of the game isn't necessarily the obtaining of absolute *certainty*, it's figuring out what to do."

PROFESSOR: "How now? That's *my* answer! Again, you're a crypto-Pragmatist."

STUDENT: "No, not quite. I'm merely trying to wean you from the idea that the object of the game can *only* be the obtaining of infallible certainty. Why are you so hung up on infallible certainty? You don't *need* it. You just need some relative subjective probabilities. You can know that lemons cure scurvy, even if you don't know whether or not you're dreaming right now, because you don't need to be infallibly certain to *know* things. You just need a little luck.

The task of philosophy is to help the scientist or the doctor to show the sailor that he should probably eat a lemon, because lemons are probably real, and they probably cure scurvy, and he probably has scurvy, and he should probably reject his irrational, superstitious belief that some god or demon will punish anyone who eats lemons, because he obtained that belief by committing a logical fallacy. The task is not necessarily to prove to him that he knows that he knows that he knows anything with infallible certainty."

PROFESSOR: "How exactly is this supposed to differ from my philosophy---what I call Pragmatism? You're always preaching my own religion to me!"

STUDENT: "Not true. Your philosophy differs because you claim Hume's skepticism is irrefutable. If that were really true, your so-called Pragmatism wouldn't work. Hume says we can't predict the future at all nor discern *any* matter of empirical fact whatsoever, even as a probability. If this were true, then nobody could ever tell whether one course of action is even *probably* more practical than any other."

Cartesian Prejudice

PROFESSOR: "I want to return for a minute to this question of certainty. The thing is, at least historically, the quest for perfectly certain knowledge has been something undertaken by the greatest philosophers."

STUDENT: "Well, I'm not going to blame them for trying. Nor would I blame a medieval alchemist for trying to turn lead into gold. There's nothing wrong with aiming high. But notice that we don't need to abandon chemistry in despair, just because it turns out we can't cheaply manufacture gold from lead.

Descartes boasted that he could prove the absolute certainty of various things including the existence of God, even if we start from a position of universal doubt, and even go so far as to positively assume that everything we now believe is false. I mean, that was really sporting of him. But his failure to pull off such an extreme and unnecessary demonstration should not scare us away from less prejudiced attempts."

PROFESSOR: "The Cartesian method is prejudiced?"

STUDENT: "Yes, prejudiced! Descartes's procedure isn't fair. He asks us to start out by accepting a dogmatic prejudice! Look at what he says. He says: 'I thought it was necessary for me to reject, *as absolutely false*, everything as to which I could imagine the least ground of doubt.' That's a completely unjustified *prejudice*. You shouldn't dogmatically *assume* that everything as to which you can *imagine* the least ground of doubt, must therefore *be* absolutely false. There's a big difference between something you can imagine might, possibly, be false, and something you should deem to be actually false. That is not a mere suspension of belief, but a mindless flight from believing *p is true* to a dogmatic conviction that *p is false*. It just trades in one set of suspected prejudices for another, less plausible, set. If it's an unprejudiced search for truth you're after, you don't begin by saddling yourself with completely dogmatic, unjustified prejudices like that. Descartes unfairly biased the contest, and tilted the playing field, toward skepticism. That's cheating."

PROFESSOR: "You misunderstand Descartes. He says he did that, as he puts it, 'in order to see if, afterwards, there remained anything in my belief that was entirely certain.' It was just an experiment, to see what would happen."

STUDENT: "I know. But the problem is that some skeptics like to pretend this Cartesian procedure is fair. That's bogus. Even if you thought that some Cartesian-style First Philosophy was the way to go, you wouldn't want to begin the process by arbitrarily assuming a completely dogmatic, unjustified, and *prima facie* implausible prejudice. Skepticism has no more right than anti-skepticism to tip the playing field in such an arbitrary and dogmatic way."

PROFESSOR: "Okay, but can't you see that he's trying to show how he can beat skepticism, even if he plays with a handicap? He says the *cogito* still works, even if you start out with a dogmatically-skeptical bias. That's cool. He says he can beat skepticism with one hand tied behind his back."

STUDENT: "But the problem is it doesn't work. He failed; as you pointed out. His *cogito* argument doesn't actually work. In the meantime, the failure of his attempt gave skepticism a new lease on life. Skepticism got an undeserved reputation for being somehow unbeatable, just because it beat Descartes by cheating on a tilted field. That's so bogus."

PROFESSOR: "How ungrateful you are. Descartes was one of the greatest souls who ever lived."

STUDENT: "I don't want to be ungrateful. If I say that Descartes was, so to speak, being unnecessarily macho, I don't mean that as criticism of him personally. As I said, it was very sporting of him. We're talking about unintended consequences. The only point I'm trying to make is that the skeptics need to understand that the failure of the *cogito* doesn't mean what they seem to think it does. Descartes thought he could beat skepticism with one hand tied behind his back, and he apparently failed. But, so what? My point is simply that I'm not offering to tie one hand behind my back. Nor should I.

The Cartesian procedure pretends to be clean, fair and neutral, while in truth it's anything but."

PROFESSOR: "Well, wait a minute. Maybe it is. I mean, the idea is that we start off with a clean slate, right? We clear the ground of all prior beliefs and then go from there."

STUDENT: "But that's not what he does! He sweeps the ground of all prior beliefs, but, then, the next thing he does is lay down a new dogmatic layer of ridiculous beliefs and then demand they be *accepted*---on faith!"

PROFESSOR: "What dogmatic beliefs?"

STUDENT: "Beliefs like that *one is, in fact, being deceived by a demon*. Read the book! He says:

> I will suppose, then...that some malignant demon, who is at once exceedingly potent and deceitful, has employed all his artifice to deceive me; I will suppose that the sky, the air, the earth, colors, figures, sounds, and all external things, are nothing better than the illusions of dreams, by means of which this being has laid snares for my credulity; I will consider myself as without hands, eyes, flesh, blood, or any of the senses, and as falsely believing that I am possessed of these; *I will continue resolutely fixed in this belief.* [6]

That's cheating! What Descartes does is not clean. It's not fair. It's

170

not neutral. It's not rational. It's biased, dogmatic, unjustified, spurious, and crazy on its face! But more to the point, it's the very definition of *prejudice*."

PROFESSOR: "Okay, okay. That's easy to fix. We'll just amend it to say that one *might---possibly---*be under the sway of a demon. Not that one *is*. But merely that it's *possible*."

STUDENT: "It's *possible*---that one is being deceived by a *demon*?"

PROFESSOR: "Yeah."

STUDENT: "You believe that? You think that's *possible*? I don't."

PROFESSOR: "Sure. I mean, well---it's *conceivable*. I mean, it's *logically* possible. I guess."

STUDENT: "Do you think that it's *physically* possible?"

PROFESSOR: "I don't know. Maybe."

STUDENT: "Well if you know so little, how could you know that such a thing *is possible*? That's a big, bold claim for one so unsure. Maybe it actually *isn't* possible."

PROFESSOR: "Well, you know, if we're just starting out right at the ground level here, then we're not supposed to be taking stuff for granted yet, like some law of physics or logic that might rule out demons as being impossible."

STUDENT: "Let me get this straight. We're supposed to be starting out, right on the ground, like newborn babes or something, and the first thing you want me to lay down on the Cartesian ground is the sentence: *'Demons are possible'*? This is supposed to come even before *I think therefore I am*? This is the first proposition that you propose we write down on our clean, freshly-wiped slate: *Demons are Possible*. Look, if I'm not allowed to take it for granted that demons are physically impossible, why are *you* allowed to take it for granted that they're *not*?"

PROFESSOR: "Okay, well, how about: *demons might be possible?*"

STUDENT: "It's possible that demons are possible?"

PROFESSOR: "Well anything is *possible.*"

STUDENT: "Is that true? Really? Is that your new *cogito* now: *Anything is Possible?* Are you saying that proposition is like, self-evident or something? Sorry, but I can't agree. I find it very hard to believe that *anything is possible.* I mean, it just seems to me that it *may* be that some things are actually impossible---especially that some things might be *physically* impossible. I suppose I could be wrong in thinking that, but at least I have to say that very far from seeming self-evident, the proposition 'anything is possible' strikes me, *prima facie*, as somewhat dubious.

More importantly, as an aspiring Cartesian *cogito*, it looks nicely self-refuting: since, *if it is true that anything is possible, then it's possible that it's not true that anything is possible.*"

PROFESSOR: "Okay, forget that. Maybe what I should have said is that what we do in a proper, reformed Cartesian procedure is to *suspend* all our former prejudices and cherished beliefs. Just suspend them. How's that?"

STUDENT: "I don't really understand. What do you mean we suspend them?"

PROFESSOR: "Well, you know we sort of put them on hold, shift them into neutral, *neither believing them, nor disbelieving them.* We put them into an mental escrow account."

STUDENT: "Okay. Sure. Fine. All of them right? All?"

PROFESSOR: "Well, yeah. Of course."

STUDENT: "Okay, no problem. But, of course, that would include all those former beliefs and prejudices such as, for example, that demons are possible, or that I once saw an electrode, or that a brain might be able to survive in a vat of fluid. So, I guess now, when you suggest that *I might possibly be an electrode-covered brain surviving in a vat of fluid*, I no longer have any good reason to believe that's remotely likely or even physically *possible*. Are you going to offer me something like a new *cogito* now, to give me some reason to think the vat story is physically possible?"

The Ubiquitous 'Burden of Proof' Cheat

PROFESSOR: "Wait a minute, now. Are you saying you think I, as the skeptic, have the burden of proof ?"

STUDENT: "No. What "burden of proof"? I fail to see why either of us should be saddled before the contest even begins with some kind of bogus handicap. It's not a criminal trial. If you must think in terms of legal analogies, think of it as a civil suit, in which the victory simply goes to the side with the better overall case. You know, the more plausible argument or the preponderance of the evidence--- however you like to phrase it. Let's be fair to each other."

PROFESSOR: "Well, maybe I should argue that you have a special burden of proof, since you're the one who claims to know things, while I don't claim to know anything."

STUDENT: "Except then you'd be claiming to *know* that I ought to suffer under some special 'burden of proof', and then I'd say that looks a little tougher to know, than that one and one is two, or that rocks exist---things you say you can't know. Anyway, then I'll just claim that you have the burden, since, as people say, extraordinary claims require extraordinary proof, and skepticism is an extraordinary claim."

PROFESSOR: "Well, Aristotle says that he who asserts must prove."

STUDENT: "So, then I guess it's up to you and Aristotle to prove that 'he who asserts must prove.' Good luck.

Aristotle's rule seems silly, since the belief of either side can be expressed as an assertion.

Is it just supposed to mean that he who speaks first must prove? That sounds like a maxim of utility or polite behavior or something like that, rather than a radical epistemological truth.

Besides, skeptical philosophers have written hundreds and hundreds of pages crammed with all sorts of assertions. They boldly claim to know that nobody really knows anything. They positively assert that we know that people have made mistakes. They claim that this proves the conclusion that every person can always be mistaken in *every* situation. (Notice the dubious validity.) They claim to know that they might be dreaming. They claim that the senses can 'lie.' They claim that reason is of dubious efficacy, etc. Skeptics are full of assertions. If Aristotle was right, and 'he who asserts must prove,' then skeptics are in big trouble."

PROFESSOR: "Not Cratylus. He was an ancient skeptic who never asserted anything. He never even spoke."

STUDENT: "If that were true, then how could anybody know he was a skeptic?"

PROFESSOR: "He wagged his finger."

STUDENT: "So?"

PROFESSOR: "Well, when he wagged his finger, he was rightly understood by his students to mean that nothing can be known."

STUDENT: "Then he asserted something. Besides, you're no Cratylus. You go so far as to positively assert something you yourself are in a position to know isn't true---namely, that *it is possible that I have no legs and am floating in a vat.* And if that weren't bad enough, then you try to convince me that, therefore, I can't possibly know anything about the external world, when you yourself know all the time that this is *not* the position I'm in, since you can see my legs! Have you no shame?"

PROFESSOR: "Oh, come now. I'm only trying to explain radical skepticism to you. Besides, how do I know you have any legs? I could be dreaming."

STUDENT: "Look, I'm offering you a level playing field. Let's agree that what we both want to find out is which side has the better overall case. If we try to saddle one side or the other with a special handicap at the outset, then we're not only cheating each other, we're also cheating ourselves.

We would be cheating ourselves of the opportunity to find out once and for all which side basically has the better overall case. Let's not try to shut down the contest before it even begins.

Besides, you're in no position to prove anything. Are you saying you think I'm *more* justified in believing that so-called 'burdens of proof' really exist, than that *rocks* exist, or that *I* exist? How are you going to be able to claim that I'm justified in believing I have a burden of proof, but not justified in believing that I have *legs*? Are you going to say that I have a good reason to believe I have a 'burden of proof,' while at the same time saying nobody ever has a good reason to believe *anything*? If I were you, I'd take the level playing field and be grateful."

The Skeptic as Kamikaze

STUDENT: "Come to think of it, this gives me an idea. I mean, the skeptic claims that no *one has a good reason to believe anything.* If so, then he himself has no good reason to believe it. He has no good reason to think that no one has a good reason to think anything. He perfectly refutes himself without any help from me! If nobody has a good reason to believe anything, then nobody has a good reason to believe that nobody has a reason to believe anything. Skepticism says no belief regarding any matter of fact is a justified belief. If so, then *that* can't be a justified belief either. No doctrine could refute itself more obviously than skepticism does. Game over. You lose. I win."

PROFESSOR: "That answer isn't sufficient."

STUDENT: "Why not?"

PROFESSOR: "Because you still need to be able to prevent the skeptic from apparently performing a *reductio ad absurdum* upon your own philosophy. If your own views can apparently be reduced to absurdity by right reason, you know *somebody* made a mistake *somewhere,* because if your philosophy is correct, that cannot happen. I mean, according to your own philosophy, somebody must have made a mistake somewhere, so you'd better figure out where. The flaw may have originated from your own philosophy.

You may compare the skeptic to a kamikaze pilot, but you'd better make sure he can't sink your ship and take you down with him. There are two kinds of Kamikazes, the kind that miss, and the kind that hit."

STUDENT: "Okay. But I don't see my ship sinking, yet. I don't even see it smoking. And you've helpfully pointed out that radical skepticism is limited to performing a *reductio* upon the premises of somebody else's philosophy, rather than supporting any claims of its own. In other words, skepticism represents not a claim in itself, but rather a coherence test for various philosophies to pass. And therefore, whenever a skeptic legitimately reduces to absurdity somebody's philosophy, then all that really proves is that *one particular* philosophy has failed, but not that all others must also fail. So, a skeptic's work is never done."

PROFESSOR: "Don't I know it."

STUDENT: "So, if my epistemology is the only one that can beat skepticism, then it must be the best one."

PROFESSOR: "Ah, youth. Do you *really* suppose, that of all the epistemologies in history, yours is likely to represent the final answer to this profound and age-old debate, a debate which has obsessed some of the world's smartest thinkers for hundreds, if not thousands, of years?"

STUDENT: "Well if there really are so very many epistemologies to choose from, then what could possibly give the skeptic reason to suppose that skepticism is powerful and cogent enough to defeat every single one of them, each one in its turn, from now until the end of time?"

Is This an Appeal to Simplicity?

PROFESSOR: "Okay, but I'm not finished with yours yet. Here's another objection. You say a chain is only as strong as its weakest link, and to the same old common sense chain, the vat story adds more links. You say however chancy the first scenario looks to us, the second scenario can only look even chancier, so we appear to have no choice but to conclude that chances are better for the one than for the other. Etc."

STUDENT: "That's right."

PROFESSOR: "Okay, so that sounds to me like you're appealing to the Epistemic Virtue of Simplicity."

STUDENT: "What's that?"

PROFESSOR: "It's an epistemic principle that says all other things being equal, go with the simpler theory. Some call it Ockham's razor. You know, you don't add more moving parts to an explanation than you need."

STUDENT: "Well, I guess that sounds okay. But, to be honest, I had no intention to appeal to any particular 'epistemic principle.' I'm just making an individual argument that strikes me as plausible. Let's just say I prefer you to take my argument the way it is, by itself. Don't yoke me to Ockham, or anybody else. Just let my argument stand or fall on its own. If you want to show me what's wrong with my argument, then just show me what's wrong with my argument, the way I framed it, myself. I'm not *appealing to* a broad, general principle, I'm just offering one individual argument. I don't even know if I believe in the existence of 'epistemic principles.' At this point, I'm still working on trying to believe in tables and chairs.

If you want to shoot down my argument, then shoot it down as an individual. I don't really know what sort of 'epistemic principles' might be gleaned from what I said, and frankly, the very notion of 'epistemic principles' seriously bothers me. I'm not that comfortable with it as a doctrine. Let's be careful not to put the cart before the horse.

And don't forget that my burden of proof is no greater than yours, so don't suppose you're somehow specially entitled to just sit back and fold your arms, and demand that I jump through burning hoops and prove all sorts of things to your skeptical satisfaction. You tell me: what's wrong with my *particular* thoughts here?"

PROFESSOR: "Well don't try to throw a special burden of proof on me, if you don't like it when I do that to you. Do unto others as you would have them do unto you."

STUDENT: "Okay, but I've given you an argument that says the mundane scenario beats the others. The ball is in your court. Your Kamikaze hasn't wounded my ship yet, so far as I can see."

PROFESSOR: "Well, I'm saying you now have an obligation to prove the validity of Ockham's Razor. You need to offer a proof of the Epistemic Principle of Simplicity, in order to support your case."

STUDENT: "No I don't. Why do I? You're so dogmatic. As I said, my argument isn't intended to 'appeal to' some supposed 'epistemic principle'; its individual cogency seems to me to be more sure, on its face, than some tedious defense of any supposed 'epistemic principle' you imagine to be embodied in it. A higher court doesn't appeal to a lower one.

Remember, I'm not claiming infallibility. Nor do I need to. Why do I need to defend Ockham? Let Ockham fend for himself. He's managed quite well for centuries without my help. Do you have some reason to complain against him? Or are you just going to sit there with your arms folded and say 'prove it' after everything I say? That's just the old Burden of Proof Cheat. Or else it's an unreasonable and unnecessary demand for absolute certainty. We've been over both of those."

PROFESSOR: "You don't need to prove the validity of Ockham's razor?"

STUDENT: "Not that I can see. Look, if you can't shake this irrational urge to collect these animals you call 'epistemic principles,' then better you should call my argument an Appeal to the Epistemic Principle of Piggyback Riding."

PROFESSOR: "Okay, then, what's the Epistemic Principle of Piggyback Riding?"

STUDENT: "I don't know. Listen, my argument is this. Here you sit, having experiences and believing you remember a rich and varied past life full of other, still more varied experiences. That's the situation in which you find yourself right now. That's not a claim, it's just my way of referring to or pointing at what you're feeling right now, *however* you feel---okay? Maybe you're asleep; maybe you're insane. Maybe all your memories are false. Maybe you're a brain in a vat, or a green alien in a coma high on drugs living in a universe with no galaxies. Maybe. Or maybe you're what you seem to be, an ordinary man on Earth, and the experiences you're having are due to the usual suspects, such as tables and chairs.

My argument was simply that the latter, mundane version of the story must be considered the most plausible contestant you've got. The alternative scenarios, as intriguing as they may be, are not quite *equal* in their *prima facie* plausibility.

Why? Because they ride piggyback on the mundane version, and between a piggyback rider and the one who carries him there can be little doubt which of the two is in the more precarious position. I mean, any delusional scenario of skepticism requires first of all that we accept our mundane beliefs, such as that *vats really can hold fluid*, and that *electrodes can stimulate brains*, and *the construction of a great supercomputer is probably possible*, and that *a mad scientist might conceivably desire to deceive somebody*, etc., etc.

There's a reason why skeptical arguments don't impress toddlers: the reason is that toddlers are too unfamiliar with *electrodes*, and *computers*. Nor have they heard of *demons*, or even brains."

PROFESSOR: "So what?"

STUDENT: "So, they don't yet have any reason to believe the scenarios are possible. They don't even have our mundane opinions about retinas, yet."

PROFESSOR: "Okay. So?"

STUDENT: "Think about it. The delusional scenarios add---to our ordinary, mundane story---additional elements, operations, and events, none of which are, of course, anywhere near being perfectly certain, even as *physical possibilities*, much less as *equal probabilities*. I mean such as that *a Cartesian evil demon is physically possible*, or that *flying robots can successfully service a Matrix jelly pod*, or that *amazing super-computers and scientists with heroically effective electrodes can really produce your rich kind of experience*.

The *possibility* that these things *might* not really be *physically possible*, and the *possibility* that even if *possible*, that they aren't *really actual*, can therefore only *subtract* from the overall likelihood of the scenarios of which they are a part.

If a chain is only as strong as its weakest link, then you can only hope to make a chain weaker by adding more links to it, especially if those links can only be relatively weaker than the original links."

PROFESSOR: "That argument reminds me of a similar one I once read by Richard Fumerton who said, 'I suspect that a purely formal justification for preferring a simple theory to a more complex theory is often available.' In fact, he offered what he called 'a *deductive* justification for preferring the simpler of two theories':

> Suppose I am considering two incompatible theories *T1* and *T2* which, relative to my evidence, are equally likely to be true. Suppose, further, that after acquiring some additional evidence (let us call my new *total* body of evidence *E*) I find it necessary to add an hypothesis *H1* to *T2*. Now provided the probability of *T1* and *T2* relative to *E* remains the same and assuming that the probability of *H1* relative to *E* is less than 1, we can *deduce* from the probability calculus that, relative to *E*, *T1* is more likely to be true than the complex theory (*T2* and *H1*). Intuitively, *T2 by itself* ran the same risk of error as *T1*, so with the addition of another hypothesis which might be false it runs a *greater* risk of error than *T1*. [7]

STUDENT: "I love it!"

PROFESSOR: "Well, don't get too excited. Fumerton is in many ways your perfect nemesis, as we shall see. But for now I'd just like to say that if mere *simplicity* is the path to victory, then I think I can win."

STUDENT: "Wait a minute now. I never said that *mere* simplicity and simplicity *alone* is what counts. Obviously not: there are simple lies and complicated truths, and what always matters first and foremost is the conformity or *fit* of a theory to the empirical data we have available. Fit is more important than mere simplicity."

PROFESSOR: "Well then why aren't you attacking the skeptical scenarios on fit to data?"

STUDENT: "Well I guess I thought the idea was supposed to be that on that account they're allegedly equal."

PROFESSOR: "Hmmm. So, does that mean you're admitting the vat theory and the mundane theory are equal in *data fit*?"

STUDENT: "No, I'm not sure I'm ready to grant they're equal on data fit. But never mind that now. If you want to show how the vat is a simpler theory, then please show me. I want to hear that argument anyway, decisive or not."

The Simple Life of a Windowless Monad

PROFESSOR: "Okay, then, forget the demon, the *Matrix,* and the brain in the vat. How about a very simple theory that says that this is all a dream, and the truth is that you're a windowless monad, asleep, dreaming that you are a human on Earth."

STUDENT: "A what?"

PROFESSOR: "A monad."

STUDENT: "I have no idea what you're saying."

PROFESSOR: "A monad---a *windowless monad.* Haven't you ever read Leibniz?"

STUDENT: "Sorry."

PROFESSOR: "A monad is a single mathematical point, having no extension in space, but possessing or constituting a conscious mind. It is a tiny little atomic soul, with no parts. This is from a book called *The Monadology,* published in the eighteenth century."

STUDENT: "How can something with no parts be conscious? How can anything that has no dimensions possibly have thoughts? It has no place for thoughts to operate---it has no parts to give rise to thoughts. So, how can it think? This is goofy. You want me to find this plausible?"

PROFESSOR: "You have to read the book. It's all explained. The only reason you find it implausible is because you're materialistic. You believe that only a healthy, active, living *brain* can think, or maybe an extremely complex machine like a computer."

STUDENT: "That's right."

PROFESSOR: "But if you're a windowless monad, then you're just wrong about that."

STUDENT: "Okay. But why should I switch horses? I've got all these experiences which lead me to believe that only complex machines or brains *can* think. It seems, looking at all this empirical evidence, that I've got the right theory going here, and Leibniz is wrong. I mean, the only reason Leibniz thought that a windowless monad *could* have experiences, is because he didn't have all the data I've got. He lived a long time ago, when people assumed that immortal souls could travel through the air and go from one body to another, while leaving their brains behind. They thought the soul was like a puff of smoke or a tiny spark housed in the pineal gland or something. But 200 years of medical experience has *driven* us to believe otherwise."

PROFESSOR: "Well, how do you know they were wrong?"

STUDENT: "Well, what about Damasio's neurology patients, and Phineas Gage, the guy who had his personality altered by an iron rod that passed through his frontal lobe. It didn't touch his pineal gland. Brain injuries, drugs, and brain surgeries radically alter consciousness in certain predictable ways. If the brain is severed with a knife, you end up with what seems like a severed *mind*. So the monad theory fails on fit to empirical data. The mind seems complicated, complex. And, what do you know, it turns out that the human brain is one of the most complicated machines on Earth. What an amazing coincidence! In the old days, some people used to think the brain was some kind of radiator for cooling the blood. But if you spend a lot of time studying brains and looking at their parts under microscopes, etc., you can't help but notice they look a lot more like computers than radiators. If the brain is a radiator for cooling the blood, it's a very poorly designed one.

So, if you look at the empirical evidence of science, it looks like you probably can't have thoughts without a brain, or something like a brain, a very complex material mechanism. And that means it looks dubious that I *could* be nothing more than a windowless monad. It doesn't necessarily seem possible *physically*. I mean, what evidence is there *for* the Leibnizian theory?"

PROFESSOR: "How do you know it's false?"

STUDENT: "I make no claim to infallibility. But, I can't understand what makes Leibniz imagine there are any 'monads' (I once saw a brain in a jar of fluid, but of course I've never seen a monad), or that such an entity could think, or that we're all monads, despite appearances to the contrary. I assure you that you don't look like a monad: you appear to have a nice healthy extension in space. And as for me, I wish I could find a way to reduce a bit my own apparent extension. Besides, you know *you* are something more than a mere figment of my windowless imagination."

PROFESSOR: "I know no such thing about *you*, though. I don't know if you are a real material substance, or merely a figment or a dream. Of course, I don't deny that this sky looks blue, and this dock feels solid beneath our feet, and this oar in my hand seems rough and cold and heavy. You know I admit all these things, and I deny no part of this world you call the world of common sense. But I'm just putting together a radically different explanation of the causes of all these mundane facts."

STUDENT: "How is this windowless monad scenario any better than the one about the brain in the vat, or the Matrix pod, or the Cartesian demon? It's got the same problems."

PROFESSOR: "This one is simpler. That makes it *better*, right?"

STUDENT: "Leibniz's *Monadology* is simpler than common sense?"

PROFESSOR: "Yeah."

STUDENT: "But you said you don't deny that this sky looks blue, and this dock fells solid beneath our feet, and this oar in your hand seems rough and cold and heavy. And therefore I suppose you don't deny the story of Phineas Gage, and the severed brains, and all the rest of all that stuff I call the empirical evidence of neuroscience."

PROFESSOR: "Certainly not. I don't think I have to deny any of the empirical data. I'm just offering a different theory to explain it all."

STUDENT: "Well, then, how is it any *simpler*?"

PROFESSOR: "It's a simpler theory."

STUDENT: "Is it? I mean, I haven't read Leibniz. I don't know how simple it is. I guess a windowless monad is supposed to be, in one sense, simpler than a brain. But if a monad contains the whole world of oars and docks and ships and neuroscience labs within itself, as it must, then I guess there are just as many items in a monadologist's ontological menagerie as there are in mine. Maybe more, if what I call *one apple* is, for him, a series of ten thousand windowless hallucinatory images, multiplied again by the number of monads involved. So much for simplicity. You're just adding some new unattractive links to the good old mundane chain. And those new links appear weaker."

PROFESSOR: "Well, the Leibnizian world has various features, of course, since it has to explain a lot of empirical evidence. There are, for example, different types of monads. It's a bit like Greek atomism. So, maybe it isn't a simpler theory after all. But, see here, I don't know why I have to saddle myself with Leibniz's explanation of life. I think I can offer one of my own, one that is really the simplest of all."

STUDENT: "What's that?"

Super Simple

PROFESSOR: "It's this: the only thing that really exists is my own experiences. Nothing else. Just the experiences, and nothing more. That's it."

STUDENT: "Hey, wait a minute, what about *my* experiences?"

PROFESSOR: "They're nothing to me. According to my theory, they don't exist."

STUDENT: "That sounds more like an autistic syndrome, than a theory."

PROFESSOR: "Ridicule is not an argument. I'm reducing your own epistemology to absurdity, so don't laugh too hard. You said go with the simpler theory, and this one is the simplest."

STUDENT: "I never said 'you should always go for the simpler theory.' When did I say that? Maybe if all other things are equal, okay, but obviously there's more to plausibility than *just* simplicity. I mean, what good is it to have the simpler theory, if it doesn't fit the data?"

PROFESSOR: "Nothing fits the data perfectly."

STUDENT: "The truth does."

PROFESSOR: "Does it?"

STUDENT: "Well, whatever doesn't fit the data, can't be true. How could it be?"

PROFESSOR: "God, your corny *naiveté* is almost touching."

STUDENT: "And your cynical corruption is depressing."

PROFESSOR: "What could possibly fit the data better than the last theory I just proposed?"

STUDENT: "What theory?"

PROFESSOR: "The theory that *your experiences are all there is.* There's no underlying 'basis' for your experiences; there's no 'cause' of your experiences, there's just the experiences themselves. That's it. End of story. It's as simple as possible, and fits the data like a glove! Voila! Indeed, it fits the data so perfectly because here the theory just *is* the data. What more could you ask for?"

STUDENT: "Well, I could ask for a *theory.*"

PROFESSOR: "That *is* the theory. The theory is just the one claim, that your experiences have no cause, and are simply all there is that exists."

STUDENT: "That's not a theory!"

PROFESSOR: "Sure it is."

STUDENT: "Well, it isn't an *explanation.* I'm looking for a theory that *explains* the data. An explanatory theory. What you're offering is just the raw data, with no explanation. But that's the given. I've already got that, thanks. Now I'm looking around for a theory that explains it. The whole point of explanatory theories is to be able to do

186

things like predict the future, in other words, to go beyond what's merely given in our immediate experience right now. I'm asking myself, why am I having all these experiences? And what's with the somewhat repetitive and orderly pattern they exhibit? Can I control them? Can I predict them? I'm wondering about it all, and looking for a plausible explanation. You haven't offered *any* explanatory theory, so it *cannot* be true that your explanatory theory is more plausible."

PROFESSOR: "Sure I have, I've offered the theory that there just is no causal basis of your experiences."

STUDENT: "That's not an explanation. That isn't an offer to explain the data. That's just a spurious, groundless, implausible claim that the data of experience *can't be explained*."

PROFESSOR: "Well, on what grounds do you reject it?"

STUDENT: "Well, for one thing, it hardly seems *possible*. If it is true that *everything* that exists is nothing more than yet another one of 'my experiences,' and everything in the world is 'in my mind,' and equally so, then how could that statement itself make any sense? Somehow, to say that *anything and everything is equally p*, seems to rob *p* of all possible meaning. I need something else, something that is *not p,* or at least *less p*, for contrast. To say 'everything is merely an experience of my mind,' is to rob the predicate of all meaning.

Also, if my experiences can't be explained, then why does my materialistic realism seem to explain them so well? With my present theory I find I can make all sorts of predictions that seem to work amazingly well. Why is that? How is that even possible?

If my experiences have no causal basis, then why do they appear to? Why the apparent order, the repetitive patterns, the seeming laws? Why does it hurt every time I hit my thumb with a hammer?

How could I be merely having experiences, if I don't actually have any material brain, nor any perceptual apparatus like sense organs, nor any actual things to look at, to affect the senses? After all, if eyeballs really exist, then something more than *mere experiences* exists. And how can I believe that all these other people, people like you, are just senseless, mindless figments of my own imagination? You appear to have your own sense experiences, just like I do. You have hands that look just like mine. You tell me that you see a full moon on the same nights that I seem to see the moon as full. Why is it that I never see a full moon, when you tell me you see a crescent moon?"

PROFESSOR: "Maybe I'm just humoring you."

STUDENT: "Well, it's worse than that, since *you* don't even have any experiences, according to your supposed "theory." You said *my* experiences are all that exist, so it's basically solipsism."

PROFESSOR: "Call it what you like."

STUDENT: "Why have I never, *ever,* had an experience of you saying you see a crescent moon when I see a full one? You're asking me to believe that this is nothing more than pure coincidence."

PROFESSOR: "I'm not saying that. I'm not saying anything about that. You keep asking why this and why that. But according to my theory, things just don't *have* causes or explanations."

STUDENT: "Well, why do things *seem* to have causes? I mean, why do I experience my experiences as, you know, so predictable? Why aren't they more like dreams, which seem so unpredictable, nonsensical, lawless, disjointed, fleeting and incoherent? Why does it *always* hurt when I stub my toe?"

PROFESSOR: "It just does."

STUDENT: "You don't know why?"

PROFESSOR: "My theory says: *there just isn't any reason why.*"

STUDENT: "Oh, come on. There's no 'theory' here at all. It's a big nothing. It's not a competing scenario or a *rival explanation* to the Cartesian demon, and the brain in the vat, the Matrix pod, and materialistic realism. It's just the absence of a competing rival. To enter the contest with a competing explanation, you first of all have to have an explanation to enter. You can't just enter your cat, or an old shoe. If you want to enter, as a rival contestant, a paranoid fantasy to explain the fact that solipsism is actually true for me, then fine. But in that case, you need some plausible story to tell about how it might work. You need to explain why things seem the way they do. If you don't have a rival explanation of experience to offer, then you can't undermine my mundane explanation of experience."

PROFESSOR: "Okay, then, I'll just flesh it a little, and say that you're in an insane asylum, asleep and dreaming while on drugs."

STUDENT: "What drugs?"

PROFESSOR: "A pint of LSD."

STUDENT: "How did I get there?"

PROFESSOR: "I'm not saying. Maybe I don't know."

STUDENT: "Well, then, where did you get this idea?"

PROFESSOR: "I'm the doctor."

STUDENT: "No you aren't. You know you're not."

PROFESSOR: "But you don't."

STUDENT: "Yes, I do."

PROFESSOR: "You don't know for *sure*."

STUDENT: "I don't need infallible certainty to know things. I just need a little luck."

PROFESSOR: "You're feeling lucky?"

STUDENT: "Where's the asylum? What year is it? What planet are we on? There's nothing simple about this one. It doesn't beat common sense in data fit, and surely not in simplicity, since it's twice the complexity that common sense is. You've got a whole second universe that needs furnishing, in addition to this one. It's no better than the Matrix, or the electrode-wielding mad scientist with the amazing vat. It's a loser."

PROFESSOR: "Okay, then how about the one where you're nothing more than one delusional, dreaming pink elephant floating all alone in a void."

STUDENT: "If I'm an elephant, I need to eat. I need air to breathe. It's not *prima facie* plausible enough to equal my common sense rival. It sounds physically impossible."

PROFESSOR: "Okay, you're one tiny windowless monad then all alone in a void."

STUDENT: "It's still more complex than common sense. Now you've got two worlds of facts to describe, this illusory one filled with a wealth of dream images, and one *extra,* the real one with the lone monad in it. That's a longer story than mine. Besides, the extra part is just an arbitrary chapter tacked on at the end of the story. You have no reason even to suggest it. It's a spurious complication."

PROFESSOR: "So what? Why should I worry about spurious complications?"

STUDENT: "For the reason your man Fumerton gave. Besides, spurious complications are too easy to gin up. That makes them suspect. What's harder is to achieve simplicity. If you have to keep loading your story down with more and more epicycles, in an endless effort to increase the fit of the theory to the data, that's not a good sign. It should raise suspicions. It's like the old saying 'Oh, what a tangled web we weave, when first we practice to deceive.' Everybody with experience knows this. If we took no notice of simplicity, the mass manufacture of capricious falsehoods would become a lot cheaper. They could be multiplied like paper clips. In which case, you'd be well-advised to favor simplicity if you're trying to find the one truth among a lot of other suspiciously over-complicated stories.

Every grownup knows what happens when people lie. One lie leads to another. And another. The story starts getting more and more complicated, and each new complication breeds more complications. Eventually the whole elaborate edifice collapses, because eventually the unbearable weight of experience is too much for it. It seems to me that's the usual outcome of a false account.

I don't mean that favoring simplicity a sure fire rule that cannot fail. But we don't need infallibility. Even if simplicity is far from a fail-proof test for the truth of a story, if you tend to favor it seems to me you'll probably do better in the long run."

PROFESSOR: "Well, you wouldn't *always* be right."

STUDENT: "No, but you'd probably increase your chances. Come on, I mean, if there were nothing wrong with tacking on spurious additions, then there would be no place to stop. You might just as well keep tacking stuff like that on forever. You'd have a windowless monad dreaming that it was an alien with fins in a coma dreaming that it was a human being on Earth. This could go on and on---why are you laughing?"

PROFESSOR: "I'm just thinking that anybody listening to us talk like this, is going to say that if we aren't already in the asylum now, maybe somebody ought to *take* us there."

STUDENT: "Yeah. Heh. I was thinking the same thing."

PROFESSOR: "I'm suddenly reminded of a passage in Hume where he refers to the speculations of philosophy as 'strained and ridiculous'."

STUDENT: "Yeah, I know. And of course it's impossible for anybody with a sense of humor not to laugh at this stuff. But, at the same time, I want also to really urge you not to use that fact as an excuse to dismiss any argument. As you yourself taught me, laughter as a way to dispose of your opponent's arguments is far more efficacious than it deserves to be. It may seem quite effective, and will surely sway the crowd, but it isn't right or just. Besides, I think that the only way to overcome the challenge of skepticism requires that it first of all be taken very seriously, and that our natural, unthinking urge to just laugh it off, amounts to little more than forfeiting the match. I'd be a lazy coward to walk away from this contest, because I can prevail, and because history suggests that something important is at stake.

So my position is that I don't think you're going to be able to beat the mundane scenario in simplicity, empirical fit, or predictive power. And anyway, if you could, then it would be rational to believe the paranoid fantasy."

PROFESSOR: "Not so! I don't have to *beat* the common sense scenario, I only need to *match* it. If I can gin up a paranoid delusional fantasy that equally matches it in plausibility, then skepticism wins."

STUDENT: "Maybe. But if you *can* do that, then why *haven't* you? I think I've shown pretty well that you haven't offered any explanatory theory of my experience that equals the mundane version in its *prima facie* plausibility. Everything you've offered so far has fallen something short of that mark, and I suspect it always will. But I could be wrong. Maybe some day you'll come to me with some more compelling evidence for a wild story about how I've been living in a jelly pod and deluded all my life, and that story will truly beat my old mundane view of things in plausibility. But then I suppose I'd have to switch to the new theory of the world, just as people did when they read Newton. Or as the boy in the *Matrix* movie does. And as soon as that happened, of course, I'd no longer be living in ignorance, so then you would lose again."

A Web of Coherence Founded on the Given

PROFESSOR: "Okay, now I think I see a chink in your armor. You're always talking about the '*prima facie* plausibility' of this or that skeptical scenario, like the vat or the *Matrix*, and comparing it to the *prima facie* plausibility of your preferred humdrum common sense rival theory that says you're a regular guy and not in a vat."

STUDENT: "Right."

PROFESSOR: "Okay, fine. I understand that. But what I don't understand is how you could possibly know or *determine* the 'relative *prima facie* plausibility' (as you like to style it) of anything in this world, until *after* you have already determined the fact that you aren't in a vat. So aren't you just begging the question? Aren't you arguing in a circle?"

STUDENT: "Not that I can see. I think maybe you're hankering after your old burden of proof ploy. Or your old excessive demand for certainty. We've been over both of those."

PROFESSOR: "Actually, what I'm thinking about now is that it seems that you must be a Coherentist, and not a Foundationalist."

STUDENT: "What's that mean?"

PROFESSOR: "Foundationalism is the doctrine that knowledge is like a building or structure which rests upon a basic foundation comprised of some self-evident or indubitable bedrock. Coherentism, on the other hand, is the doctrine that knowledge is more like a logically consistent or internally coherent 'web' of beliefs which depend on sense-experience only along the periphery."

STUDENT: "I don't understand. They sound the same. Where's the conflict? If the logically coherent web of belief must conform to sense-experience along the edges, and the foundational edifice requires and possesses an interconnected logical coherence, what's the difference? Cut the web in one spot and stretch it out straight and you've got the Foundationalist's edifice, stretch the Foundationalist edifice around into a circular shape and you've got the Coherentist web. What's the difference?"

PROFESSOR: "The difference is that according to Foundationalism, thought proceeds in one direction only, from the bottom up, proceeding carefully from a first indubitable and self-evident bedrock, whereas in the Coherentist's version, you're allowed to challenge any part of the system, and to make a change in any place, in order to achieve overall coherence. Wilfrid Sellars argued for Coherentism in a famous essay in which he argued that empirical knowledge "is rational not because it has a *foundation* but because it is a self-correcting enterprise which can put *any* claim in jeopardy, though not *all* at once.'[8]"

STUDENT: "Well that sounds okay. Maybe I'll go for something like Coherentism then. Certainly, I don't want to make the mistake of saying that you can't know anything at all until you first know something else that logically entails it. If that were true then a child could never even begin to learn anything. The process has to get going somehow. But I see there in your book that Sellars also says he doesn't mean empirical knowledge 'has no foundation,' or to suggest that we 'put it in a box with rumors and hoaxes.' In fact, he says: 'There is clearly *some* point to the picture of human knowledge as resting on a level of propositions---observation reports---that do not rest on other propositions in the same way as other propositions rest on them.'[9]

So, even Sellars admits that it's not necessarily the case that all beliefs are created equal, nor that it doesn't matter where the adjustments are made. Some beliefs are more, shall we say 'foundational,' or basic, relative to others, in *some* sense, even if something like Coherentism is right. Some claims depend upon others for support. You can't prove that the Bible is true by quoting a line from the Bible that says "everything in this book is true." And no web of belief can whirl like a castle in the air. If it "must answer to the tribunal of experience," then it's an anchored web that cannot float away. The way you described it, it needs to be supported by the data of experience around the 'periphery.' So perhaps the right paradigm is some happy compromise between two extremes here. I can imagine either side wrongly going too far. Can't you?"

PROFESSOR: "Maybe."

STUDENT: "I mean, while I don't feel attracted to a rigid model in which rational support must always proceed in a one-way, bottom-up fashion, neither am I comfortable agreeing that we can just as well make any change in any place, just so long as we achieve coherence. I don't know about *that*. I'm not going to allow myself to pretend I do not seem to see a pillar of fire, or the sea parting, just because biblical miracles may not *cohere* with my atheism. I'm obliged to try to *explain* what I seem to see and feel. Is it a volcano, a tsunami, a dream? I'm not going to pretend that I'm not *having* any experience. And given sufficient evidence, I'm going to need to alter my beliefs. If I saw miracles, if I saw the Ten Commandments blazing across the sky in ancient Hebrew script and witnessed the dead come back to life, I'd give up my atheism in a heartbeat. It's the task of theory to defer to experience, not the task of experience to defer to theory.

So in that sense, experience is the *given*. You're having experiences. What you say and think has to face up to your experience. I mean, you can't just *ignore* your experience and pretend you're not having it. Maybe you can try to explain your experience as being somehow misleading, but in that case you must have some reason grounded in and consistent with experience to think that it's really possible and/or probable that you're being misled in some respect. But, isn't it the job of the web of beliefs to find a coherent way to explain *the given*, i.e., experience?"

PROFESSOR: "Well, the problem we might have with Coherentism is what happens if more than one theory of the world is coherent? What do we do then? Like what about some lunatic who has a really far-out, bizarre theory of the world that's no less coherent than your own world view?"

STUDENT: "You mean, like the theory that he's a brain floating in vat of fluid hooked up to electrodes connected to the super computer of a mad scientist who feeds him all his experiences?"

PROFESSOR: "Well, yeah. Er---no, I guess we've beaten that one to death. But, look, are you going to try to deny that there might be two different theories of the world that both seem coherent enough to be justified for us?"

STUDENT: "No, I mean, I guess I can think of some examples like the theory of evolution and the theory of relativity. Those two both seem coherent, as far as I know, though I'm no expert there. But, so what? As long as they don't contradict each other or conflict, I accept them both. Unless and until something better looking comes along, or somebody shows me some problem, like some unnoticed conflict."

PROFESSOR: "Okay, but what about a case in which two coherent theories *do* conflict?"

STUDENT: "Pick the one that's more plausible. One of them is bound to at least a *little* better, to be *more* consistent than the other, like to fit more of the data, or to fit the data more precisely."

PROFESSOR: "Ah, so you'll help yourself to a new, second criteria to break a tie in coherence?"

STUDENT: "*Data-fit* isn't a new, second criteria! It's part and parcel of coherence. A theory has got to be consistent with the data, obviously. A theory that isn't consistent with the data isn't a coherent theory."

PROFESSOR: "Hmm…well, how do you know this Coherentism of yours is the right way to get to your precious Truth and Rationality?"

STUDENT: "Isn't that something that's just true by definition? I mean, doesn't being *rational* or *reasonable* mean trying to avoid contradicting yourself; and doesn't your theory being *true* basically mean its being in conformity or consistency or correspondence with things as they are, out there in the real world outside your addled brain and its half-baked notions?"

PROFESSOR: "Well, if I'm not a *realist*, then that's not what I claim *truth* is."

STUDENT: "One of many things wrong with you."

The Problem of the Criterion

PROFESSOR: "Ah, but not so fast. What about the Problem of the Criterion?"

STUDENT: "What's that?"

PROFESSOR: "It's from Sextus Empiricus. He was an ancient Greek skeptic, member of a philosophical school called Pyrrhonism. You might say they were the original postmodernists, if you can pardon the anachronism. Pyrrhonism is where Hume got a lot of his ideas. In *The Outlines of Pyrrhonism*, Sextus Empiricus explained the problem of the criterion by arguing that:

> Proof always requires a criterion to confirm it, and the criterion also a proof to demonstrate its truth; and neither can a proof be sound without the existence of a true criterion nor can the criterion be true without the previous confirmation of the proof. So in this way both the criterion and the proof are involved in circular process of reasoning, and thereby both are found to be untrustworthy; for since each of them is dependent on the credibility of the other, the one is lacking in credibility just as much as the other.[10]

STUDENT: "I don't quite get it. Am I doing what he says I am? Am I using a "criterion"? And if not, do I need one? I don't quite know what he means. I didn't think we were trying to do Euclidean geometry. I mean, the way I see it, we're just offering up various overall worldviews or explanations of life and talking about which one so far seems most plausible, all things considered. Aristotle had a worldview different from that of Sextus, and you have one different from Aristotle, and I have one different from yours. My claim is that my overall explanation of things looks more plausible---more likely to be more true---than the competition I've seen so far, all things considered. But if I've overlooked something, I'm ready to hear about it. I'm not pretending to be infallible."

PROFESSOR: "Let me try to say this a different way. Look, you can't tell me you think there's nothing wrong with arguing in a circle. Right? I mean, you admit you don't condone question-begging. You call it a fallacy."

STUDENT: "True."

PROFESSOR: "So, the problem is, however you proceed, you have to rely on some principles, some standards, or some method. For example, if you hold up reason, logic, or rationality as your standard, then by what other standard do you support that one? What can you say to somebody who doesn't recognize *reason* as a legitimate standard?"

STUDENT: "I'm not sure I understand. You mean what do I say to somebody who feels free to logically contradict himself?"

PROFESSOR: "Yeah. I mean, by what right are you telling him that it's wrong for him to logically contradict himself?"

STUDENT: "I don't. If he's a poet, I might even encourage it."

PROFESSOR: "So you don't think there's anything wrong with contradicting yourself?"

STUDENT: "Not if you're writing poetry, no. But if you're writing laws, or science books, or philosophy, or giving directions to an ambulance driver, then it's probably not good. Normally, it results in a failure to communicate. If you tell somebody one thing and then turn around and contradict yourself and deny it, you're hardly saying anything at all. But if you're just writing poetry or comedy or singing a song, then the purpose is to please or amuse, and not necessarily to communicate a fact, or state anything clearly. If you contradict yourself when talking to somebody, usually they will become confused and ask you to explain what you mean, unless there's some obvious joke you're making, or something like that."

PROFESSOR: "Okay, then what about the evidence of the senses? Here's something you merely take for granted---the reliability of sense perception."

STUDENT: "No I don't---you do. You're the one who needs to take it for granted as an unquestionable dogma that your senses were telling you the truth when you thought you once really saw a real vat, and an actual electrode. I don't share that problem. I take no claims for granted as unquestionable dogmas. I'm wide open to all your questions. I'm not afraid---I'm ready to follow this crazy philosophical discussion wherever it may take us. Have I not given you perfect freedom to challenge any and all my beliefs? Have I not welcomed all your questions and objections and insisted they be heard, and taken seriously, and have a fair trial? Have I not insisted that no bogus "burden of proof" be laid unfairly upon you, any more than upon myself? How unjust you are to accuse me of dogmatism! You and Rudd, and Hume and Sextus, are the *dogmatic* ones."

PROFESSOR: "Well now you're contradicting yourself. A *skeptic* can't be *dogmatic*. That's impossible by definition. It's a contradiction in terms."

STUDENT: "Well you're a contradictory bunch. Listen, I already told you that I'm not at all keen on the notion of *epistemic principles*. But neither do I see that I'm taking any such animals for granted anywhere as unquestionable dogmas. You're the one who likes to tout epistemic principles---not me. You're the extreme foundationalist who imagines our beliefs to be like some kind of single-file stack of bricks, where each brick represents some indubitable certainty which obtains its infallibility from the fact that it solidly rests upon another such brick, etc. etc."

PROFESSOR: "Well, there you go. That's just the problem. The buck has to stop someplace. How do you prove the *bottom* brick is true?"

STUDENT: "I just said that's *your* picture---not mine. I'm not such an extreme foundationalist. As I just said, the way I see it, we're basically offering up various overall theories of life, various rival *explanations* of experience, and thinking about which one so far seems the most believable. I'm not claiming to have *originally obtained* my explanation of life by some infallible process. I don't pretend to have consciously built it up step by step from the ground floor by logical inferences. To tell you the truth, I'm not sure, exactly, *how* I came by it originally. Nor am I demanding that you be able to demonstrate that your brain in the vat story was originally created as a result of some infallible process of step-by-step deduction. I suppose you read it in some book, or that it came from a science fiction movie. The point is that you don't need to be able to demonstrate an *infallible pedigree* before you enter your story in the contest, and neither do I. Anybody is free to enter any hypothesis he likes, no matter how ridiculous it is, or where he *got* it. I don't care if it came to you in a dream, I'm willing to entertain your nutty hypothesis. The whole point of the contest is that it obviates the need to wring our hands over *infallible pedigrees*. My position is merely that my overall explanation of things is more plausible---more likely to be more true---than the vat story, or the demon story, or any of the others I've seen so far. But if I've overlooked something, I'm ready to be corrected. My mental arena is open to all contestants, and never closes its doors. Nothing is ever final---I mean, nothing is ever carved in stone. I'm not pretending to be infallible, and I take nothing for granted."

PROFESSOR: "The trouble is, if you *take nothing for granted*, then your worldview *has no basis*. If you take nothing as *given*, then you have nothing to *go* on."

STUDENT: "No---well---I didn't mean it that way. I only meant that I take no *claim*, no *statement*, no *English sentence*, for granted. But, of course, there *is* a pre-linguistic "basis," in the sense of a "given," as I said before. You know what I mean---experience, or "raw feels," or whatever you choose to name the situation in which you find yourself. But that doesn't mean that we're given a bunch of *English sentences*, or a book about particle physics, that we can take for granted. Of course, that isn't what I mean when I say that there's something that's *given*. Come on. Kant himself, and even Sellars, admitted that there's *something* that is, as Sellars put it, in *some* sense *given*."[11]

The 'No Basis' Gambit

PROFESSOR: "I don't think you understand. Let me express this objection in a different way. Here's a recent passage from Anthony Rudd:

> The…skeptic is not necessarily driven by a neurotic obsession with absolute certainty. The serious skeptical argument does not assert that there is a minuscule possibility that I am being deceived by the Cartesian demon, and so (because knowledge involves certainty) I can't say I really *know* anything about my physical environment. The argument is rather that I have no basis for asserting or denying any of the indefinitely large number of hypotheses that can be presented to explain the experience that I have. There is no basis for

the calculation of any probabilities at all. …The skeptical challenge is to show why I should suppose that any of these hypotheses is better justified than any of the others.[12]

STUDENT: "First of all, that's a *self-refuting* claim. Look, if there's no basis at all upon which *anything* can be justifiably preferred as relatively more or less worthy of belief, then there's no basis upon which Rudd himself could possibly have justifiably come to believe *that*."

PROFESSOR: "To believe what?"

STUDENT: "To believe that there's no basis upon which anything can be worse or better justified than anything else. Right? I mean, if there's no basis upon which any beliefs can be worse or better justified than any others, then there's no basis upon which Rudd himself could possibly have justifiably come to believe that there's no basis upon which any beliefs can be worse or better justified than any others. Could a claim be more nicely self-refuting?

What is this? Is it just a spurious challenge to the anti-skeptic which is merely meant to express the old Burden of Proof Cheat? Is it iterative skepticism? We've been over that ground."

PROFESSOR: "I don't think you understand my point here."

STUDENT: "No, I don't. You're right about that."

PROFESSOR: "Look, ask yourself, *relative to what* do you judge one explanatory hypothesis, i.e., my brain in the vat story, to be *worse off* than another explanatory hypothesis, i.e., your mundane, commonsensical story?"

STUDENT: "Relative to *each other*, and relative to *experience*. The vat story is worse off relative to the mundane rival, because unless the mundane story is actually true, the vat story has nothing whatsoever to recommend it even as a (physical) *possibility*. When one of the rival philosophical contestants depends upon the other for support, and its merits are hopelessly parasitic upon the other being the winner of the contest, that's a contestant with a problem."

PROFESSOR: "The point is, I'm trying to say that you need something like a *foundation* or *underlying basis* upon which you can rest your judgment that my hypothesis looks worse off than yours."

STUDENT: "You mean something *given*, something sort of 'self-evident,' like raw experience?"

PROFESSOR: "No, I mean you need a *sentence*, something *linguistic*, something *propositional*, like 'I think therefore I am.' You need a proposition, so that other propositions can be logically deduced from it."

STUDENT: "Okay. *That's your claim.* Now what I need is an argument to go with that claim. It's an important claim, but it seems to be perfectly self-defeating. According to your own version of infallibilist Foundationalism, there's no good reason to believe in your version of infallibilist Foundationalism. Again we see the philosophy you refute so nicely is not mine, but your own. Are you again playing the kamikaze pilot here?

If you're a kamikaze, then you must take aim at me with a *reductio ad absurdum* which reveals the hidden contradiction secretly festering in the heart of my own philosophy. Here I am. Come and get me. You seem to feel little obligation to really argue your side of things. You just want to fold your arms and sit back and demand that I do all the work. You're too lazy. Unless you have some *new argument* you want to offer here, I can only suppose this is nothing other than the same old Burden of Proof Cheat. You try to win by pretending I have some special burden of proof that you don't share. But that seems bogus to me. Like a kind of cheating.

I mean, I'm saying please tell me why I should *believe* that I actually have nothing whatsoever to go on. You say I have, as you put it, "no basis." Do I possess no kind of information whatsoever? *Is that true?* I doubt that claim. It looks dubious to me. I mean, you make it sound like I must be a deaf, blind baby in the womb, with nothing to go on. Don't I have my experiences to go on? Don't I therefore have a mountain of raw data to go on?"

PROFESSOR: "Raw sense-data?"

STUDENT: "I don't care what you call it; you know what I mean. I'm talking about...you know...just whatever you feel or seem to see right now. Never mind what you *call* it. Call it what you like. I don't mean the things we *say about* it, like the sentences of our theories. You have something that you had even long before you ever tried to say anything about it."

PROFESSOR: "Raw feels?"

STUDENT: "Whatever."

PROFESSOR: "You say you have a mountain of information, but you don't. I mean, not if you're a deluded brain in a vat. Maybe your whole life is a dream. Maybe all your memories are nothing but false delusions, and you really were born only a *moment* ago, and the evil scientist's computer implanted you with a bunch of false memories."

STUDENT: "Well in that case, you're still offering a theory, or an hypothesis, to explain my seeming memories, this seeming conversation, this seeming world. So the data or information we're dealing with is the same. It has to be. Because the whole *point* of a paranoid skeptical hypothesis is that it's supposed to be able explain the *same* raw data in an alternative way. If it didn't purport to explain the *same* data as the mundane commonsense hypothesis does, then it wouldn't be a *rival* hypothesis.

Rudd can't mean to deny that he *has experience*. Look at the passage: he himself says that various hypotheses 'can be presented to explain *the experience that I have*.' That's what he says. The key word there is *have*. It makes no sense to pretend you're not having any experiences. The point is to find some explanation that completely fits this ineffable raw experience that you cannot deny you *have*. The data to be explained is just the situation in which you now find yourself: these sensations, this life-world, this Matrix, this scene-image, this illusion, this whatever it is. This prickly, pungent, blooming, buzzing *da kine*. It doesn't matter what you *call* it, you know what I'm talking about: look around, reach out your hand and I'll slap it for you."

PROFESSOR: "Ouch! What are we a Zen master now?"

STUDENT: "There. You feel something. You're 'having experience.' It's true of a rock that it has no feelings and therefore has nothing to go on. And maybe a tiny embryo has nothing to go on. But you have something to go on. I mean, it's already a part of the situation in which you now *find* yourself, no matter what---no matter what you *say* about it, or which *language* you adopt, or how you finally end up, in the end, theoretically, trying to explain *why* you're having this particular experience. The skeptics try to offer up alternative explanations to rival common sense, but we don't have a *rival* explanation unless it purports to explain the *same* empirical data."

PROFESSOR: "Well, some philosophers think you can't get here from there. They say the first thing you have to do is run that raw data through your own arbitrary conceptual scheme first, before you can arrive at any kind of knowledge at all. And therefore, our knowledge is never clean, but always biased and polluted by our preconceived notions which we impose upon the data."

STUDENT: "That sounds like a Kantian hangover or something. As a vulgar realist, I don't really understand that claim. I mean, for example, I can imagine how it might be possible, even for a speechless caveman, without any language, to arrive at an explanatory theory that he himself has *eyes* and that this is the reason he seems to *see* far away things. Perhaps he can't see his own eyes, but he can see his own feet, and he can see that other people have feet and eyes, and that they seem to see with their eyes. Etc. And, so, he comes up with the 'hypothesis' that the reason he seems to see things, even things far away from himself, is because he likewise has *eyes* which can actually see far away things. Perhaps, if he was clever enough, he could even come up with this hypothesis all by himself, just by looking at his face reflected in a still pond and experimenting, even if he never saw another human or animal with eyes, nor ever heard the word *eye*."

PROFESSOR: "What's that supposed to prove?"

STUDENT: "I thought you suggested that maybe a person can't bootstrap his way into an *explanation of experience* from the ground up, *without* irrationally taking something dubious for granted. I think my clever hominid can do it all by himself, and never need be closed-minded or dogmatic. He can do this while remaining laudably open-minded the entire time."

PROFESSOR: "Well, even if he doesn't use words or language, he'll have to impose the concept of an *eye* on the raw data. I mean, if he never mentally ties together the various patches of blue and pink and white and brown which go into making up his notion of one particular 'eye,' then he'd never arrive at the theory. Would he?"

STUDENT: "But, he's not *arbitrarily* putting together the eye, the whole reason why the blue and the pink and the white always travel together is because they're all a part of the same object in reality. He didn't 'tie' or 'put' them together arbitrarily, capriciously. He found them together. He didn't invent eyes, he found them ready-made, out there, in nature. Eyes have certain amount of objective natural integrity, as physical objects. It's only your mental ability to abstract that causes you then come along and take them apart.

Besides, my caveman is staying open-minded: there's nothing to stop him from changing his mind later, and adopting some radically new conceptual scheme. He can be perfectly prepared to decide one day in the future that there aren't really any eyes after all, because actually he's a windowless monad in a vat, or whatever. He can change his mind. He can remain forever ready to keep following the evidence wherever it may lead. He might even read too much canonical philosophy, and become thoroughly bamboozled. That would be sad. But it can happen."

Hume's Riddle of Induction

PROFESSOR: "Well, okay, maybe you think you're riding high now, my boy, but I'm afraid I've saved the best for last. You remember a while back you said you liked Richard Fumerton's 'deductive argument for simplicity,' and I warned you that Fumerton is for you more nemesis than ally?"

STUDENT: "Yes."

PROFESSOR: "Well consider what he says a couple pages after that part you liked. He then says:

> The traditional problem of perception, incidentally, is a different matter. If reasoning to the best explanation really does collapse into inductive reasoning (or even if inductive reasoning underlies reasoning to the best explanation), then one still has to tell Hume how to get beyond his sensations to a world logically but not causally independent of them. The sort of complex inductive reasoning discussed above does not seem available to us at this early stage of our attempt to reconstruct the foundations of empirical knowledge, for not having gone beyond sensation yet, it is not clear how anything we can correlate would be in any way relevant to establishing the existence of physical objects. Here I suspect that as long as one works within the framework of radical empiricism, one is faced with the extremely difficult task of choosing between Humean skepticism and the complexities of a phenomenalistic analysis.[13]

How do you like Fumerton now?"

STUDENT: "I see what you mean."

PROFESSOR: "Well?"

STUDENT: "Well…that just sounds like all the same old fallacies. He's imbibed all the old canards: the false dilemma between anti-realism and skepticism, the unnecessary demand for infallible certainty, the old burden of proof ploy, extreme infallibilist Foundationalism, the Brain in the Vat challenge, etc. etc. He's obviously a fan of Hume, and seems to assume all those old arguments are winners. But I already refuted all that stuff. Why do I have to do it again?"

PROFESSOR: "Because you did not address them all. You haven't refuted Hume's Riddle of Induction."

STUDENT: "What's that?"

PROFESSOR: "Hume's Riddle of Induction is a doozy. As a matter of fact, many if not most philosophy professors consider it to be quite devastating, if not irrefutable."[14]

STUDENT: "Oh dear. How does it go?"

PROFESSOR: "Well, to make it short and sweet, the argument is that there are two kinds of beliefs we can have. One concerns mere *relations of ideas*, such as that 'no bachelor is married,' and that 'twice two is four,' and the other concern *matters of fact and existence*, such as that 'no bachelor is twenty feet tall,' and that 'bread is nourishing to humans.' But the thing is, when it comes to our beliefs about matters of fact and existence, our knowledge of their truth must always rest upon experience.

So what, you say? Well, the problem is that it is possible, says Hume, that we might wake up tomorrow only to discover that what held good in our past experience, no longer holds. We might, for example, meet a bachelor who is twenty feet tall, or we might find out that bread no longer nourishes us, or even that the sun has failed to rise as it always used to do. Now, if you try to argue that we have some probable estimation about such things, based upon past experience, Hume can show that this begs the question. It begs the question, because, if you are arguing that the future must continue to resemble the past, you can't base this claim on the fact that it has always done so in the past, and therefore it will continue to do so. That begs the question, because it takes for granted the very point at issue: namely, whether or not the future must indeed really continue to resemble the past. But I'll let Hume say it in his own words:

> All reasonings may be divided into two kinds, namely, demonstrative reasoning or that concerning *relations of ideas*, and moral reasoning, or that concerning *matter of fact and existence*. That there are no demonstrative arguments in the case seems evident; since it implies no contradiction that the course of nature may change, and that an object, seemingly like those which we have experienced, may be attended with different or contrary effects. May I not clearly and distinctly conceive that a body, falling from the

clouds, and which, in all other respects, resembles snow, has yet the taste of salt or feeling of fire? Is there any more intelligible proposition than to affirm, that all the trees will flourish in December and January, and decay in May and June? Now whatever is intelligible, and can be distinctly conceived, implies no contradiction, and can never be proved false by any demonstrative argument or abstract reasoning *a priori.*

If we be, therefore, engaged by arguments to put trust in past experience, and make it the standard of our future judgment, these arguments must be probable only, or such as regard matter of fact and real existence, according to the division above mentioned. But that there is no argument of this kind, must appear, if our explication of that species of reasoning be admitted as solid and satisfactory. We have said that all arguments concerning existence are founded on the relation of cause and effect, that our knowledge of that relation is derived entirely from experience, and that all our experimental conclusions proceed upon the supposition that *the future will be conformable to the past.* To endeavour, therefore, the proof of this last supposition by probable arguments, or arguments regarding existence, *must be evidently going in a circle, and taking that for granted, which is the very point in question.*[15]

STUDENT: "Hmmm."

PROFESSOR: "What do you say now, eh?"

STUDENT: "Well, first of all, I don't understand why he says that anything we can imagine, or that implies no logical contradiction, is therefore *possible.*"

PROFESSOR: "Well, the point is that such things are *logically* possible. Because what's logically impossible implies a contradiction."

STUDENT: "Okay, but what about something that, while in that sense logically possible, is nevertheless *physically* impossible. For example, it might be *logically* possible for me to lift a fifty ton rock with one hand, but it isn't *physically* possible."

PROFESSOR: "Well that's not going to get you anywhere. If you want to prove that's physically impossible, you'll have to show why it's impossible for you to wake up tomorrow and suddenly be able to do it. How do you know this won't happen? You don't."

STUDENT: "It doesn't strike me as likely."

PROFESSOR: "Nor me. But you need to prove that. And then you run into the second part of Hume's argument, which says you can't prove it's improbable. He says you can't prove it's *impossible*, and you can't prove it's *improbable* either. He's got you blocked at both exits. Checkmate."

STUDENT: "You said this was a new move."

PROFESSOR: "It is! This is a different skeptical strategy."

STUDENT: "No it isn't."

PROFESSOR: "What do you mean?"

STUDENT: "It's the same old play. It's the Cartesian Demon, the *Matrix*. It's the same old Brain in the Vat."

PROFESSOR: "No it isn't! This is the Riddle of Induction."

STUDENT: "It's the same old gambit, and it suffers from the same old problems. It contains all the same old fallacies, only this time, they're all rolled up into a tight little ball. It tries to deploy, first of all, the same old Burden of Proof Cheat. Secondly, it relies on the same old unreasonable and unnecessary demand for perfect infallible certainty, and perhaps iterative certainty too. And thirdly, it depends upon my accepting, as an *equal* contestant, a relatively less plausible piggyback-riding claim about what really, truly is *physically* possible.

After all, the whole point of the *demon* and the *vat* and the *Matrix* is to prove that for all you know you could wake up tomorrow in a world very different from this one. You could wake up in the Matrix pod, or in the vat, or whatever. You might suddenly find that your whole life has been a dream, and then the sun stops rising, and moon crashes into the sea, and pigs can fly, and you can lift huge boulders with one hand.

The only difference is that the demon stories flesh the argument out a bit more, that's all. In fact, those versions *improve* upon this one, by offering at least a little story to explain *how* such unprecedented events might be not just *logically* possible, but also *physically* possible. Hume's Riddle of Induction is just a Cartesian demon with one leg missing.

Look, Hume says:

> We can at least conceive a change in the course of nature; which sufficiently proves that such a change is not absolutely impossible. To form a clear idea of any thing, is an undeniable argument for its possibility.[16]

Could a claim be more obviously wrong? Skepticism---including Hume's version---always depends upon this wrongheaded assumption that to prove a thing *logically possible* is sufficient to prove it *physically possible*. And that just isn't true. It's not only logically invalid, it's pretty obviously false as a matter of fact. Anything which just happens as a matter of fact to be physically impossible--- regardless of whether we know that it's physically impossible---is, as a matter of fact, whether we know it or not, *impossible*. And all the apparent *logical* possibility in the world cannot change that matter of fact. If something is *physically* impossible, then it's impossible. Period.

Hume's burning snow that tastes like salt, the Cartesian Demon, the Brain in the Vat---they all suffer from this same error. Look, if any weird scenario isn't physically possible, then a mere logical possibility isn't enough, since for anything to be really possible, it must be both logically and physically possible. That's why the Brain in the Vat is superior to your so-called Riddle of Induction. This one suffers from all the vices of those, but has less to offer in its favor. So all the answers I just gave to those, can be re-applied to this new one.

For example, it's just as I said before, if electrodes cannot actually do what the vat story requires of them, then goodbye to the vat story. If a brain cannot, after all, survive in a vat of fluid, then goodbye to the vat story. If it isn't physically possible for snow to taste like salt and burn you, then goodbye to possibility that it can. However uncertain we may be of our mundane beliefs, we can only view these weird scenarios as even *less* certain. However chancy the mundane scenario looks to us, the other scenarios can only look chancier. That's why we have no choice but to conclude that chances are better for the mundane scenario than for those others.

Think about it: if you *are* a brain in a vat, then you have to conclude that, despite appearances, you've never actually seen any *vats*, nor any *electrodes*, nor *computers*. In other words, you no longer have any reason to believe there are any such things. So, you no longer have any reason to think the Brain in the Vat scenario is physically possible. In other words, if the Vat scenario is true, then you have no reason to think it physically possible, and the only case in which you could know it to be physically possible, would be if it was actually false."

PROFESSOR: "What about Hume's claim that you beg the question? He says you reason in a circle. Look, just tell me this. How do you know you won't wake up tomorrow and find that things have changed? You have a mindless expectation that they won't, but that's just a blind animal prejudice."

STUDENT: "No it isn't! First of all, I don't expect everything to remain the same; I expect some things to change, and others not. I expect some things to change in some ways, and not in others. I don't have a mindless, knee-jerk expectation of an unmitigated lack of change. What I have is a lot of complex theories and beliefs about how things work and what's likely to happen based upon the natures of various things in themselves and their differences from each other. And I have my mundane realist theory that I'm an observer of these things, rather than a brain in a vat. If all I had was a stupid, mindless, brute expectation that things won't change, how could I expect *tomorrow morning* to come at all?"

PROFESSOR: "Well, you can't just take all that stuff for granted. You have to prove it."

STUDENT: "Ah, yes. Here we go again. Time for the old Burden of Proof Cheat. Every skeptic's favorite move."

PROFESSOR: "Well it's every anti-skeptic's favorite ploy, too!"

STUDENT: "So it is. You're right about that. It's everybody's favorite way to cheat at philosophy. So let's resolve, both of us, once and for all to renounce that unsportsmanlike conduct. But, now, I'm experiencing an unmistakable *déjà vu*, and I'm sure you are too. We're right back where we started. If you want my answers, just rewind the tape. This is a re-run, and the outcome will be the same. Why do it twice? Already, I can predict your next move, which will be to point out my own personal fallibility, and to demand a perfect unimpeachable certainty, immune from any possibility of error, etc., etc. We've been there and done that."

PROFESSOR: "Okay, but wait a minute. Not so fast. You said we don't need certainty, because all we need is probability, and you said we can have that. But now here I've got an argument that says you can't get *probability* either."

STUDENT: "No you don't, because it bases that claim on the same old fallacies. It bases the claim that I can't get probability on the same old Burden of Proof cheat, and the same egalitarian Piggyback Rider fallacy, and merely adds to these old fallacies the palpably false claim that I suffer from a blind, irrational expectation of unrelieved monotony, which actually I don't, since in truth I expect to experience not only various and sundry changes, but even the occasional unprecedented novelty. If you want to give me an argument that I can't obtain probabilities, you need to give me an argument that's plausible. You need an argument that's cogent, but you don't have one."

PROFESSOR: "Okay, but don't try to put a special onus on me. You don't like it when I try to do that to you. You know, you seem to have a lot of probabilistic stuff going on here. But I wonder if you really know what you're talking about. Can you explain to me how all this stuff is supposed to operate? Because, I'd like to know."

STUDENT: "Well, I'll confess that I don't consider myself an expert in those kinds of things. I'm no logician, nor skilled in probability theory, and I confess I never heard the word 'abduction' before I met you. But I'm sure we could go and read about such things in the library, or consult some experts."

PROFESSOR: "What if you find out it's an infant field?"

STUDENT: "Well then maybe we should give it a chance to grow and develop, before we take it upon ourselves to rule out the project as hopeless."

PROFESSOR: "Maybe."

Why Did the Demon Go Out of Style?

PROFESSOR: "But I just thought of something else. I wonder, regarding my skeptical scenarios---you know, that tomorrow the sun fails to rise as usual, or snow begins to taste like salt, or feel like fire, or you wake up in a *Matrix* pod---why should I care if I have no reason to think they're *physically* possible?"

STUDENT: "Well, it's not enough just to say they're *logically* possible, since there are things logically possible that aren't physically possible, aren't there? Like me flying to Mars in the next ten seconds simply by flapping my arms."

PROFESSOR: "No, you're missing the point. The point is that, as a skeptic, I can just say that we don't know what's *physically* possible and what isn't. Therefore it's enough for me simply to point out the sheer *logical* possibility of the paranoid scenario. Because *my* position is that *for all you really know* all kinds of crazy things may be physically possible."

STUDENT: "That shamelessly begs the question. Besides, you really don't have the luxury of taking the 'position' that we don't know. You're a radical epistemological skeptic, so the only 'position' available to you is an untenable, *self-refuting* one, as you yourself admit. You're a Kamikaze pilot. Skepticism isn't coherent enough to constitute a rival position like that. Skepticism, as skeptics admit, can't really aspire to being something more than merely an attempt to reduce to absurdity somebody else's philosophy. And my philosophy doesn't render demons very plausible, physically."

PROFESSOR: "When did I ever try to say you might be deceived by a demon? I never said that. Descartes said that. But that's not what *I* said. I said you might be a brain floating in a vat hooked up via myriads of electrodes to a supercomputer whose software feeds all your sensations to you. There was no *demon* in that story. You believe in *vats*, don't you?"

STUDENT: "Yes, I believe in vats."

PROFESSOR: "Okay, then. There you go."

STUDENT: "My point exactly."

PROFESSOR: "What point?"

STUDENT: "Why do you eschew the demon?"

PROFESSOR: "I just dropped him, that's all."

STUDENT: "For no reason?"

PROFESSOR: "Call it fashion."

STUDENT: "So, then, you could just as well have used a demon, instead of a vat?"

PROFESSOR: "Let's just say I choose not to."

STUDENT: "You don't want to."

PROFESSOR: "I choose not to."

STUDENT: "Why? Why do you choose not to?"

PROFESSOR: "I don't know. If you're so smart, you tell me."

STUDENT: "I say you dropped the demon because down deep you sensed the fact that you need to put up an *equal* contestant to rival the mundane scenario of common sense. You knew you needed an equal contestant since anything less wouldn't work. You need equal plausibility, and you know it. I admit that you'd really have something there, if you *did* spin me a convincing paranoid tale for which I could really and truly say that it appears that, for all I think I know, I really have not one jot more reason to find my mundane world a more likely story than your paranoid tale of delusion.

But you failed to do that. I say that we can see, on closer inspection, that your demonic tales are never really *quite* equal in plausibility to the mundane world. They never really *quite* come up to that bar of *equal* credibility."

PROFESSOR: "Okay. Fine, then, let's ditch the demon. Now, why doesn't the *vat* tale give me perfect equality?"

STUDENT: "I answered that already. The vat scenario is a loser. It's a piggyback rider. Because a chain is only as strong as its weakest link, and to the same old mundane, common sense chain (I once saw a real vat; computers really exist; electrodes really exist) the vat scenario adds more links, and the links it adds can only appear to be relatively weaker ones, (a brain can survive in a vat of fluid; electrodes can deliver rich experiences to a brain; electrodes can be attached to a wet brain without falling off; a future super-computer would be able to perform amazing feats; an evil scientist wishes to deceive me). Therefore, we cannot help but consider the vat story to be a weaker chain, overall.

If it turns out that brains can't survive in vats, *or* that electrodes aren't up to the task, *or* that computers can't pull it off, then the whole scenario collapses. So the mundane theory is more plausible. The mundane scenario possesses the same chance of failure as the vat scenario *minus the chance of failure associated with the dubious add-ons.* Therefore, unless the add-ons are *perfectly infallible*---and neither of us could think that---the mundane theory wins. Bingo!

For any s whose probability is less than perfectly certain, it must be the case that s *and* c is less likely than c alone. Let s stand for 'a brain can survive in vat of fluid,' and c stand for 'brains exist.' The mundane theory requires only that brains exist, while the vat story requires *more* than that: both that they exist, *and* that they can survive in a vat of fluid, disconnected from a body. We don't really even know if this is *physically possible*. Besides, we can't view the two as equals, because if the mundane scenario *isn't true*, then the skeptical one loses all its support, and all its plausibility. If I *am* a brain in a vat, then despite appearances, I've never truly *seen* any vats, and therefore I no longer have any reason to suppose it's *physically possible* that vats can preserve brains. The vat story aims to shoot a hole in its own boat."

PROFESSOR: "Well, you said the skeptic is a Kamikaze. So then we agreed that his game isn't to float a boat of his own, but merely to perform a *reductio ad absurdum* upon the particular beliefs of some actual non-skeptic."

STUDENT: "That's right. But, then, stop trying to pretend that you have a boat of your own that floats. Just a second ago, you said: 'as a skeptic, *I can just say that we don't know what's physically possible* (and therefore it's enough simply to point out the sheer logical possibility of the disturbing scenario).' You can't put forward positive claims like that. For a skeptic, that's a question-begging dogma he can't defend, on peril of self-refutation. You agreed that in order to avoid self-refutation, skeptics are limited merely to performing a *reductio* on somebody else's doctrines.

As a skeptic, you don't have the option of setting up your own alternative skeptical system of belief in opposition to mine, because it would refute itself. That's no contest. To undermine my system of beliefs, the radical skeptic must do so from within, employing a *reductio* strategy. You need to deal with the fact that according to my belief system, demons probably aren't *physically possible*, and that I'm far from knowing or claiming that a brain really *can* be given rich experiences by being hooked up to *electrodes* while floating in a vat of fluid."

PROFESSOR: "What's this supposed to have to do with Hume's Riddle of Induction?"

STUDENT: "Hume's thinks it's enough for him show that wild events are *logically* possible. But it isn't enough for a skeptic to offer some disturbing scenario that's nothing more than a *logical* possibility. Hume's Riddle of Induction makes the amazing claim that it '*is possible*' for snow to taste like salt, or burn you. But, no matter how logically possible they may be, nevertheless, things which are not *physically* possible *are not possible.*

Therefore Hume's Riddle of Induction needs to add some plausible story, some imaginary scenario, a story like the *Matrix*, or the vat, in order to say it might really be *physically* possible for snow to taste like salt or burn us tomorrow. Then we're back to the same old Brain in a Vat contest, and skepticism loses.

I'm not saying the skeptic has some bogus burden of irrefragable proof. But neither can he foist any such upon his opponent. Nor do I claim to be infallible. But neither do I need to be.

Besides, if tomorrow something white began to fall from the sky, and it tasted like salt, and burned, I don't know what makes Hume think we should call it *snow.*"

PROFESSOR: "Okay, but, I'm not sure you completely appreciate Hume's position. Hume said:

> The mind can always conceive any effect to follow from any cause, and indeed any event to follow upon another: whatever we conceive is possible: at least, in a metaphysical sense: but wherever a demonstration takes place, the contrary is impossible, and implies a contradiction. There is no demonstration, therefore, for any conjunction of cause and effect.[17]

STUDENT: "Possible in a *metaphysical* sense? But not in a *physical* sense? Why should I care if some weird thing is 'metaphysically' possible? If we have no reason to suppose it's *physically* possible, then we have no reason to think it's *possible*. Period. In which case, all the 'metaphysical' possibility in the world avails you nothing. The only way I can have a reason to consider something *possible*, is if I have reason to consider it *both* physically *and* logically possible. Real possibility requires both logical *and physical* possibility. Hume failed to see that. Face it, your idol made a mistake."

PROFESSOR: "Let me try putting it to you this way. There are two possibilities. One can defend induction deductively or inductively. It can't be defended deductively, but defending it inductively begs the question."[18]

STUDENT: "Don't be such an old-fashioned foundationalist. You might just as arbitrarily insist that *deduction* is bogus, unless we can offer some infallible *non-deductive* argument to support it. There might be something wrong with your unspoken premises here. After all, haven't you just performed a nice little *reductio ad absurdum* upon them? So, something's gone wrong somewhere.

But please notice that you're showing that there's something wrong with *your* philosophy, not *mine*. You're assuming that I need to defend *what Hume calls* 'induction.' But in truth you and Hume are tilting at some imaginary windmill, some straw man you call 'induction.' Does Hume's creature really stalk the land? I don't accept Hume's caricature of empirical reasoning. What about Mill's methods? What about Hempel's account of childbed fever? I don't think scientific rationalism operates the way Hume claims it does. I mean, I don't recognize real empirical thinking in Hume's cartoon. So, besides your other problems, you and Hume are committing the fallacy of the Straw Man.

You like to call my method *abduction*. I don't know if that's a good name or not, but, in any case, if you want to show me that some hidden absurdity lies coiled in the heart of *my* philosophy, you need to get yourself a new riddle. A riddle of *abduction*.

If you still feel the need for a *deductive* argument that supports my approach, please remember that I already showed why it appears to be a logically necessary truth that *some things might be physically impossible*, since if it is true---as you and Hume claim---that anything non-contradictory is logically possible, then it follows that it must be logically possible that some things are *physically impossible*.

In addition to that one, let's also remember that beautiful little gem from my nemesis, your man Fumerton. I mean the gem he called 'a *deductive* argument for preferring the simpler of two theories.' I love that thing:

> Suppose I am considering two incompatible theories *T1* and *T2* which, relative to my evidence, are equally likely to be true. Suppose, further, that after acquiring some additional evidence (let us call my new *total* body of evidence *E*) I find it necessary to add an hypothesis *H1* to *T2*. Now provided the probability of *T1* and *T2* relative to *E* remains the same and assuming that the probability of *H1* relative to *E* is less than 1, we can *deduce* from the probability calculus that, relative to *E*, *T1* is more likely to be true than the

complex theory (*T2* and *H1*). Intuitively, *T2 by itself* ran the same risk of error as *T1*, so with the addition of another hypothesis which might be false it runs a *greater* risk of error than *T1*. [19]

As I said before, for any *s* whose probability is less than a perfectly certain, it must be the case that *s and c* is less likely than *c* alone. If what you crave are some *deductive* arguments to support a good *non-deductive* style of empirical reasoning, how about these two, for starters?"

Is This Too Negative?

PROFESSOR: "Well, it's refreshing to hear you give an argument or two in support of your side, because I was just about to complain that you spend most of your time refuting my philosophy, rather than laying out positive arguments or evidence *for* yours."

STUDENT: "What do want me to do, wave my hands in front of you like G. E. Moore, or kick a rock, like Johnson did? Should I hit you with a snowball?"

PROFESSOR: "No, of course not. That doesn't prove anything."

STUDENT: "Why not?"

PROFESSOR: "Well, because it just takes realism for granted. It's like begging the question. It proves nothing!"

STUDENT: "Okay, but why? If you stub your toe on a rock, and it really hurts, why shouldn't an idealist count that as providing at least some amount of evidence in *favor* of realism?"

PROFESSOR: "Because, silly, the idealist offers an alternative explanation for that same empirical data. As Fichte put it, *the idealist destroys this proof by explaining experience in another way: thus he denies precisely what the realist relies upon.* [20] And likewise for the skeptic, whose argument is that a delusional alternative explanation is equally plausible."

STUDENT: "So, now you should understand why my arguments have to be so 'negative.' As you've just shown, it would not be enough for me to hit you with a snowball and tell you the story of Phineas Gage. Instead, what I need to do is to challenge your claim to be able to formulate *an equally plausible rival explanation* of the same empirical data."

PROFESSOR: "Okay, but then, it sounds like you have no new philosophical system of your own to offer."

STUDENT: "Well, ironically it was Hume who suggested philosophy might aspire to nothing more than 'common sense, methodized and perfected.' That sounds okay to me. So maybe I'm not trying to create a 'new philosophical system,' whatever that means. Let's just say I'm trying to make room for philosophy to improve, after it breaks out of the dark postmodern prison-house where it's languished for so long."

Is This Epistemological Conservatism?

PROFESSOR: "Okay, but, you know looking back over some of the things you've said, I'm wondering if you're claiming to enjoy a special advantage according to *epistemic conservatism*."

STUDENT: "What's that?"

PROFESSOR: "That's a doctrine that says that when pitting a wild new *Matrix*-like scenario up against the mundane, commonsense alternative, the commonsense alternative ought to be given the trophy in case of a tie. The claim is that the mere fact that the commonsense alternative is the one we, or you, already believe at the outset, that therefore it should be enjoy a little privilege for that reason alone."

STUDENT: "That sounds too much like the old burden of proof cheat. We both agreed not to cheat like that. That's not my argument."

PROFESSOR: "Are you sure? I mean, you were just telling me that I should have some reason to believe that it's physically possible to wake up tomorrow and find that snow suddenly tastes like salt and burns. You say it isn't enough for us merely to show that it's logically possible, but we ought to have a reason to think it physically possible too."

STUDENT: "Yeah. I mean, we need to have some reason to think it physically possible. It seems to me that it's probably not physically possible. So, if you want me to take it seriously, I need to be able to think that, in spite of appearances to the contrary, really, it *is* physically possible for that to happen."

PROFESSOR: "Well, I mean, anything is, you know, *possible*."

STUDENT: "Is it? I doubt that. Experience seems to suggest that many things appear to be, perhaps, *impossible*, actually."

PROFESSOR: "There! You see what I mean?"

STUDENT: "What?"

PROFESSOR: "You're always being too dogmatic. You're just taking your anti-skeptical realism *for granted* in this whole debate! You always do that. You can't do that!"

STUDENT: "Do what?"

PROFESSOR: "You're...you're begging the question."

STUDENT: "No I'm not. You are!"

PROFESSOR: "Well there it is. You see? It's just like I told you before. Fichte had it right. He said: the realist is a dogmatic materialist who takes realism on faith, but the idealist takes idealism on faith also. Fichte said that between your 'dogmatism' and idealism,

> Reason provides no principle of choice; for we deal here not with the addition of a link in the chain of reasoning...but with the beginning of the whole chain...as an absolutely primary act... Hence the

choice is governed by caprice, and since even a capricious decision must have some source, it is governed by inclination and interest.[21]

STUDENT: "Well there's a loser's song. God, you're a follower of Nazi creeps!"

PROFESSOR: "Who's a Nazi creep? Fichte? Spare me the *ad hominems*. How about answering the argument?"

STUDENT: "I already did! What have we been doing all this time? I'm not taking anything *for granted*. Yes, I have certain ordinary beliefs, anti-skeptical notions, realist beliefs, etc. I have a lot of beliefs, which seem to me to be pretty good. I think I have good reasons for them. Yet, I'm perfectly willing to entertain any and all reasons you *claim* to have for doubting these. I'm far from closed-minded, and I'm no hothouse flower. I'm wide open to hear your stories.

Show me an alternative that flies. *Offer me a rival that rivals common sense. Or reduce my complacent worldview to absurdity on its own terms.* You boasted that you could, so go for it. Knock yourself out. Bring it on. Here I am. You seem incapable of doing it. I think that's pretty interesting. Pretty telling. Nothing looks quite as good as a theory whose enemies can't shoot it down, but not for lack of trying."

PROFESSOR: "You're not listening. I'm suggesting maybe it's inherently a stalemate."

STUDENT: "I understand. You're losing the fight, so now you want to call it a draw. To heck with that, I'm the winner and you're the loser. Your kites don't fly and mine does. You lose and I win. It's no draw. Besides, what's this new line about a stalemate? You're obviously backing down. Your old favorite philosophers claimed that my beliefs are losers. They fire off an incredible barrage of supposed *refutations* of my 'naive' realism and my anti-skeptical 'dogmatism.' Russell says 'science, if true, shows naive realism is false.'[22] Hegel claims that philosophical 'reflection can confound common sense,' and that 'in the face of speculation' the truths of common sense 'vanish.'[23] Hume boasted that his philosophy 'leaves not the lowest degree of evidence in any proposition, either in philosophy or common life.'[24]   Those are some big, bold claims.   But pressed to the wall, you've been forced to admit that all this stuff is a self-refuting, self-contradicting kamikaze, whose only hope is to appear to reduce to absurdity somebody else's philosophy.   Now, lo and behold, what have we found?   The philosophy reduced to absurdity by the skeptical kamikaze is merely his own philosophy---a philosophy which he himself admits isn't shared by ordinary people he therefore disparages as naive!

But then, when faced with the challenge of performing a similar *reductio* upon the beliefs of the vulgar and naive, you can't do it.

So, now, after failing the attempt, you want to tell the ordinary, vulgar, and naive anti-skeptical realist winner of the contest they should abandon their beliefs and stop taking them 'for granted?' You've got a lot of nerve!"

PROFESSOR: "Well, wait a minute now. Don't change the subject. If I recall, you admitted that if a skeptical scenario could merely *tie* the mundane alternative, then that's a *win* for skepticism."

STUDENT: "For *skepticism*, not *idealism*. Idealism doesn't get paid on a tie. Fichte's claim is that idealism and realism are as a matter of fact equally plausible. But I already showed why that's not believable, when I argued against idealism. Besides, the very claim that realism and idealism are stalemated is a claim which itself seems to take idealism for granted. I mean, nobody but an anti-realist would say that. The claim itself presupposes there are no mind-independent facts to get in the way of our 'capricious' choice. Let's just say no realist would mistake Fichte for a *neutral* party."

PROFESSOR: "Okay, fine. Never mind idealism. Let's stick to skepticism. So, if skepticism gets paid on a *tie*, then doesn't that mean there *is* a 'burden of proof,' after all, and it burdens *your side?*"

STUDENT: "No. Skepticism is not the same thing as a skeptical *scenario*. The skeptic gets paid if he can show a tie between the *Matrix* scenario and the mundane alternative. But that doesn't mean the *Matrix* story wins---that means *skepticism* wins. *If* the Matrix can *tie* the mundane world. Skepticism isn't the claim that you *are* in the Matrix. It's the claim that *it's a toss up*. It's the claim that for all you can tell you might *just as plausibly* be in the *Matrix* as out of it (and therefore you can't know anything, etc.).

Skepticism claims that there is a tie between paranoia and common sense, and therefore skepticism gets paid if there really *is* such a tie. In other words, there's no special 'burden of proof' on either side. The skeptic has to argue his side of it, i.e., he has to pull his own weight, and try to tell us why we should think the contest (between his favorite paranoid alternative and the sane world) *is* an even bet. He's not entitled to just sit there with arms folded and demand that the anti-skeptic do all the work. Just because somebody offers to pay a tied hand of cards doesn't mean you don't have to show your cards to prove you really *have* a tie. I mean, I say you have no tie. I think your cards are losers. Unless you can show me some better-looking cards, I'd be wrong to consider your hand a 'tie' and pay it. I'm calling your hand. Your cards are worse than mine. I win."

PROFESSOR: "Now it sounds like you think the burden is on me."

STUDENT: "Not at all. There's no more burden of proof on you than on me. I'm not claiming any special advantage in the name of a knee-jerk conservatism. I don't need to cheat. I'm not taking common sense 'for granted.' I'm open. I'm always ready to suddenly wake up in the jelly pod and discover I was wrong after all and I'm really in the Matrix, or whatever. Or even that I *might just as well* for all I know be a brain in a vat.

But that doesn't mean I owe you some Euclidean system of proofs to demonstrate that I really do know with absolute infallible pedigreed certainty that I know that I know that I know that lemons cure scurvy and I can't be wrong. That's your old iterative skepticism, with an excessive and unreasonable demand for a perfect infallible certainty, and we've been over that. You need to get over this obsessive demand for an infallibility. Nobody needs it. Think ordinal probability, or comparative plausibility, or relative justification. Certainty is a *more or less* kind of thing, not an *all or nothing* kind of thing.

The point is that I have a rational, plausible, reasonable, sensible, coherent, mundane, commonsensical, compelling explanation of experience that holds water, while you're apparently unable so far to offer even a single alternative that's merely *equal*. That means I win. It's no stalemate, mate, it's checkmate. You lose. I get the chips."

PROFESSOR: "Well, now, wait a minute. Are you going to give those chips back to me if tomorrow we wake up in jelly pods?"

STUDENT: "Consider it a promise."

What If Only Strings Exist?

PROFESSOR: "But aren't you being too dogmatic? I mean, what if tomorrow you read in the newspaper that physicists have discovered that the only things that really exist are subatomic strings, like incredibly tiny packets of energy randomly gyrating in a universe of a dozen dimensions, only three or four of which dimensions we are able to perceive? Then what?"

STUDENT: "I don't know, what?"

PROFESSOR: "Well, wouldn't that go some way towards making you suspect that rocks and chairs really do exist in the mind alone, after all?"

STUDENT: "Wouldn't it be more natural, or make more sense, to say that if this new theory is true, then it just means that rocks and chairs are *made out of* these things? After all, if atoms and molecules shouldn't make us say that rocks and chairs don't exist, then why should some even smaller little building blocks make us say it?"

PROFESSOR: "Well, if, say, physicists proved that there were a dozen dimensions, even though we only perceive three, wouldn't it mean that Kant may have been right about the three-dimensionality of the world being a feature of our minds, rather than a feature of reality as it is in itself?"

STUDENT: "No, because then the three we perceive would be real. It would just mean that there were some more *in addition to them* that we don't perceive. If you want me to become an admirer of Kant, you'll have to have the physicists saying that there are *fewer* dimensions than we perceive, not more. Just as you'll have to have them proving that rocks and chairs don't exist, which is something different from having them say that rocks and chairs are made out of atoms, or strings, or whatever."

PROFESSOR: "What if they start saying that there are multitudes of parallel universes, in which multitudes of other versions of you exist unperceived and unperceivable?"

STUDENT: "Well, that would be pretty wild."

PROFESSOR: "Doesn't it pose a problem for your philosophy?"

STUDENT: "Not that I can see. In fact, it seems that it poses a problem for Kant's admirers, rather than for me. After all, Kant says we ought 'never dream of seeking to inform ourselves about the objects of our senses as they are in themselves, that is, out of all relation to the senses.'[25] According to Kant, you should to stop trying to discover the hidden inner forces *behind* the taste and color of apples, and instead become like a painter or gourmet, who merely notes their taste and color. Likewise C. S. Peirce, who sounds like he denies the possibility of turkey ham."

What About Mysticism?

PROFESSOR: "Well, in rejecting my old philosophy, you may be leaving the door open to more than just chemistry and physics. I think you may be opening the door to all sorts of kooky, mystical claims."

STUDENT: "How so?"

PROFESSOR: "Well, according to my philosophy, you can categorically rule out a lot of mystical stuff like claims of receiving direct revelations from above, unmediated by the five senses."

STUDENT: "Well what good does it do me to categorically rule out mysticism, if that's going to rule out chemistry and physics? I don't see the need to *categorically* rule out certain types of claims, anyway. Let a hundred flowers bloom. I'm not afraid that I won't be able to explain what it is about each kooky claim *in particular* that I find implausible. If a claim strikes us as implausible, then we ought to be able to explain why that individual claim, in particular, seems implausible. To the extent that kooky claims are kooky, they're kooky for good reasons. To the extent that we don't have any reason to consider a claim kooky, to that extent we should take it seriously, and give it a fair trial, and not try to dismiss it without a hearing, or categorically rule it out of court. If somebody claims that God is talking to him inside his head, then let him show us why we shouldn't conclude he's just a schizophrenic who hallucinates, just like any other schizophrenic does. If the voice in his head can predict the future, I mean like precisely predict every stock market number, and solve famous math puzzles too, then that's really impressive. What are you going to do, refuse to notice that this guy can predict the stock market?"

PROFESSOR: "Now who's encouraging the crazies?"

STUDENT: "Well it's going to be worse if you try to put up some kind of wall between science and mysticism. To the extent that you do that, you're ceding more to the mystics than I am. Just as I welcome the claims of the mystics to be heard and debated by science, at the same time I deny their claims any special protection from critical examination. That philosophic *wall* you've built to contain the claims of mysticism, has served just as much to protect mysticism from science, as it has to protect science from mysticism."

PROFESSOR: "Well at least the wall allowed our side to breathe for the last few hundred years. I'm not so quick to abandon the truce. Let's not provoke the old enemy. Remember what happened to Galileo."

STUDENT: "Let's just say I'm less worried than you are, that we would lose the battle."

PROFESSOR: "Nothing could better show your ignorance of both history and the human race."

What About Tolerance?

STUDENT: "Well, as long as we're talking about history, I'd like to point out that Jonathan Edwards, the fire-breathing preacher who took the country by storm during the Great Awakening with sermons like "Sinners in the Hands of an Angry God," was inspired by the anti-realism of the eighteenth century, and used Berkley's idealism to bolster his arguments in favor of irrational, fanatical, religious emotionalism. According to my interpretation of history, I blame skeptical anti-realism for entailing a Romantic, totalitarian backlash against the liberal Age of Reason."

PROFESSOR: "Well, if that's your interpretation of history, I can assure you it's a minority view! Most of the people I know see skepticism as a philosophy that leads to tolerance, while they see realism leading to intolerance."

STUDENT: "I disagree."

PROFESSOR: "Well, if you're operating on the belief that there's only one Truth, one Reality with a capital R, then it follows that when two sides disagree, then at least one side is *wrong*. And if there's only one True Reality, and we can also have *knowledge* of it, as you insist we can, then why should we respect the false beliefs of people who deny this True Reality? They may as well be forced to conform to the One True and Known Reality. Right?"

STUDENT: "No, because they might both be wrong. Good Heavens, what a gross caricature. There's a happy medium, between radical Humean despair and dogmatic closed-mindedness. As a matter of fact, history shows that radical epistemological skepticism, far from being what we call 'healthy skepticism,' leads only to the blind submission of fideism, as Hume pointed out more than once! I never said we should suppose our beliefs about the world to be infallible, or complete, or perfect, or eternal, or even very good. I take nothing for granted. I admitted that we're fallible and ignorant in all sorts of ways, and may very well---let's hope---be looked down upon, by our descendants, as relative fools.

But when you decide there's no truth, no reality, for us to have differing beliefs about, then you end up with the conclusion that for us even to discuss or debate our disagreements must be a farcical exercise. You end up where the postmodern hordes are, those followers of yours you keep trying to disavow. For example, they say there's nothing more to the adversarial process of reasoned debate than a naked grab for power. Yet, who can blame them for thinking that? If I suggest that you and I are trying to figure out what the objective truth is, they say that's baloney, because there's no such animal as objective, realist truth for us to be seeking. It's *you* that taught them that!"

PROFESSOR: "Well, why can't we just explain that what we're seeking is simply beliefs that work, in practice? We can take our stand as Pragmatists looking for a useful theory."

STUDENT: "No, because that leads to Orwell's dystopia. Maybe social convenience is all you claim to be after, but I for one am still naive enough to suppose that what we're seeking is truth. Things as they really, actually *are*. And by that I don't just mean a theory that works, unless you flesh out the word 'works' so far that you end up with it meaning something like 'corresponds to and conforms with the real facts of external reality as it is in itself.'

I want to know what the truth is about the world, even if I haven't a prayer of ever achieving more than a small slice of knowledge, or a modest degree of increased accuracy. A little bit of knowledge is better than none. I'm not claiming to have, or to be able to get, anything close to omniscience or infallibility. But I do think I ought to try my level best to make as much progress as a fallible creature can. And I think somewhere in your heart of hearts, you feel the same way---or did, until the cynical and perverse David Hume corrupted your soul."

PROFESSOR: "You're incredibly unjust. According to you, Hume takes the blame for things that were already there, almost two hundred years earlier in Montaigne, to say nothing of Berkeley, Locke or Sextus Empiricus. Yet it's always Hume that you blast."

STUDENT: "That's because it was Hume that really swayed

everybody, it was Hume that made it stick. Berkeley was laughed at, and the Greeks are often ignored, but Hume is simply revered."

PROFESSOR: "Do you deny he was brilliant?"

STUDENT: "I don't deny it. He was devilishly clever."

PROFESSOR: "What about his great argument against miracles?"

STUDENT: "Maybe I just used it against his skepticism. We have to prefer the lesser miracle."

PROFESSOR: "Come, saith the Lord, let us reason together."

STUDENT: "Exactly. But how strange it is, that you once supposed it might help to defeat radical skepticism to swallow, hook, line and sinker, the anti-realist dogmas of history's greatest radical skeptic.

Hume was no *friend* of science. His epistemology blew science out of the water! No sooner had physics, medicine, astronomy, geology, and chemistry enjoyed a most wonderful rebirth, when along came Hume and Kant with their skeptical idealism to outlaw the whole project, and usher in the irrational and destructive Romantic movement. Hume is to this day the leading attorney for the Romantic reaction, bringing back the blind submission of al-Ghazali to end the liberal Age of Reason."

PROFESSOR: "Well, I'm afraid I still can't dismiss those concerns about tolerance. I mean, how do you know freedom of religion would have been established in the world, if not for my kind of philosophy?"

STUDENT: "Just a minute ago you wondered if rejecting your tradition wasn't going to lead to too *much* tolerance. You can't have it both ways. I don't think a more commonsensical philosophy would be either too tolerant or too intolerant. Besides, I think it's true, and that's more important. But, let's look at the history of idealism. The liberalism of Milton and Locke came first, before the idealism of Berkeley. Berkeley represented the religious reaction. Jonathan Edwards reads Berkeley, and the next thing you know his followers are burning books."

PROFESSOR: "What are you talking about? You mean Savonarola? That was Renaissance Italy."

STUDENT: "I'm talking about James Davenport, in Connecticut, in 1743."

PROFESSOR: "You have an eccentric view of history."

STUDENT: "Look at the logic. Look at the facts. Look at the timeline. Notice that after Berkeley's idealism and Hume's skepticism, we get the irrational Great Awakening and Romantic totalitarianism. Radical skepticism is the opposite of the healthy kind. It doesn't conduce to tolerance or freedom. History shows the opposite is the case. What do we get after Sextus Empiricus? The Dark Ages! Who loves Sextus Empiricus? Savonarola. Who loves al-Ghazali? Islamic fundamentalists. Who adores Hume? Nazis!"

PROFESSOR: "Feh. You're data-mining."

STUDENT: "Anti-skeptical realists like me who think they've found knowledge aren't afraid to debate. It's the skeptical cynics, who say truth is a social construction, who have a *reason* to burn books. And they do! Look at your postmodernists---they enacted campus speech codes. They're always flirting with totalitarianism. They say it's all a power struggle and nothing more. So, what remains after one concludes that, other than to win, in the struggle for power? They say political expedience is the only arbiter of truth.

It was anti-skeptics like Milton and Locke who gave birth to liberalism, not skeptics like Hume and Burke, or totalitarian idealists like Fichte and Hegel. Once you reject that we can see and know about an actual real world of things independent of us, there's no *purpose* to be served by freedom of thought and speech. Milton and Jefferson said the purpose of freedom is to let Truth emerge victorious from the fray. But truth means nothing to you people!"

PROFESSOR: "Sure it does. Truth means that which the community finds expedient in the way of belief."

STUDENT: "This is a philosophy that supports freedom? I don't think so! Maybe it bolsters absolute majority rule, as in democratic totalitarianism, but it sure doesn't support the freedom of the individual. Can't you see that it's no *coincidence* that Heidegger, DeMan and Habermas were Nazis, and that postmodernists still take totalitarianism's side against classical liberalism and the free world?"

PROFESSOR: "Oh please, this is too much. Spare me the fallacies *ad nazium*."

STUDENT: "Yeah, I know. You want me to believe that Rorty and Dewey's socialism, Putnam's Marxist-Leninism,[26] Hegel's state-worship, Sartre's Communism, and Heidegger and DeMan's Nazism, were all merely coincidental and had nothing to do with their philosophy. But to these sheer coincidences would have to be added a lot of similar coincidences, for example, that it was none other than Kant's disciple and Hegel's inspirer Fichte who laid down the tenets not only of racist German nationalism, but also of national socialism. Their buddy Hamann used to say *Hume is always my man,*[27] and that's exactly what's wrong with Hume. I mean, these German Idealists were a bunch of Nazis before even Jefferson was president, for crying out loud! Fichte's nationalist socialism dates to 1800. That beats the socialism of Fourier, Owen, and even Saint-Simon.[28] Why do I always find you over there on the totalitarian side of the English Channel? That's the wrong side of history. You need to come back over to the free side."

PROFESSOR: "*Hamann the Humean*, it almost rhymes."

STUDENT: "It's not funny!"

PROFESSOR: "It's a silly, anachronistic, hyperbolic *ad hominem*. A sloppy smear, and in any case pointless. Should we go for a flat Earth just because Goebbels believed in a round one? Get serious.

Besides, your hick view of history makes no sense. Hume was a liberal and no Continental. He has some really fine arguments for free trade. He was a friend of Adam Smith, a forerunner for utilitarianism and even evolution. And as for Kant, have you never read his beautiful essay on enlightenment? You of all people should appreciate Hume and Kant. Your ingratitude knows no shame. And speaking of nationalism, what is your blinkered view of history but merely an expression of your own corny Anglo-American prejudices inherited from Locke and Reid? Don't be such a hayseed."

STUDENT: "Better a hayseed than a jaded totalitarian creep!"

PROFESSOR: "Oh, grow up."

STUDENT: "Okay, look, maybe you have some valid points there. But, on the other hand, maybe a philosopher shouldn't get as much credit for the ideas he inherits from others, as for the effects his input has on later history. I mean, I think Kant and Hume merely inherited the sweet liberalism of England, and for that I give credit to Locke, the man who set us all free. Locke and Newton worked wonders in the Age of Reason, but Hume, Kant and Fichte planted the seeds of its destruction."

Because It Works?

PROFESSOR: "Sorry, but I really don't see how your vulgar anti-skeptical realism does much for freedom."

STUDENT: "Well, for one thing, notice that reason, evidence, double-blind placebo-controlled experiments and fair, well-mannered debating are the sorts of things that appeal to *naïfs* like me, who suppose that the object of the game is to find the mind-independent truth, whoever's ox gets gored. Your followers, on the other hand, say truth is whatever works for the community, and 'isn't found but made.' What else is left to do then, but defeat the Enemies of the People, by any means necessary? If truth is not found but made, then it no longer seems that a fair and impartial inquiry should conduce to finding it. If truth is made, then it's *made up.* You say truth is just the fiction that works, for now, to serve whatever purposes the Community has in mind. And the Community can't be wrong!"

PROFESSOR: "Now who's caricaturing? Look, what if you think

one thing, and yet everybody else in the world insists that you're quite wrong? Is it really going to be reasonable and rational for you to conclude you're right? Maybe not. Don't be like Lewis Carroll's Humpty-Dumpty."

STUDENT: "It depends on the evidence. It depends on the situation. Your problem is that you seem to be in a position where you have to say that one person being right against the conventional wisdom is practically a *logical impossibility*."

PROFESSOR: "I find it amusing that here you are, reading me the riot act, on the grounds that my epistemology is liable to conduce to certain consequences harmful to the interests of the community. Can you not see the delicious irony? You practically contradict yourself."

STUDENT: "No I don't. I'm not saying we shouldn't care what the consequences are. We should care. Of course. I'm just saying that cannot be all there is to *truth*. I'm saying they aren't the same thing. I'm saying there's something more to being true, than merely being expedient, and I'm also saying that to think otherwise isn't expedient."

PROFESSOR: "I'm loving this."

STUDENT: "What I mean is, you should stop saying 'if it works, then it's true,' and instead say if it's true, then it will (usually) work (better, in the long run). You're doing it backwards."

PROFESSOR: "Okay, but Rorty would just say if it's freedom you're after then just take care of freedom and let truth take care of itself, as his book title says. You're telling me to pursue your philosophy for the sake of the social consequences. But in that case, why shouldn't I take a shortcut? Why don't we cut to the chase, and just pursue the good social consequences directly? Why detour?"

STUDENT: "Maybe it's a means-end thing. Maybe it's an act vs. rule utility issue. Why be virtuous? Why be honest? If the purpose is simply to maximize utility? Because if we cynically abandon honesty and virtue, those good consequences won't actually materialize. Virtue works. Attempted shortcuts fail. Experience proves it. If you don't know the truth, you *can't* pursue the good consequences, because a lying map will sooner or later wreck the ship."

PROFESSOR: "Realist truth-seeking works?"

STUDENT: "Yes. But that isn't my argument that realism is true. I argued that it was true independently of its consequences. But, now, I'm arguing that it doesn't necessarily have bad consequences, and may even have good ones. A Pragmatist will be tempted to see that as a sufficient argument for its being true, but, of course, I don't see it that way, or I'd truly be guilty of the sort of irony that made you laugh.

And as far as tolerance goes, I'll admit that I do think it's permissible to convict murderers and put them in jail, on the basis of my anti-skeptical realism, which makes me think that criminal guilt can be truly and objectively known by mere mortals. But what would you do? Let everybody out of jail, on the grounds that there's no ready-made world? After all, if there's no independent world in which things in themselves are a certain way rather than being another way, how can anybody be known to be objectively guilty?

Even worse, how can anybody be known to be objectively *innocent*? Anti-realists can and have persecuted innocents on the grounds that whatever works for the community is not only expedient but also *true*. You know, I mean Orwell's point. If there's no such thing as a useful lie, according to the logic of your philosophy, then nothing useful can be accused of being a lie, because that's a logical impossibility."

PROFESSOR: "Well you're not going to be able to get away completely from the arbitrary authority of the community. You're not going to get away with being like Humpty-Dumpty, who says that his words mean whatever he says they mean regardless of the way those words are used by the rest of his linguistic community. Nor would you let me do it! Remember, you wouldn't let me get away with saying that it's true by definition that things in themselves cannot be perceived. You pointed out that I had no right to disregard the authority of the ordinary linguistic community, and highjack those words, and give them a new, non-ordinary definition which rendered my Kantian claim trivially true by definition. You said that was cheating."

STUDENT: "So I did. I guess I have to admit that when it comes to the definition of words, there is a certain authority enjoyed by the linguistic community as against the renegade. But you talk as if that social authority also covers substantial disputes over all and sundry matters of fact, and not just over the definition of words. You can't make it true by definition that the Party invented the airplane. And don't give me that stuff again about how you can turn a freight train into a raisin by changing the speech habits of the community. We've been over that ground. There's a difference between merely changing the language, and changing the facts on the ground."

PROFESSOR: "Well, are we sure there's a hard, bright line between the two? Sometimes it seems difficult to resolve disputes over matters of fact, without getting caught up in what you like to dismiss as a purely semantic quibble over the meaning of words. This tends to happen a lot at the cutting edge of physics. Remember the *atom* case. I mean, sometimes it's hard to come to any agreement over matters of fact, without first ironing out some kind of agreement about the use of the words.

And philosophy necessarily involves disputes over how we should speak, because as philosophers we're rightly concerned with various propositions which may flow, logically, from certain statements we accept. That's a part of our job. Besides, you yourself said the question of a word's definition or meaning ultimately comes down to a question of an empirical matter of fact, to wit, a matter of fact about how people actually use the word."

STUDENT: "Yes, but there's a crucial difference between merely altering our use of a word, as opposed to altering the facts on the ground to which our words refer. Look, your so-called 'pragmatism' is anything but pragmatic. According to your own doctrines, it cannot possibly work---you can't truly know which beliefs work and which don't. Besides being Orwellian, it also doesn't work because it bases everything upon being able to tell which beliefs *as a matter of fact* work and which *as a matter of fact* don't, and that's a need for what you and Hume call "knowledge of matters of fact and existence" and claim we can't have.

Would a brain in a vat be able to tell which of his beliefs as a matter of fact and existence 'work,' or are even 'better for him to believe?' According to your own philosophy, you might just as well be a deluded victim of an evil scientist who is tricking you into destroying yourself just when you think you're doing yourself good. Hume says we have to rely upon mindless habit and custom, precisely because we cannot rely upon 'Reason,' nor 'the Evidence of the Senses.' He claims to have 'shewn' that reliance upon reason and evidence 'entirely subverts itself, and leaves not the lowest degree of evidence in any proposition, either in philosophy or common life.'[29] But that would have to include propositions like that *it works to believe x,* or *it's better for us to believe p*, or that *by doing y, I really am as a matter of fact following custom."*

PROFESSOR: "Well, I seem to get along pretty well in the world, and yet I'm a follower of Hume. It sure seems to me like it works!"

STUDENT: "So, is that not something you know, as a matter of fact and existence, to be in reality true? To the extent you get along, it's because, contrary to Hume's claims, you can and do know things! It's because, contrary to Hume's claims, you're *not* weak or blind, and Reason and the Evidence of Senses *aren't* bogus. The reason why it "works" to follow Hume's advice is because Hume's advice says you ought to reject his philosophy and forget about it---if you can!

Look, if reason and empirical evidence *were* bankrupt, then you would have no reason to believe, nor empirical evidence to suggest, that they were. Nor would you have reason to believe nor evidence to suggest that any other way of thinking or living is even possible, much less practical or conducive to anything. If you can't know anything, then you can't know *anything*. Not even that. So how could you even know what's practical and what isn't? There's nothing more impractical than this folderol you unjustly call "Pragmatism." If it were true, it wouldn't work. Your so-called Pragmatism does not and could not solve or in any way overcome the fallacious skepticism that motivates it. A Humean can only function because he disregards his own philosophical claims and just ignores them."

PROFESSOR: "Exactly! You finally understand Hume. Come to Daddy."

STUDENT: "No! Look, the reason why mindlessly disregarding skeptical arguments seems to work is because those arguments are fallacious and false---not because *reason* is false! What's false is your Humean campaign against reason. You keep teaching your students that nothing and nobody can refute Hume, and Hume teaches them that the only answer is for us all to become proudly irrationalist, embracing a 'blind submission' to thoughtless customs, mindless habits, powerful emotions, and animal instincts. [30]

I mean, okay, maybe this is good advice for stupid people, if they're unlikely to be able to improve upon the conventional wisdom in any way. But we can't all be Humeans, and even an idiot can't be a Humean all the time. We can't all follow each other around like brainless lemmings unable to depend at all on reason or glean any empirical matters of fact from our experience.

Look, just ask yourself, *why* is it, according to Hume, that we're supposed to abandon my naive kind of philosophy? It's supposedly because 'we have...no choice left, but betwixt a false Reason and none at all,'[31] and because the evidence of the senses 'leaves not the lowest degree of evidence in any proposition, either in philosophy or common life.'[32] You teach your students that 'Reason is incapable of dispelling these clouds,'[33] and that 'the observation of human blindness and weakness is the result of all philosophy, and meets us at every turn, in spite of our endeavors to elude or avoid it.'[34] That's a travesty! It's wrong. It's false. It's corrupting and debilitating, and historically it's been very harmful.

It's no wonder postmodern philosophy books like *Farewell to Reason* have been so popular---these militant irrationalists are good students of your teachings. Now they're ready to follow in the footsteps of the Romans and ring down another thousand-year Dark Age on us all!"

PROFESSOR: "Oh, good heavens. Well, if that's the case, it was certainly no part of my intention. I'm just trying to do the best I can. Really, I don't see how I could have done much differently. I really don't know what you expect from me."

STUDENT: "I just want you to admit that Hume's arguments for skeptical idealism are fallacious and beatable. Then you can't be tempted by the dubious charms of a bunch of Nazis. You can become for the first time a true friend to science, instead of an enemy to it. You can become for the first time a loyal defender of right and good and freedom and the American Way---a heartfelt champion of Reason, Reality, and Truth. You can live in peace and harmony with the "naive" realism of ordinary common sense, a prosperous and happy Jack, back on the farm, like me."

PROFESSOR: "Well now you sound like Rorty, who says we should just give up epistemology."

STUDENT: "No, no! On the contrary, I think epistemology has plenty of valuable work to do. Besides making amends for all the harm it's done, it ought to try to get out of this rut by working out a good philosophy of probability and 'abduction' if that's what you like to call it. Giving up on philosophy---now---would be like giving up on medical science at that point in history just before it began to cure more patients than it killed. It would be like leaving a dangerous highway overpass half-built, perfectly designed to send all the cars sailing off the end. We can't give up now, and walk away, and leave everything in such a state. Rorty says:

> I hope that people will never stop reading, e.g., Plato, Aristotle, Kant and Hegel, but also hope that they will, sooner or later, stop trying to sucker freshmen into taking an interest in the Problem of the External World and the Problem of Other Minds.[35]

That's the *worst* thing we could possibly do. He's saying he hopes everybody keeps catching the disease, but stops looking for a cure."

It's All in Your Head

Citations for a Problematic Tradition

Sextus Empiricus

"Although, no doubt, it is easy to say what nature each of the underlying objects appears to each man to possess, we cannot go on to say what its real nature is, since the disagreement admits in itself of no settlement. For the person who tries to settle it is...in one of the aforementioned dispositions... And if he is to judge the sense impressions while he is in some one disposition...he will not be an impartial judge of the external underlying objects owing to his being confused by the dispositions in which he is placed."[1]

"Proof always requires a criterion to confirm it, and the criterion also a proof to demonstrate its truth; and neither can a proof be sound without the existence of a true criterion nor can the criterion be true without the previous confirmation of the proof. So in this way both the criterion and the proof are involved in circular process of reasoning, and thereby both are found to be untrustworthy; for since each of them is dependent on the credibility of the other, the one is lacking in credibility just as much as the other."[2]

Michel de Montaigne

"The senses do not comprehend the foreign object, but only their own impressions."

"We no longer know what things are in truth; for nothing comes to us except falsified and altered by our senses."

"The uncertainty of the senses makes everything they produce uncertain...the conception and semblance we form is not of the object, but only of the impression and effect made on the sense; which impression and the object are two different things...And as for saying that the impressions of the senses convey to the soul the quality of the foreign objects by resemblance, how can the soul make sure of the resemblance, having itself no communication with foreign objects? Just as a man who does not know Socrates, seeing his portrait, cannot say that it resembles him."[3]

"Things do not lodge in us in their own form and essence...Thus, external objects surrender to our mercy; they dwell in us as we please."[4]

"I must see at last whether it is in the power of man to find what he seeks, and whether that quest that he has been making for so many centuries has enriched him with any new power and any solid truth. I think he will confess to me...that all the profit he has gained from so long a pursuit is to have learned to acknowledge his weakness. The ignorance that was naturally in us we have by long study confirmed and verified."[5]

Nicolas Malebranche

"One must not confuse the ideas of things with the things themselves. Remember, that we do not see bodies in themselves, and that it is only through their ideas that they are visible."[6]

"Faith alone can convince us that bodies actually exist."[7]

John Locke

"Our knowledge [is] conversant about our ideas only. Since the mind, in all its thoughts and reasonings, hath no other immediate object but its own ideas, which it alone does or can contemplate, it is evident that our knowledge is only conversant about them."[8]

George Berkeley

"All that we know or conceive are our own ideas."[9]

"The things I perceive are my own ideas, and...no idea can exist unless it be in a mind."[10]

"Nothing is perceived by the senses beside ideas."[11]

"With all my heart, retain the word *matter*, and apply it to the objects of sense, if you please, provided you do not attribute to them any subsistence distinct from their being perceived...You talked often as if you thought I maintained the non-existence of sensible things: whereas in truth no one can be more thoroughly assured of their existence than I am...though indeed I deny they have any existence distinct from being perceived; or that they can exist out of all minds whatsoever.

I might as well doubt of my own being, as of the being of those things I actually see and feel...

My endeavours tend only to unite and place in a clearer light that truth, which was before shared between the vulgar and the philosophers: the former being of opinion, that *those things they immediately perceive are the real things:* and the latter, that *the things immediately perceived are ideas which exist only in the mind.* Which two notions put together, do in effect constitute the substance of what I advance."[12]

"Sensible things are all immediately perceivable; and those things which are immediately perceivable, are ideas; and these exist only in the mind."[13]

David Hume

"Philosophy informs us that everything which appears to the mind is nothing but a perception, and is interrupted and dependent on the mind."[14]

"Properly speaking, 'tis not our body we perceive, when we regard our limbs and members, but certain impressions, which enter by the senses."[15]

"The slightest philosophy...teaches us that nothing can ever be present to the mind but an image or perception."

"The mind has never anything present to it but the perceptions, and cannot possibly reach any experience of their connexion with objects. The supposition of such a connexion is, therefore, without any foundation in reasoning."[16]

"The only existences, of which we are certain, are perceptions, which being immediately present to us by consciousness, command our strongest assent, and are the first foundation of all our conclusions. The only conclusion we can draw from the existence of one thing to that of another, is by means of the relation of cause and effect, which shews, that there is a connexion betwixt them, and that the existence of one is dependent on that of the other. The idea of this relation is derived from past experience, by which we find, that two beings are constantly conjoined together, and are always present at once to the mind. But as no beings are ever present to the mind but perceptions; it follows that we may observe a conjunction or a relation of cause and effect between different perceptions, but can never observe it between perceptions and objects. It is impossible, therefore, that from the existence or any of the qualities of the former, we can ever form any conclusion concerning the existence of the latter, or ever satisfy our reason in this particular.

...Let it be taken for granted, that our perceptions are broken, and interrupted, and however like, are still different from each other; and let any one upon this supposition shew why the fancy, directly and immediately, proceeds to the belief of another existence, resembling these perceptions in their nature, but yet continued, and uninterrupted, and identical; and after he has done this to my satisfaction, I promise to renounce my present opinion. ...Whoever would explain the origin of the common opinion concerning the continued and distinct existence of body, must take the mind in its common situation, and must proceed upon the supposition, that our perceptions are our only objects, and continue to exist even when they are not perceived.

Though this opinion be false, it is the most natural of any, and has alone any primary recommendation to the fancy.

...For as the philosophical system is found by experience to take hold of many minds, and in particular of all those, who reflect ever so little on this subject, it must derive all its authority from the vulgar system; since it has no original authority of its own."[17]

"When we press one eye with a finger, we immediately perceive all the objects to become double, and one half of them to be removed from their common and natural position. But as we do not attribute to continued existence to both these perceptions, and as they are both of the same nature, we clearly perceive, that all our perceptions are dependent on our organs, and the disposition of our nerves and animal spirits. This opinion is confirmed by the seeming increase and diminution of objects, according to their distance; by the apparent alterations in their figure; by the changes in their colour and other qualities from our sickness and distempers: and by an infinite number of other experiments of the same kind; from all which we learn, that our sensible perceptions are not possessed of any distinct or independent existence."[18]

"It is universally allowed by philosophers, and is besides pretty obvious of itself, that nothing is ever really present with the mind but its perceptions or impressions and ideas."[19]

"That our senses offer not their impressions as the images of something distinct, or independent, and external, is evident; because they convey to us nothing but a single perception, and never give us the least intimation of any thing beyond."[20]

"It seems evident, that men are carried, by a natural instinct or prepossession, to repose faith in their senses; and that, without any reasoning, or even almost before the use of reason, we always suppose an external universe, which depends not on our perception, but would exist, though we and every sensible creature were absent or annihilated. Even the animal creation are governed by a like opinion, and preserve this belief of external objects, in all their thoughts, designs, and actions.

It seems also evident, that, when men follow this blind and powerful instinct of nature, they always suppose the very images, presented by the senses, to be the external objects, and never entertain any suspicion, that the one are nothing but representations of the other. This very table, which we see white, and which we feel hard, is believed to exist, independent of our perception, and to be something external to our mind, which perceives it. Our presence bestows not being on it: our absence does not annihilate it. It preserves its existence uniform and entire, independent of the situation of intelligent beings, who perceive or contemplate it.

But this universal and primary opinion of all men is soon destroyed by the slightest philosophy, which teaches us, that nothing can ever be present to the mind but an image or perception, and that the senses are only the inlets, through which these images are conveyed, without being able to produce any immediate intercourse between the mind and the object. The table, which we see, seems to diminish, as we remove farther from it: but the real table, which exists independent of us, suffers no alteration: it was, therefore, nothing but its image, which was present to the mind. These are the obvious dictates of reason; and no man, who reflects, ever doubted, that the existences, which we consider, when we say, *this house* and *that tree*, are nothing but perceptions in the mind, and fleeting copies or representations of other existences, which remain uniform and independent...

By what argument can it be proved, that the perceptions of the mind must be caused by external objects, entirely different from them, though resembling them (if that be possible) and could not arise either from the energy of the mind itself, or from the suggestion of some invisible and unknown spirit, or from some other cause still more unknown to us?

...It is a question of fact, whether the perceptions of the senses be produced by external objects, resembling them: how shall this question be determined? By experience surely; as all other questions of a like nature. But here experience is, and must be entirely silent. The mind has never anything present to it but the perceptions, and cannot possibly reach any experience of their connexion with objects. The supposition of such a connexion is, therefore, without any foundation in reasoning.

...This is a topic, therefore, in which the profounder and more philosophical sceptics will always triumph, when they endeavour to introduce an universal doubt into all subjects of human knowledge and enquiry.

... Reason...can never find any convincing argument from experience to prove, that the perceptions are connected with any external objects."[21]

"The mind can always *conceive* any effect to follow from any cause, and indeed any event to follow upon another: whatever we *conceive* is possible: at least, in a metaphysical sense: but wherever a demonstration takes place, the contrary is impossible, and implies a contradiction. There is no demonstration therefore, for any conjunction of cause and effect."[22]

"We can at least conceive a change in the course of nature; which sufficiently proves that such a change is not absolutely impossible. To form a clear idea of any thing, is an undeniable argument for its possibility."[23]

"I am ready to reject all belief and reasoning, and can look upon no opinion even as more probable or likely than another."[24]

"If we believe that fire warms or water refreshes, it is only because it costs us too much pains to think otherwise."[25]

"Reason is incapable of dispelling these clouds."[26]

"Philosophy has nothing to oppose to them [i.e., skeptical humors]..."[27]

"We have...no choice left, but betwixt a false reason and none at all. For my part, I know not what ought to be done in the present case. I can only observe what is commonly done; which is, that this difficulty is seldom thought of."[28]

"I may, nay I must yield to the current of nature, in submitting to my senses and understanding; and in this blind submission I shew most perfectly my sceptical disposition and principles."[29]

"I have already shewn, that the understanding, when it acts alone, and according to its most general principles, entirely subverts itself, and leaves not the lowest degree of evidence in any proposition, either in philosophy or common life. We save ourselves from this total scepticism only by means of that singular and seemingly trivial property of the fancy, by which we enter with difficulty into remote views of things."[30]

"This sceptical doubt, both with respect to reason and the senses, is a malady, which can never be radically cured, but must return upon us every moment, however we may chase it away, and sometimes may seem entirely free from it. 'Tis impossible upon any system to defend either our understanding or senses; and we but expose them farther when we endeavour to justify them in that manner. As the sceptical doubt arises naturally from a profound and intense reflection on those subjects, it always increases, the farther we carry our reflections, whether in opposition or conformity to it. Carelessness and inattention alone can afford us any remedy. For this reason I rely entirely upon them."[31]

"The observation of human blindness and weakness is the result of all philosophy, and meets us at every turn, in spite of our endeavors to elude or avoid it."[32]

Immanuel Kant

"It still remains a scandal to philosophy and to human reason in general that the existence of things outside us...must be accepted merely on *faith*, and that if anyone thinks good to doubt their existence, we are unable to counter his doubts by any satisfactory proof."[33]

"All objects of an experience possible for us are nothing but appearances, i.e., mere representations, which...have outside our thoughts no existence grounded in itself. ...The realist...makes these modifications of our sensibility into things subsisting in themselves, and hence makes mere representations into things in themselves."[34]

"The senses...never and in no single instance enable us to know things in themselves."[35]

"Things in themselves...cannot be objects of experience." [36]

"Matter...is nothing other than a mere form or a certain mode of representation of an unknown object."[37]

"Nothing intuited in space is a thing in itself...what we call outer objects are nothing but representation of our sensibility the form of which is space. The true correlate of sensibility, the thing in itself, is not known, and cannot be known, through these representations; and in experience no question is ever asked regarding it."[38]

"External objects (bodies)...are mere appearances, and are therefore nothing but a species of my representations, the objects of which are something only through these representations. Apart from them they are nothing."[39]

"The objects with which we have to do in experience are by no means things in themselves but only appearances."[40]

"Appearances are not things, but rather nothing but representations, and they cannot exist at all outside our minds."[41]

"Phenomena are not things in themselves, and are yet the only thing that can be given to us to know."[42]

"Things as objects of our senses existing outside us are given, but we know nothing of what they may be in themselves, knowing only their appearances, that is, the representations which they cause in us by affecting our senses."[43]

"The non-sensible cause of these representations is entirely unknown to us."[44]

"As we have just shown that the senses never and in no manner enable us to know things in themselves, but only their appearances...we conclude that all bodies together with the space in which they are, must be considered nothing but mere representations in us, and exist nowhere but in our thoughts."[45]

"Your object is merely in your brain."[46]

"It is also false that the world (the sum total of all appearances) is a whole existing in itself...appearances in general are nothing outside our representations."[47]

"Since space is a form of that intuition we call outer...we can and must regard the beings in it as real; and the same is true of time. But this space and this time, and with them all appearances, are not in themselves things; they are nothing but representations and cannot exist at all outside our minds."[48]

"The understanding itself is the lawgiver of Nature; save through it, Nature would not exist at all."[49]

"If I remove the thinking subject, the whole corporeal world must at once vanish."[50]

"If then, as this critical argument obviously compels us to do, we hold fast to the rule above established, and do not push our questions beyond the limits within which possible experience can present us with its object, we shall never dream of seeking to inform ourselves about the objects of our senses as they are in themselves."[51]

"I had to deny knowledge in order to make room for faith."[52]

G. E. Schulze

"Where do the representations that we possess originate, and how do they come to be in us? This has been for a long time one of the most important questions in philosophy. Common opinion has rightly held that, since the representations in us are not the objects themselves being represented, the connection between our representations and the things outside us must be established above all by a careful and sound answer to this question. It is in this way that certitude must be sought regarding the reality of the different components of our knowledge."[53]

J. G. Fichte

"That there is nothing whatever but my presentations is, to the natural sense of mankind, a silly and ridiculous conceit which no man can seriously entertain and which requires no refutation. To the well-informed judge, who knows the deeper grounds for this opinion, grounds which cannot be removed by mere reasoning, this thought is one of despair and annihilation."[54]

"In all seriousness, and not only in a manner of speaking, the object shall be posited and determined by the cognitive faculty and not the cognitive faculty by the object."[55]

F. W. J. Schelling

"It can be demonstrated, indeed, to the most obstinate dogmatists, that the world consists only in presentations."[56]

Bertrand Russell

"The view which I should wish to advocate is that objects of perception do not persist unchanged at times when they are not perceived, although probably objects more or less resembling them do exist at such times."[57]

"Among the objects with which we are acquainted are not included physical objects (as opposed to sense-data), nor other people's minds. These things are known to us by what I call 'knowledge by description'."[58]

W. V. O. Quine

"I do not see that we are farther along today than where Hume left us. The Humean predicament is the human predicament."[59]

Hilary Putnam

"Realism is an impossible attempt to view the world from Nowhere."[60]

"The mind never compares an image or word with an object, but only with other images, words, beliefs, judgments, etc."[61]

Donald Davidson

"The approach to the problem of justification we have been tracing must be wrong. We have been trying to see it this way: a person has all his beliefs about the world---that is, all his beliefs. How can he tell if they are true, or apt to be true? This is possible, we have been assuming, only by connecting his beliefs to the world, confronting certain of his beliefs with the deliverances of the senses one by one, or perhaps confronting the totality of his beliefs with the tribunal of experience. No such confrontation makes sense, for of course we can't get outside our skins to find out what is causing the internal happenings of which we are aware."[62]

"The ultimate source (not ground) of objectivity, is in my opinion, intersubjectivity. If we were not in communication with others, there would be nothing on which to base the idea of being wrong, or, therefore, of being right, either in what we say or in what we think."[63]

"If I did not know what others think, I would have no thoughts of my own and so would not know what I think."[64]

Richard Rorty

"A number of contemporary philosophers, including myself, do their best to complicate the traditional distinctions between the objective and the subjective, reason and passion, knowledge and opinion, science and politics. We offer contentious reinterpretations of these distinctions, draw them in nontraditional ways. For example, we deny that the search for objective truth is a search for correspondence to reality and urge that it be seen instead as a search for the widest possible intersubjective agreement."[65]

"Paul de Man was one of the most beloved and influential teachers of recent times. He was the person primarily responsible for the movement which we now call 'deconstruction.' The special twist de Man put on Heideggerian and Derridean themes has been the single most influential contribution to what is sometimes called, by its enemies, 'the politicization of the humanities' in American universities."[66]

"What people like Kuhn, Derrida, and I believe is that it is pointless to ask whether there are really mountains or whether it is merely convenient for us to talk about mountains."[67]

"There is no procedure called 'turning to the facts'...there is no procedure of 'justification in light of the facts' which can be opposed to concilience of one's own opinion with those of others."[68]

"The claim that we are responsible to reality is as hopeless as the idea that true sentences correspond to reality....we have no responsibilities except to fellow-players of what Sellars and Brandom call 'the game of giving and asking for reasons.'"[69]

"We understand knowledge when we understand the social justification of belief, and thus have no need to view it as accuracy of representation."[70]

"The notion of 'accurate representation' is simply an automatic and empty compliment which we pay to those beliefs which are successful in helping us to do what we want to do."[71]

"Justification is not a matter of a special relation between ideas (or words) and objects, but of conversation, of social practice."[72]

"Philosophers on my side of the argument answer that objectivity is not a matter of corresponding to objects but a matter of getting together with other subjects---that there is nothing to objectivity except intersubjectivity."[73]

"Nature itself is a poem that we humans have written."[74]

"There is no enclosing wall called 'the Real.' There is nothing outside language to which language attempts to become adequate."[75]

"If one reinterprets objectivity as intersubjectivity, or as solidarity...then one will drop the question of how to get in touch with 'mind-independent and language-independent reality.' One will replace it with questions like 'What are the limits of our community?' ...Dewey seems to me to have given us the right lead when he viewed pragmatism not as grounding, but as clearing the ground for, democratic politics."[76]

"My rejection of traditional notions of rationality can be summed up by saying that the only sense in which science is exemplary is that it is a model of human solidarity."[77]

"We need to think of reason not as a truth-tracking faculty but as a social practice---the practice of enforcing social norms on the use of marks and noises, thereby making it possible to use words rather than blows as a way of getting things done. To be rational is simply to conform to those norms. This is why what counts as rational in one society may count as irrational in another. The idea that some societies are more rational than others presupposes that we have some access to a source of normativity other than the practices of the people around us."[78]

"What we cannot do is to rise above all human communities, actual and possible. We cannot find a skyhook which lifts us out of mere coherence---mere agreement---to something like 'correspondence with reality as it is in itself.' ...Pragmatists would like to replace the desire for objectivity---the desire to be in touch with reality which is more than some community with which we identify ourselves---with the desire for solidarity with that community."[79]

"I do not think there are any plain moral facts out there in the world, nor any truths independent of language, nor any neutral ground on which to stand and argue that either torture or kindness are preferable to the other. So I want offer a different reading of Orwell.

...In the view of *1984* that I am offering, Orwell has no *answer* to O'Brien, and is not interested in giving one. Like Nietzsche, O'Brien regards the whole idea of being "answered," of exchanging ideas, of reasoning together, as a symptom of weakness...[Orwell] does not view O'Brien as crazy, misguided, seduced by a mistaken theory, or blind to the moral facts....I take Orwell's claim that there is no such thing as *inner* freedom, no such thing as an "autonomous individual," to be the one made by historicist, including Marxist, critics of "liberal individualism." This is that there is nothing deep inside each of us, no common human nature, no built-in human solidarity, to use as a moral reference point. There is nothing to people except what has been socialized into them."[80]

"For pragmatists, the question should always be 'What use is it?' rather than 'Is it real?'"[81]

"The difference between myself and Conant is that he thinks that someone like Winston, trapped in such a society, can turn to the light of the facts. I think that there is nowhere for Winston to turn."[82]

> "The authority of a thousand is not worth the humble reasoning of a single individual."[1]
>
> ---Galileo

BIBLIOGRAPHY

Abela, Paul, *Kant's Empirical Realism*, Oxford University Press, 2002.

Allison, Henry E., *Kant's Transcendental Idealism: An Interpretation and Defense*, Yale University Press, revised and expanded, 2004.

Alston, William P., *Realism & Antirealism*, Cornell University Press, 2002.

Aronowitz, Stanley, *Science as Power*, University of Minnesota, 1988.

Armstrong, D. M., *Perception and the Physical World*, Routledge & Kegan, 1961.

Audi, Robert, *Epistemology: a Contemporary Introduction*, second edition, Routledge, 2003.

Aune, Bruce, *Knowledge of the External World*, Routledge, 1991.

Austin, J.L., *Sense and Sensibilia*, Oxford University Press, 1964.

Avramides, Anita, *Other Minds*, Routledge, 2001.

Ayer, A. J., *The Problem of Knowledge,* Pelican, 1956.

Beiser, Frederick C., *German Idealism: The Struggle Against Subjectivism*, 1781-1801, Harvard University Press, 2002.

Berlin, Isaiah, *The Magus of the North: J.G. Hamann and the Origins of Modern Irrationalism*, Farrar, Straus, & Giroux, 1994.

_____, *Three Critics of the Enlightenment,* Princeton University Press, 2000.

_____, *Freedom and Its Betrayal: Six Enemies of Human Liberty,* Vintage UK, 2001.

Booth, Wayne C., *Modern Dogma and the Rhetoric of Assent,* University of Chicago Press, 1974.

Brandom, Robert, ed., *Rorty and His Critics*, Blackwell Publishing, 2000.

Brewer, Bill, *Perception and Reason,* Oxford University Press, 1999.

Chisholm, Roderick, *Perceiving*, Cornell University Press, 1957.

Coates, Paul, *Current Issues in Idealism,* St. Augustine's Press, 1996.

Collins, Arthur, *Possible Experience: Understanding Kant's Critique of Pure Reason,* University of California, 1999.

Dancy, Jonathan, ed., *Perceptual Knowledge*, Oxford University Press, 1988.

Dancy, Jonathan, *Introduction to Contemporary Epistemology*, Blackwell Publishing, 1985.

Davidson, Donald, *Subjective, Intersubjective, Objective,* Oxford University Press, 2001.

DeRose, Keith, and Warfield, Ted A., eds., *Skepticism: a Contemporary Reader*, Oxford University Press, 1999.

Devitt, Michael, *Realism and Truth*, second edition, Princeton University Press, 1996.

DeVries, Willem A., and Triplett, Timm, *Knowledge, Mind and the Given: Reading Wilfrid Sellars's "Empiricism and the Philosophy of Mind," Including the Complete Text of Sellars's Essay,* Hackett Publishing Company, 2000.

Dicker, Georges, *Kant's Theory of Knowledge: An Analytical Introduction*, Oxford University Press, USA, 2004.

Dummett, Michael, *Truth and Other Enigmas*, Harvard University Press, 1978.

Fichte, J.G., *Science of Knowledge*, translated by Peter Heath & John Lachs, Appleton Century Crofts, 1970.

Flew, Antony, *Hume's Philosophy of Belief*, Routledge, 1961.

_____, *David Hume, Philosopher of Moral Science*, Blackwell Publishing, 1986.

_____, *Introduction to Western Philosophy: Argument and Ideas from Plato to Popper*, revised edition, Thames and Hudson, 1989.

Fumerton, Richard A., "Induction and Reasoning to the Best Explanation," *Philosophy of Science* 47, 1980: 589-600.

_____, *Metaphysical and Epistemological Problems of Perception,* Lincoln: University of Nebraska Press, 1985.

_____, "Skepticism and Reasoning to the Best Explanation," in Enrique Villanueva ed., *Philosophical Issues 2: Rationality in Epistemology*, 1992: 149-169.

_____, *Metaepistemology and Skepticism,* Rowman & Littlefield Publishers, 1995.

_____, *Realism and the Correspondence Theory of Truth,* Rowman & Littlefield Publishers, Inc., 2002.

_____, "The Challenge of Refuting Skepticism," *Contemporary Debates in Epistemology*, Matthias Steup and Ernest Sosa, eds., Blackwell Publishing, 2005.

_____, *Epistemology*, Blackwell Publishing, 2006.

Gardner, Sebastian, *Kant and The Critique of Pure Reason,* Routledge, 1999.

Gendler, Tamar Szabo and Hawthorne, John, eds., *Perceptual Experience*, Oxford University Press, 2006.

Goodman, Nelson, *Of Mind and Other Matters*, Harvard University Press, 1987

Guyer, Paul, *Kant and the Claims of Knowledge,* Cambridge University Press, 1987.

Hanson, Norwood R., *Patterns of Discovery*, Cambridge University Press, 1961.

Haack, Susan, *Evidence and Inquiry: Towards Reconstruction in Epistemology*, Blackwell Publishing, 1995.

Hicks, Stephen, *Explaining Postmodernism: Skepticism and Socialism from Rousseau to Foucault*, Scholargy Publishing, 2004.

Hildebrand, David L., *Beyond Realism and Idealism*, Vanderbuilt University Press, 2003.

Howson, Colin, *Hume's Problem: Induction and the Justification of Belief*, Oxford University Press, 2000.

Huemer, Michael, *Skepticism and the Veil of Perception*, Rowman & Littlefield Publishers, 2001.

Hume, David, [1739-40] (1978) *A Treatise of Human Nature*, edited by L. A. Selby-Bigge, revised by P. Nidditch, Oxford: Clarendon, second edition.

_____, [1748] (1972) *An Enquiry concerning Human Understanding*, in *Enquiries...by David Hume*, edited by L. A. Selby-Bigge, Oxford: Clarendon, Second edition.

Jeffry, R. *The Logic of Decision*, second ed., Chicago, University of Chicago Press, 1983.

Jones, W. T., *A History of Western Philosophy, Vol. IV: Kant and the Nineteenth Century*, second ed., revised and expanded, Harcourt Brace, 1980.

Kant, Immanuel, *Critique of Pure Reason*, [1781] trans. Paul Guyer and Allen Wood, Cambridge University Press, 1999.

Kelley, David, *The Evidence of the Senses: A Realist Theory of Perception*, Louisiana State University, 1986.

Khlentzos, Drew, *Naturalistic Realism and the Antirealist Challenge*, MIT Press, 2004.

Kuhn, Thomas, *The Structure of Scientific Revolutions*, second edition, Chicago University Press, 1970.

Kulp, Christopher B., ed., *Realism/Anti-realism and Epistemology*, Rowman & Littlefield Publishers, 1997.

Kusch, Martin, *Knowledge by Agreement*, Oxford University Press, 2002.

Latour, Bruno, *Science in Action*, Harvard University Press, 1987.

Landesman, Charles, *Skepticism: The Central Issues,* Blackwell Publishing, 2002.

Landesman, Charles, and Meeks, Roblin, eds., *Philosophical Skepticism*, Blackwell Publishing, 2003.

Langton, Rae, *Kantian Humiltiy: Our Ignorance of Things in Themselves,* Oxford University Press, 1998.

Lemos, Noah, *An Introduction to the Theory of Knowledge*, Cambridge University Press, 2007.

Lipton, Peter, *Inference to the Best Explanation*, Routledge, 1991.

Lyotard, Jacques, *The Postmodern Condition: A Report on Knowledge*, University of Minnesota, 1979.

Macdonald, G. F., ed., *Perception and Identity: Essays Presented to A. J. Ayer with His Replies*, Cornell University Press, 1979.

Maia Neto, Jose R., and Popkin, Richard H., eds., *Skepticism in Renaissance and Post-Renaissance Thought: New Interpretations,* Humanity Books, 2004.

Malachowski, Alan, *Richard Rorty*, Princeton University Press, 2002.

Maund, Barry, *Perception*, McGill-Queen's, 2003.

McDowell, John, *Mind and World*, Harvard University Press, 1994.

Mensch, James R., *Intersubjectivity and Transcendental Idealism*, State University of New York Press, 1988.

Musgrave, Alan, *Common Sense, Science and Scepticism: A Historical Introduction to the Theory of Knowledge,* Cambridge University Press, 1993.

Orwell, George, *1984*, 1949.

Pinkard, Terry, *German Philosophy 1760-1860: The Legacy of Idealism*, Cambridge University Press, 2003.

Pols, Edward, *Radical Realism: Direct Knowing in Science and Philosophy*, Cornell University Press, 1992.

Popkin, Richard H., *The History of Scepticism: from Savonarola to Bayle*, Oxford University Press, 2003.

Price, H. H., *Perception*, London: Methuen & Company Ltd.,1932.

Putnam, Hilary, *Reason, Truth and History*, 1981.

_____, *Realism and Reason*, Cambridge Univeristy Press, 1983.

_____, *The Many Faces of Realism*, Open Court, 1987.

_____, *Representation and Reality*, Bradford Book, 1988.

_____, *Realism With a Human Face*, Harvard University Press,1990.

_____, *Words & Life*, Harvard University Press, 1994.

_____, *The Threefold Cord*, Columbia University Press, 1999.

Quine, Willard Van Orman, *Ontological Relativity and Other Essays*, Columbia University Press, 1969.

Robinson, Howard, *Perception*, Routledge, 1994.

Reid, Thomas, *An Inquiry into the Human Mind on the Principles of Common Sense*, Edinburgh: Edinburgh University Press, 1997.

Rorty, Richard, *Philosophy and the Mirror of Nature*, Princeton University Press, 1979.

_____, *Consequences of Pragmatism: Essays, 1972-1980*, University of Minnesota, 1982.

_____, *Contingency, Irony, and Solidarity*, Cambridge University Press, 1989.

_____, *Objectivity, Relativism, and Truth: Philosophical Papers, Volume 1*, Cambridge University Press, 1991.

_____, *Essays on Heidegger and others: Philosophical Papers, Volume. 2*, Cambridge University Press, 1991.

_____, *Truth and Progress*, Cambridge University Press, 1998.

_____, *Take Care of Freedom and Truth Will Take Care of Itself*, Stanford University Press, 2006.

_____, & Pascal Engel, trans. William McCuaig, Patrick Savidan, ed., *What's the Use of Truth?* Columbia University Press, 2007.

_____, *Philosophy as Cultural Politics*, Cambridge University Press, 2007.

Rudd, Anthony, *Expressing the World*, Open Court, 2003.

Scheffler, Israel, *Science and Subjectivity*, 2nd edition, Hackett Publishing Company, 1982.

Schwartz, Robert, ed., *Perception*, Blackwell Publishing, 2003.

Sellars, Wilfrid, *Empiricism and the Philosophy of Mind: With an Introduction by Richard Rorty and a Study Guide by Robert Brandon*, Harvard University Press, 1997.

Smith, A. D., *The Problem of Perception*, Harvard University Press, 2002.

Smith, Norman Kemp, *A Commentary to Kant's Critique of Pure Reason*, Macmillan, 1918.

Sosa, Ernest, and Villanueva, Enrique, *Skepticism (Philosophical Issues)*, Blackwell Publishing, 2000.

Stace, W.T., *The Philosophy of Hegel: A Systematic Exposition*, Dover, 1955.

Steup, Matthias, and Ernest Sosa, eds., *Contemporary Debates In Epistemology,* Blackwell Publishing, 2005.

Stove, David, *The Plato Cult and Other Philosophical Follies,* Blackwell Publishing, 1991.

Strawson, P.F., *The Bounds of Sense: An Essay on Kant's Critique of Pure Reason,* Routledge, 1966.

Stroud, Barry, *The Quest for Reality*, Oxford University Press, 2000.

_____, *The Significance of Philosophical Scepticism*, Oxford, 1984.

Swartz, Robert J., ed., *Perceiving, Sensing, and Knowing*, London: University of California Press, 1965.

Thompson, Garrett, *Bacon to Kant: An Introduction to Modern Philosophy*, second edition, Waveland Press, 2002.

Unger, Peter, *Ignorance: A Case for Scepticism*, Oxford University Press, 1975.

Urban, Wilbur Marshall, *Beyond Realism and Idealism,* George Allen, 1949.

Warnock, G. J., ed., *Philosophy of Perception,* Oxford University Press, 1967.

Williams, Michael, *Unnatural Doubts: Epistemological Realism and the Basis of Scepticism,* Princeton University Press, 1996.

Wood, Allen W., *Kant*, Blackwell Publishing, 2004.

Zahavi, Dan, *Husserl & Transcendental Intersubjectivity*, trans. Elizabeth A. Behnke, Ohio University Press, 2001.

Acknowledgments

Thank you to those who read drafts and helpfully commented: Antony Flew, William H. Shaw, Sterling Harwood, Deborah Savage, and Timothy Kneale. Thank you also to Jeannie and Denise, without whom there would be no book, and to my husband for earning my living, without which there'd have been no affording Jeannie and Denise. (So, darling, I forgive you for resenting every minute I spent on this, and hope you likewise forgive me for the occasionally empty sock drawer.)

Some friends have asked why I wrote this book, and I can only answer as a person who might be asked why did you throw up: some things you just can't help. As to why I published it myself, I would of course have preferred to publish a respectable book. But, being a person of no position higher than sock washer, I wasted only a little time offering it to serious philosophy publishers. I didn't ask anybody's opinion before writing it, and, as their websites explain, you're really not supposed to write a philosophy book and then send it to them to see if they approve of it. What's required is first of all to submit a formal proposal, and then wait patiently in hopes of one day receiving permission to write a philosophy book. To dream that such would be granted to a laundress of no account would be naive.

Anyway, having already done what's not allowed by writing a philosophy book without permission, I figured I was on my own and may as well cast my lot with all the other cranks who have without permission constituted the sweet land of liberty since a handful of crackpots braved a howling wilderness for no good reason besides the fact they had a problem with getting permission.

"Enlightenment is man's release from his self-incurred tutelage. Tutelage is man's inability to make use of his understanding without direction from another. Self-incurred is this tutelage when its cause lies not in lack of reason but in lack of resolution and courage to use it without direction from another. *Sapere aude* [dare to know] 'Have courage to use your own reason!' — that is the motto of Enlightenment."

---Immanuel Kant, 1784

Notes

[1] Hume, *Enquiry Concerning Human Understanding,* [1748] Section XII, part I, 118-119, in Selby-Bigge ed., p. 152-153.

[2] Quine, *Ontological Relativity and Other Essays,* (Columbia University Press, 1969), p. 72.

[3] Frankfurt, *On Bullshit,* Princeton University Press, 2005, p. 1.

[4] See Daniel Dennett, "The Case for Rorts," in Robert Brandom, ed., *Rorty and His Critics,* (Blackwell, 2000) p. 91.

[5] See Charles Guignon, *Richard Rorty,* (Cambridge University Press, 2003), back cover.

[6] Richard Malachowski, *Richard Rorty,* (Princeton University Press, 2002) back cover.

[7] "Pragmatism and Romanticism," in *Philosophy as Cultural Politics,* (Cambridge University Press, 2007) p. 107.

[8] Rorty, *Philosophy and the Mirror of Nature,* (Princeton University Press, 1979) p. 10.

[9] Rorty, "Pragmatism and Romanticism," in *Philosophy as Cultural Politics*, (Cambridge University Press, 2007) p. 109.

[10] Rorty, Nov. 18, 2003 lecture: "Putnam, Pragmatism, and Parmenides."

[11] Rorty, *Objectivity, Relativism and Truth,* (Cambridge University Press, 1991) pp. 38-39.

[12] Rorty, *Philosophy and the Mirror of Nature,* p. 170.

[13] Rorty, *Philosophy and the Mirror of Nature,* p. 10.

[14] John Heil, "Recent Work in Realism and Anti-realism," *Philosophical Books,* (1989) p. 65, cited in Michael Devitt, *Realism and Truth,* second ed., (Princeton University Press, 1996) p. vii.

[15] John Foster, *The Nature of Perception,* (Oxford University Press, 2000) p. 226-227.

[16] Putnam, *The Threefold Cord,* (Columbia University Press, 1999) p. 11.

[17] Some candidates for a pack of twenty: Berkeley, Hume, Kant, Leibniz, Fichte, Schopenhauer, Hegel, Kierkegaard, Heidegger, Husserl, Mill, Dewey, Wittgenstein, Sellars, Kuhn, Rorty, Putnam, Dummett, Davidson, Goodman. Those who would point to G. E. Moore as an example of a good champion of common sense realism might remember his "Defence of Common Sense" defended an exotic and misbegotten creature foreign to common sense, i.e., the *sense-datum.* Though Moore didn't invent the term, he endorsed it and popularized his version of it as something that you might see two of, if your eyes are crossed. (In 1889 we can find John Venn explaining "what are known as 'after images' being a modification of the present sense-datum by those which had gone before." (Venn, *The Principles of Empirical or Inductive Logic,* London: Macmillan & Co., 1889, p. 150.)

[18] Charles Taylor, "Sense Data Revisited," in Macdonald, G. F., ed., *Perception and Identity: Essays Presented to A. J. Ayer with His Replies,* Cornell University Press, 1979, p. 99.

[19] Richard Malachowski, *Richard Rorty,* (Princeton University Press, 2002) back cover.

[20] Rorty, *Contingency, Irony, and Solidarity,* (Cambridge University Press, 1989) pp. 176-177, emphasis altered.

[21] In a supreme irony, this is a phrase made famous by Hume, who did so much to sabotage the possibility.

[22] David Detmer, *Challenging Postmodernism: Philosophy and the Politics of Truth*, (Humanity Books, 2003) p. 67.

[23] Even Kant: "Idealism---I mean material idealism---is the theory which declares the existence of objects in space, without us, as *either doubtful only and not demonstrable, or* as false and impossible." (*Critique of Pure Reason*, B274, emphasis added.) Likewise, when Jean Baudrillard expresses what most professional philosophers might call idealism or anti-realism, he himself refers to it as "hyper-skepticism." ("Yes, hyper-skepticism. Intellectuals must stop legitimizing the notion that there is some 'ultimate truth' behind appearances.")

[24] Rorty, "Realism, Anti-realism and Pragmatism," in *Realism/Anti-realism and Epistemology*, Christopher Kulp, ed., 1997, p. 150. Support for Rorty's claim is easy to find. See Davidson, in Kulp, p. 109, Drew Khlentzos, *Naturalistic Realism and the Antirealist Challenge*, (MIT Press, 2004) pp. 6, 19-20, 24; Sebastian Gardner, *Kant and the Critique of Pure Reason* (Routledge, 1999) p. 33-37; Anthony Rudd, *Expressing the World*, (Open Court, 2003) p. 91; P. F. Strawson, in Jonathan Dancy, ed., *Perceptual Knowledge*, (Oxford University Press, 1988) p. 94-95; Henry E. Allison, *Kant's Transcendental Idealism*, p. 15; and Paul Abela, *Kant's Empirical Realism*, (Oxford University Press, 2002) p. 92.

[25] D. M. Armstrong, *Perception and the Physical World*, (Routledge & Kegan, 1961) p. 101.

[26] Anthony Rudd, *Expressing the World*, (Open Court, 2003) p. 2.

[27] Colin Howson, *Hume's Problem: Induction and the Justification of Belief*, (Oxford University Press, 2000) p.116.

[28] Rorty, *Philosophy and the Mirror of Nature*, (Princeton University Press, 1979) p. 294.

[29] G. R. G. Mure, *Retreat from Truth*, 153.

[30] Hume, *Treatise*, Book I, Part IV, Section VII, in Selby-Bigge, p. 269.

CHAPTER 1: What Can Be Realism

[1] Ernst Mach, *The Analysis of Sensations* [1886], Chapter 1, reprinted Patrick Gardiner, ed., *Nineteenth-Century Philosophy*, The Free Press, 1969, p. 383.

[2] Dickinson S. Miller, "Naive Realism: What is It?" in C. A. Strong, ed., *Essays Philosophical and Psychological in Honor of William James*, (Longmans Green, & Co. 1908) pp. 234, 240. "Naive realism is the view of the great mass of civilized humanity..." Oswald Kulpe, *Introduction to Philosophy: a Handbook for Students of Psychology, Logic, Ethics, Aesthetics, and General Philosophy*, first published in German in 1895. See also Robert G. Olson, *A Short Introduction to Philosophy*, (Dover, 1967) p. 7, 21, and Douglas Clyde Macintosh, *The Problem of Knowledge*, (G. Allen & Unwin ltd., 1916) p. 213. For some echoes in fields outside philosophy, see Mary Henle, *1879 and All That*, (Columbia 1986) pp. 3-4, Gordon B. Moskowitz, *Social Cognition: Understanding the Self and Others*, (Guilford Press, 2005) p. 22, James J. Schuerich, *Research Method in the Postmodern*, (Routledge, 1997) p. 30, and Tapio Luoma, *Incarnation and Physics: Natural Science in the Theology of Thomas F. Torrance*, (Oxford, 2002) p. 62.

[3] See H. H. Price, *Perception*, (London: Methuen & Company Ltd., 1932) p. 26. John Dewey, *Essays in Experimental Logic*, (Chicago: University of Chicago Press, 1916) pp. 254-255, C. A. Strong, ed., *Essays Philosophical and Psychological in Honor of William James*, (Longmans Green, & Co. 1908) pp. 177-178.

[4] These literal quotations are sampled from various leading lights, including Sellars, Putnam, and Kant. For chapter and verse, and lots more of the like, see Appendix.

[5] Hume, *Treatise of Human Nature*, Book I, Sect. II, in Selby-Bigge ed., 1888, p. 193.

[6] Hume, *Enquiry*, Section XII, part I, 118, in Selby-Bigge ed., p. 152.

[7] See Howard Robinson, *Perception*, 1994, p. 34, for the standard view, which identifies as "naive realism" the "vulgar" stance convicted by Hume's "slightest philosophy." (Hume's *Enquiry*, Selby-Bigge, p. 119.) "By naive realism we mean the attitude of the ordinary mind towards the external world." Dickinson S. Miller, "Naive Realism: What is It?" in C. A. Strong, ed., *Essays Philosophical and Psychological in Honor of William James*, (Longmans Green, & Co. 1908) pp. 234, 240. "*Naive* realism is the view of the great mass of civilized humanity..." Oswald Kulpe, *Introduction to Philosophy: a Handbook for Students of Psychology, Logic, Ethics, Aesthetics, and General Philosophy,* first published in German in 1895. See also Robert G. Olson, *A Short Introduction to Philosophy*, (Dover, 1967) p. 7, 21, and Douglas Clyde Macintosh, *The Problem of Knowledge*, (G. Allen & Unwin ltd., 1916) p. 213.

[8] *Critique of Pure Reason*, A492/B520.

[9] *Critique of Pure Reason*, A370.

[10] *Critique of Pure Reason*, B520.

[11] *Prolegomena to Any Future Metaphysics*, Part One, Remark II, 288-289.

[12] *Critique of Pure Reason*, A484/B512.

[13] Kant, *Critique of Pure Reason,* A126.

[14] Kant, *Critique of Pure Reason,* A383.

[15] Berkeley, *Three Dialogues*, in Locke, Berkeley, Hume, *The Empiricists*, (Anchor Books) p. 274, 303, 305, 253.

[16] Kant A285/B341. Arthur Collins (1999) tried to make the case that Kant, even though he constantly referred to himself as an idealist, was really "not an idealist," on account of the fact that he never denied that there were actual things in themselves subsisting outside the mind. Completely invisible, unknowable, and unimaginable things like, for example, God. Kant merely denied that rocks, trees, houses, tables, chairs, bananas, cannonballs, mountains, ships, planets, or anything else "with which we have to do" in all our experience, could "by any means" or "in any manner whatsoever" actually exist outside us. But, of course, Berkeley, the definitive idealist, had treated things more or less the same way, since Berkeley likewise allowed God to exist outside the mind, while relegating all the rocks, trees, houses, tables, chairs, and cannonballs to the mind. As Strawson put it, "Kant is closer to Berkeley than he acknowledges." Peter Strawson, *The Bounds of Sense*, (Methuen, 1966) p. 22. See also Norman Kemp Smith, *A Commentary to Kant's Critique of Pure Reason*, (Macmillan, 1918) p. 298-321. Thus Collins seems merely to be pointing out that Kant and Berkeley are not quite as absolute, in their idealism, as the later absolute idealists.

[17] Galileo, "The Assayer," [1623] in Richard H. Popkin, ed., *Philosophy of the 16th and 17th Centuries.* (New York: The Free Press, 1966) p. 58.

[18] Hobbes, *Leviathan*, in Richard H. Popkin, ed., *Philosophy of the 16th and 17th Centuries.* (New York: The Free Press, 1966) p. 190.

[19] Daniel Dennett, "Wondering Where the Yellow Went," *The Monist*, Vol. 64, No. 1, January 1981, p. 102.

[20] Wilfrid Sellars, 1956 essay "Empiricism and the Philosophy of Mind," reprinted in DeVries & Triplett, *Knowledge, Mind and the Given* (Hackett, 2000), p. 253, emphasis added.

[21] Strawson, "Perception and Its Objects," in Dancy, ed., *Perceptual Knowledge*, Oxford University Press, 1988, p. 111.

[22] Strawson, "Perception and Its Objects," in Dancy, ed., *Perceptual Knowledge*, Oxford University Press, 1988, pp. 100-101.

[23] Putnam, *The Many Faces of Realism*, (Open Court, 1987) p. 4.

[24] Putnam, "Why There Isn't a Ready-Made World," 1981, in *Realism and Reason*, (Cambridge Univ. Press, 1983) pp. viii, 207, and "The Question of Realism," *Words & Life*, (Harvard, 1994), p. 297.

[25] Fumerton, *Realism and the Correspondence Theory of Truth*, (Rowman and Littlefield, 2002) p. 73.

[26] Devitt, *Realism and Truth*, second ed., (Princeton, 1991), p. 331.

[27] Drew Khlentzos, *Naturalistic Realism and the Antirealist Challenge*, (MIT Press, 2004) p. 190, quoting Hilary Putnam, "Reply to Miller," Philosophical Topics, 20: *The Philosophy of Hilary Putnam*, (Christopher Hill issue ed.,) no. 1, 1992, p. 373.

[28] D. M. Armstrong, "Perception, Sense Data and Causality," in Macdonald, G. F., ed., *Perception and Identity: Essays Presented to A. J. Ayer with His Replies*, (Cornell University Press, 1979) p. 84.

[29] A. J. Ayer, *The Problem of Knowledge*, (1956) pp. 79, 82, 97, and Ayer, "Reply to John Foster," in Lewis Edwin Hahn, ed., *The Philosophy of A. J. Ayer*, (Open Court, 1992) pp. 198-200. See also Richard Fumerton, *Metaphysical and Epistemological Problems of Perception*, (University of Nebraska, 1985) p. 73, and Avrum Stroll, *Twentieth Century Analytic Philosophy*, (Columbia, 2000) p. 49. In Jonathan Dancy, *Introduction to Contemporary Epistemology*, (Blackwell Publishing, 1985) p. 155, Dancy's menu is generous enough to offer realists a choice labeled "naive indirect realism." Be warned, however, that there's a strange and unappetizing concoction ready to serve as definition, should any *naifs* feel tempted to check that box. Suffice it to say Dancy doesn't exaggerate when he calls it "grossly implausible."

[30] DeVries, and Triplett, *Knowledge, Mind and the Given,* Hackett, 2000, p. 9.

[31] Kant, *Critique of Pure Reason*, B276-277.

[32] Charles Taylor, "Sense Data Revisited," in Macdonald, G. F., ed., *Perception and Identity: Essays Presented to A. J. Ayer with His Replies*, (Cornell University Press, 1979) p. 99.

[33] See for example G. A. Paul, "Is There a Problem About Sense-Data?" reprinted in Robert J. Swartz ed., *Perceiving Sensing, and Knowing*, (London: University of California Press, 1965), p. 271- 287.

[34] DeVries and Triplett, *Knowledge, Mind and the Given* , 2000, p. 4.

[35] Daniel Dennett, *Consciousness Explained* (Little, Brown & Co., 1991), p. 369.

[36] Maund, *Perception*, (McGill-Queen's, 2003), p. 92.

[37] Richard Fumerton, *Metaphysical and Epistemological Problems of Perception*, (Nebraska, 1985) p. 76.

CHAPTER 2: ## The Same Waking that Dreaming

[1] Edmund Spenser, *The Faerie Queene.*

[2] Hume, Treatise, Book I, Part IV, sect. vii, in Nidditch ed., p. 272.

[3] Keynes, *The General Theory of Employment, Interest, and Money.* 1936, (New York: Harcourt, Brace and World), pp. 383-384.

[4] See Rorty, Nov. 18, 2003 lecture: "Putnam, Pragmatism, and Parmenides." and *Philosophy and the Mirror of Nature*, (Princeton University Press, 1979) p. 10.

[5] In 1856, Albert Schwegler's *History of Philosophy in Epitome*, had Jacobi, Fichte, Herbart, Schelling, and Hegel under the sectional heading "the post-Kantian philosophy." In 1858, John Stuart Mill spoke of "the post-Kantian movement as represented by Schelling and Hegel." David Masson in 1866 referred to "the post-Kantian movement, as represented in Fichte, Schelling, and Hegel." Robert Adamson (1881) talked about Fichte as "post-Kantian," explaining that "The philosophy of Fichte attaches itself, by a kind of natural necessity, to that of Kant, of which it is an extension and development." In 1896 Thomas Acland listed "Fichte, Schelling, and Hegel" as "post-Kantians." (Albert Schwegler, *A History of Philosophy in Epitome*, second edition, translated from the original German by Julius Seelye, New York: D. Appleton and Co., 1856, p. 268. John Start Mill, *A System of Logic: Ratiocinative and Inductive*, Harper & Bros., 1858, p. 40n. David Masson, *Recent British Philosophy: A Review with Criticisms*, New York: D. Appleton and Co., 1866, p. 87. Robert Adamson, *Fichte*, London: William Blackwood and Sons, 1881, pp. 105-107. Thomas Dyke Acland, *Knowledge, Duty, and Faith*, London: Kegan Paul, Trench, Trubner & Co., 1896, p. 217.)

[6] Adrian Moore, Oxford philosopher interviewed on BBC's "Western Philosophy" series, 2005.

[7] Randall, in Allen Wood ed., *Basic Writings of Kant*, (New York, Modern Library, 2001) front cover.

[8] David Fate Norton, ed., *The Cambridge Companion to Hume*, (Cambridge University Press, 1993), back cover.

[9] Anita Avramides, *Other Minds*, (Routledge, 2001) p. 140. "The more one reads in Reid the more philosophical power one finds there. I think he would have maintained his status throughout, had he been as inscrutable as Hegel." Daniel N. Robinson, *The Great Ideas of Philosophy*, first edition, Part IV, Lecture 32, "Thomas Reid and the Scottish School," (The Teaching Company, 1997). Benjamin Rush, who suggested "Common Sense" as the title for Tom Paine's pamphlet, had been in Edinburgh and friendly with Thomas Reid's cousin. "Now here's the first major jurisdictional dispute of the Supreme Court [Chisholm v. Georgia, 1793] and the decision given by a justice of the Supreme Court citing Reid's *Inquiry into Human Mind* as authoritative. I've often said to students, show me a place where the Supreme Court is citing Reid's *Inquiry* and that's a place I'd like to live." Daniel N. Robinson, *American Ideals: the Founding of a "Republic of Virtue,"* Lecture 8: "The Constitution of the United States, Part 1," (The Teaching Company, 2004).

[10] Reid, *An Inquiry into the Human Mind on the Principles of Common Sense* (Edinburgh: Edinburgh University Press, 1997), pp. 75-76.

[11] Kuhn, *The Structure of Scientific Revolutions*, (2nd edition, Chicago, 1970) p. 135, 150. See also Norwood R. Hanson, *Patterns of Discovery*, (Cambridge, 1961) Chapter I.

[12] Kuhn, p. 148.

[13] Kuhn, p. 150.

[14] p. 151.

[15] p. 152.

[16] p. 170.

[17] p. 135.

[18] p. 159.

[19] p. 170.

[20] Nelson Goodman, *Of Mind and Other Matters*, (Harvard University Press, 1984) p. 29.

[21] W. T. Stace, *The Philosophy of Hegel: a Systematic Exposition*, (Dover, 1955), p. 42.

[22] Rorty, "Reply to Conant," in *Rorty and His Critics*, (Blackwell, 2000), pp. 342-343.

[23] Reid, *Essays*, II, Chapter x, 179, quoted in Antita Avramides, *Other Minds*, (Routledge, 2001) p. 141.

[24] "The threat of solipsism nagged Husserl. The question of the status of others occupied him during the last years of his life and remained a question that seemed to challenge to the foundation of his life's work. ...Having adopted transcendental idealism, he became increasingly aware of the problem it raised with regard to intersubjectivity. How, within the idealistic standpoint, do I acknowledge the independent existence of Others---of fellow subjects?" James R. Mensch, *Intersubjectivity and Transcendental Idealism*, (State University of New York Press, 1988) p. 1, back cover.

[25] Rorty, *Objectivity, Relativism, and Truth*, Philosophical Papers, vol. 1 (Cambridge: Cambridge University Press, 1991) p. 13.

[26] Rorty, *Objectivity, Relativism and Truth*, (Cambridge University Press, 1991) pp. 38-39.

[27] Davidson, 1997 essay "Indeterminism and Anti-realism," reprinted in *Subjective, Intersubjective, Objective*, (Oxford University Press, 2001) p. 83. It was ironic that Hume, who did so much to shoot down the anti-skeptical realism of common sense, once said that philosophy should be "common sense methodized and perfected." In a similar irony, we find Kant beautifully expressing a laudable motto to which his own fans eventually came to lead the opposition: "Enlightenment is man's release from his self-incurred tutelage. Tutelage is man's inability to make use of his understanding without direction from another. Self-incurred is this tutelage when its cause lies not in lack of reason but in lack of resolution and courage to use it without direction from another. *Sapere aude!* [dare to know] 'Have courage to use your own

reason!' — that is the motto of enlightenment." (Kant, "What is Enlightenment?" 1784, translation by Lewis White Beck, from Immanuel Kant, On History, ed., with an introduction, by Lewis White Beck Indianapolis: Bobbs-Merrill, 1963, p. 3.)

[28] *Critique of Pure Reason*, A370.

[29] *Prolegomena to Any Future Metaphysics*, Part One, Remark II, 288-289.

[30] Kant, *Prolegomena to Any Future Metaphysics*, Part One, Remark II, 288-289.

[31] Putnam, *Realism with a Human Face*, (Harvard, 1990) p. 248.

[32] Michel de Montaigne, "Apology for Raymond Sebond," (1576) in Richard H. Popkin, ed., *The Philosophy of the 16th and 17th Centuries.* (New York: The Free Press, 1966) p. 80-81.

[33] Hume, *Enquiry Concerning Human Understanding*, Section XII, part I, 118-119, Selby-Bigge ed., pp. 152-153.

[34] Hume, *Treatise of Human Nature*, Book I, Sect. II, Selby-Bigge ed., p. 189.

[35] G. E. Schulze, *Aenesidemus*, [1792] 94, translated by George di Giovanni and H. S. Harris, eds., *Between Kant and Hegel*, revised edition, (Hackett Publishing, 2000), pp. 105-106

[36] Putnam, *Realism and Reason*, (Cambridge Univ. Press, 1983), p. viii.

[37] McDowell, *Mind and World*, (Harvard University Press, 1996) pp. 16, 42.

[38] Davidson, 1983 essay, "A Coherence Theory of Truth and Knowledge," reprinted in *Subjective, Intersubjective, Objective,* (Oxford University Press, 2001) p. 144.

[39] Richard Rorty, *Philosophy and the Mirror of Nature*, (Princeton, 1979), p. 10 .

[40] Ibid.

[41] Davidson, 1983 essay, "A Coherence Theory of Truth and Knowledge," reprinted in *Subjective, Intersubjective, Objective,* (Oxford University Press, 2001) p. 144.

[42] Rorty, *Philosophy and the Mirror of Nature*, (Princeton University Press, 1979) p. 170.

[43] *Philosophy and the Mirror of Nature*, p. 170.

[44] Rorty, Nov. 18, 2003 lecture: "Putnam, Pragmatism, and Parmenides."

[45] W. T. Stace, *The Philosophy of Hegel: a Systematic Exposition*, (Dover, 1955), p. 43-45.

[46] Ibid.

[47] Rorty, 2003.

[48] Hegel, [1830] *Lectures on the Philosophy of World History*, (Cambridge University Press, 1975), p. 94.

[49] Hegel, *Philosophy of History*, [1837], 41.

[50] J. G. Fichte, *Characteristics of the Present Age*, 1806, trans. W. Smith, 2nd edition, (London: John Chapman, 1859) p. 36.

[51] Hegel, *Philosophy of Right*, [1821], 258.

[52] Hegel, *Philosophy of History*, 68.

[53] Hegel, *Philosophy of Right*, [1821], 319, Remark.

[54] Hegel, *Lectures on the History of Philosophy*, second edition, [1840] reprinted in *Hegel Selections*, edited by M. J. Inwood, Macmillan Publishing Company, 1989, pp. 439-440.

[55] Schopenhauer, *The World as Will and Representation*, Volume 2, Haldane-Kemp translation, (1891) p. 20-22.

[56] Heidegger, cited in *Heidegger and Nazism*, Victor Farias, trans. Paul Burrell, (Philadelphia: Temple Univ. Press, 1989) p. 118.

[57] Frederich Engels, *The New Moral World*, third series, no. 21, November 18, 1843.

[58] Orwell, *1984*, Chapter 3, (Penguin, 1990) p. 266.

[59] Rorty, *Contingency, Irony, and Solidarity*, (Cambridge University Press, 1989) pp. 176-177, emphasis altered.

[60] Martin Kusch, *Knowledge by Agreement*, (Oxford University Press, 2002) pp. 1, 245, and back cover.

[61] Martin Kusch, *Knowledge by Agreement*, (Oxford University Press, 2002) pp. 245.

[62] Orwell, *1984*, (Penguin, 1990), p. 81.

[63] Stanley Aronowitz, *Science as Power*, (University of Minnesota, 1988), back cover.

[64] See William James, "Pragmatism's Conception of Truth," from *Pragmatism: A New Name for Some Old Ways of Thinking*, (Longmans, 1907), reprinted in Simon Blackburn & Keith Simmons, eds., *Truth* (Oxford University Press, 1999) p. 62.

[65] Kusch, *Knowledge by Agreement*, (Oxford University Press, 2002) pp. 248-249, 258.

[66] Ibid.

[67] Ibid.

[68] Paul Feyerabend, *Farewell to Reason*, (Verso, 1987), back cover.

[69] Ibid.

[70] Feyerabend, *Farewell to Reason*, p. v.

[71] *Farewell to Reason* , p. viii.

[72] Jacques Lyotard, *The Postmodern Condition: A Report on Knowledge*, (University of Minnesota, 1979).

[73] Rorty, *Take Care of Freedom and Truth Will Take Care of Itself*, (Stanford, 2006), p. 21.

[74] Wittgenstein, *Tractatus Logico-Philosophicus*, 1921, 1.1, 1.13, 5.6-5.61, trans. Pears and McGuinness, (Routledge, 1961) p. 56-57.

[75] Goodman, *Ways of Worldmaking*, p. 6.

[76] Jacques Derrida, *Of Grammatology*, (Johns Hopkins University Press, 1977) p. 158.

[77] John McDowell, *Mind and World*, (Harvard University Press, 1996) p. 114.

[78] Sellars, *Empiricism and the Philosophy of Mind*, (Harvard University Press, 1997), p. 63.

[79] This is Rorty explaining Sellars's view in Wilfrid Sellars, Robert Brandom, and Richard Rorty, *Empiricism and the Philosophy of Mind*, (Harvard University Press, 1997), p. 4.

[80] Rorty, "Pragmatism and Romanticism," in *Philosophy as Cultural Politics*, (Cambridge University Press, 2007) p. 107.

[81] Rorty, "Pragmatism and Romanticism," in *Philosophy as Cultural Politics*, (Cambridge University Press, 2007) pp. 114-115.

[82] Rorty, "Pragmatism and Romanticism," in *Philosophy as Cultural Politics*, (Cambridge University Press, 2007) p. 113.

[83] Isaiah Berlin, *The Age of Enlightenment*, (New York: New American Library, 1956) p. 273.

[84] Hamann, quoted in Isaiah Berlin, *The Magus of the North: J. G. Hamann and the Origins of Modern Irrationalism,* (New York: Farrar, Straus, and Giroux, 1993) p. 77.

[85] Hamann, quoted in Berlin, *The Age of Enlightenment*, (New York: New American Library, 1956) p. 274.

[86] *Critique of Practical Reason*, Part I, Book I, Chap. I, sec. II, 54.

[87] *Prolegomena to Any Future Metaphysics*, Part One, Remark II, 288-289.

[88] Nelson Goodman, *Of Mind and Other Matters* (Harvard University Press, 1984) p. 42. See also Goodman, *Ways of Worldmaking*, (Hackett, 1978).

[89] Goodman, *Of Mind and Other Matters*, pp. 36, 37.

[90] Film "What the Bleep Do We Know?" directed by Betsy Chasse and Mark Vicente, Fox Home Entertainment, 2004.

[91] Kant, *Critique of Pure Reason*, B2.

[92] J. G. Fichte, "First Introduction to the Science of Knowledge," I 421, in *Science of Knowledge*, translated by Peter Heath & John Lachs, (Appleton Century Crofts, 1970) p. 4.

[93] Fichte, "First Introduction," 433-434. Like his postmodern followers, Fichte claimed that, in the choice between realism and idealism, "Reason provides no principle of choice...the choice is governed by caprice, and since even a capricious decision must have some source, it is governed by inclination and interest." (I 432-433.)

[94] Fichte, *The Vocation of Man*, [1800], Book Two, ed. and trans. Roderick Chisholm, (Bobbs-Merrill, 1956) pp. 38, 75-76.

[95] Rorty, "The Quest for Uncertainty," in *Take Care of Freedom and Truth Will Take Care of Itself: Interviews with Richard Rorty,* edited by Eduardo Mendieta, (Stanford University Press, 2006) p. 15.

[96] Hume, *An Enquiry Concerning Human Understanding*, Section IV, part I, 26.

[97] W. V. O. Quine, *Ontological Relativity and Other Essays,* (Columbia University Press, 1969), p. 72.

[98] Hume, *Treatise,* Book I, Part IV, Section VII, in Selby-Bigge ed., p. 269

[99] Hume, *Dialogues Concerning Natural Religion,* edited by Norman Kemp Smith, (New York: Macmillan & Co.) 1947, p. 228.

[100] Hume, *Dialogues Concerning Natural Religion,* edited by Norman Kemp Smith, (New York: Macmillan & Co.) 1947, p. 228. Though published in 1779, Hume's *Dialogues* were composed closer to 1750.

[101] Richard H. Popkin, *The History of Scepticism, from Savonarola to Bayle,* revised and expanded, Oxford, 2003, pp. 3-27., and D. P. Walker, *The Ancient Theology,* London: Duckworth,1972, p. 60.

[102] Erasmus, "In Praise of Folly," in Richard H. Popkin, ed., *The Philosophy of the 16th and 17th Centuries.* (New York: The Free Press, 1966) p. 32.

[103] Henry Cornelius Agrippa von Nettesheim, *Of the Vanitie and Uncertaintie of Artes and Sciences,* Englished by James Sanford (London, 1569) p. 183v, in Popkin, Richard H., *The History of Scepticism from Erasmus to Spinoza,* (University of California Press, 1979) p. 24.

[104] Loyola, in Richard H. Popkin, *The History of Scepticism from Erasmus to Spinoza,* (University of California Press, 1979) p. 4.

[105] Michel de Montaigne, "Apology for Raymond Sebond," (1576) in Richard H. Popkin, ed., *The Philosophy of the 16th and 17th Centuries.* (New York: The Free Press, 1966) p. 73.

[106] Montaigne, "Apology for Raymond Sebond," in Popkin ed., p. 72.

[107] Montaigne, in Popkin ed., p. 74.

[108] Montaigne, in Popkin ed., pp. 80-81.

[109] In Popkin ed., p. 72.

[110] Bayle, "Pyrrho," in *Historical and Critical Dictionary,* (1702).

[111] Hume, *Treatise,* Part IV, sections I & II.

[112] Hume, *A Treatise of Human Nature,* (1740) Book I, Part IV, Sect. VII, in Selby-Bigge ed., p. 267-268.

[113] Hume, *Treatise,* Book I, Part IV, Sect. VII, in Selby-Bigge ed., p. 268.

[114] *Treatise,* in Selby-Bigge ed., p. 269.

[115] See Isaiah Berlin, *The Magus of the North: J.G. Hamann and the Origins of Modern Irrationalism.* (Farrar, Straus, & Giroux, 1994), p. 33.

[116] Kant, *Critique of Pure Reason,* Bxxx.

CHAPTER 3: Seeing Things

[1] Fichte, *The Vocation of Man,* (1800) Book III, ed. and trans. Roderick Chisholm, (Bobbs-Merrill, 1956) p. 83.

[2] Fumerton, *Metaphysical and Epistemological Problems of Perception,* (Nebraska University Press, 1985) p. 73.

[3] David Hume, *Treatise,* in Selby-Bigge edition p. 191.

[4] Compare Hume, *Enquiry Concerning Human Understanding,* Section XII, part I, 118-119, in Selby-Bigge ed., p. 152-153.

[5] Compare "...the reality is objective, but the objects aren't." Hilary Putnam, "The Vision and Arguments of a Famous Harvard Philosopher," in Andrew Pyle, ed., *Key Philosophers in Conversation,* (Routledge, 1999) p. 52.

[6] For an interesting discussion of this point, see Paul Guyer, *Kant and the Claims of Knowledge* (Cambridge University Press, 1987) Chapter 15, especially p. 339.

[7] Kant, *Critique of Pure Reason,* B519.

[8] Charles Sanders Peirce, "How to Make Our Ideas Clear," *Popular Science Monthly*, January 1878, 286-302.

[9] *Critique of Pure Reason*, B520.

[10] *Prolegomena to Any Future Metaphysics*, Part One, Remark II, 288-289.

[11] *Critique of Pure Reason*, A484/B512.

[12] B522.

[13] *Critique of Pure Reason*, A383.

[14] A484/B512

[15] *Critique of Pure Reason*, B521/A493.

[16] Hume, *Enquiry*, Section XII, part I, 118-119, in Selby-Bigge ed., p. 152-153, emphasis altered.

[17] Kant, *Critique of Pure Reason*, A380.

[18] *Critique of Pure Reason*, A370.

CHAPTER 4: Doubting Skepticism

[1] René Descartes, *Meditations,* end of Meditation I, 1901 trans. John Veitch.

[2] See Richard Fumerton, "Skepticism and Reasoning to the Best Explanation," in Enrique Villanueva ed., *Philosophical Issues, 2: Rationality in Epistemology*, 1992, p. 163-165.

[3] See Richard Fumerton, "Skepticism and Reasoning to the Best Explanation," in Enrique Villanueva ed., *Philosophical Issues, 2: Rationality in Epistemology*, 1992, p. 163-165.

[4] Peter Unger, *Ignorance*, (Oxford University Press, 1975) p. 132.

[5] See Roderick Firth, "Coherence, Certainty, and Epistemic Priority," in Jonathan Dancy ed., *Perceptual Knowledge*, (Oxford, 1988) p. 171, "There is no logical inconsistency in asserting that someone has a false belief which he cannot rationally doubt, and which he is not in a position to correct; consequently there is no inconsistency in asserting that expressive judgments are indubitable and incorrigible, while at the same time granting that some of them may be false."

[6] René Descartes, *Meditations,* end of Meditation I, 1901 trans. John Veitch, emphasis added.

[7] Richard A. Fumerton, "Induction and Reasoning to the Best Explanation," in *Philosophy of Science*, Volume 47, 1980, p. 598.

[8] Sellars, *Knowledge mind and the Given*, DeVries and Triplett, eds. (Hackett, 2000) p. 250.

[9] Ibid.

[10] Sextus Empiricus, *Outlines of Pyrrhonism,* (Harvard University Press, 1993) Chapter III-IV.

[11] Wilfrid Sellars, Robert Brandom, and Richard Rorty, *Empiricism and the Philosophy of Mind*, (Harvard University Press, 1997), p. 13.

[12] Anthony Rudd, *Expressing the World*, (Open Court, 2003) p. 98.

[13] Richard A. Fumerton, "Induction and Reasoning to the Best Explanation," in *Philosophy of Science*, Volume 47, 1980, p. 600.

[14] "No one has been able to knock Hume's argument down." Colin Howson, *Hume's Problem: Induction and the Justification of Belief*, (Oxford University Press, 2000) p. 109. "To many people, justifying induction seems rather like squaring the circle. It has so often been shown to be impossible that anyone who attempts it risks the suspicion of being mildly insane." J. L. Mackie, "A Defence of Induction," in Macdonald, G. F., ed., *Perception and Identity: Essays Presented to A. J. Ayer with His Replies*, Cornell University Press, 1979, p. 113. Howson also cites C. D. Broad, "The Philosophy of Francis Bacon," in *Ethics and the History of Philosophy*, (London, Routledge and Kegan Paul, 1952) p. 142-143.

[15] Hume's *Enquiry*, 30, in Selby-Bigge, pp. 35-36..

[16] Hume, *Treatise*, Book I, Part IV, Sect. VI, in Selby-Bigge ed., p. 89.

[17] David Hume, "Abstract of the Treatise," *A Treatise of Human Nature*, [1740], edited by L. A. Selby-Bigge 1888, second edition, revised by P. H. Nidditch, (Oxford: Clarendon Press, 1978) p. 650.

[18] William H. Shaw phrased it this way in private correspondence, July 2006.

[19] Richard A. Fumerton, "Induction and Reasoning to the Best Explanation," in *Philosophy of Science*, Volume 47, 1980, p. 598.

[20] Fichte, "First Introduction to the Science of Knowledge," I 431, in *Science of Knowledge*, translated by Peter Heath & John Lachs, (Appleton Century Crofts, 1970) p. 13.

[21] Fichte, "First Introduction to the Science of Knowledge," I 432-433, in *Science of Knowledge*, translated by Peter Heath & John Lachs, (Appleton Century Crofts, 1970) pp. 14-15.

[22] Russell, *An Inquiry Into Meaning and Truth*, (London: Unwin, 1950), p. 15.

[23] Hegel, *The Difference Between Fichte's and Schelling's System of Philosophy*, H.S. Harris and Walter Cerf eds., (SUNY, 1977) p. 99.

[24] Hume, "Conclusion of this Book," *Treatise*, Book I, part IV, sect. vii, Selby-Bigge ed., p. 267-268.

[25] Kant, *Critique of Pure Reason*, A380.

[26] Putnam, *Realism with a Human Face*, (Harvard, 1990) , p. 189.

[27] Berlin, p. 33.

[28] Fichte, "Addresses to the German Nation," 1806, Fichte, *The Closed Commercial State*, 1800.

[29] Hume, *A Treatise of Human Nature*, (1740) Book I, Part IV, Sect. VII, in Selby-Bigge ed., p. 267-268.

[30] Hume, *Treatise*, "Conclusion of this Book," Book I, Part IV, Sect. VII, in Selby-Bigge ed., p. 269.

[31] Ibid, p. 268.

[32] Ibid, pp. 267-268.

[33] Ibid, p. 269.

[34] Hume, *Enquiry*, Section IV, Part I, 26, in Selby-Bigge ed., p. 31.

[35] Rorty, "Hilary Putnam and the Relativist Menace," *Truth and Progress*, (Cambridge University Press, 1998) p. 47.

Appendix

[1] Sextus Empiricus, *Outlines of Pyrrhonism*, Book I, Chapter XIV.

[2] Sextus Empiricus, *Outlines of Pyrrhonism*, Book I, 116-117.

[3] Michel de Montaigne, "Apology for Raymond Sebond," (1576) in Richard H. Popkin, ed., *The Philosophy of the 16th and 17th Centuries*. (New York: The Free Press, 1966) p. 80-81.

[4] Montaigne, in Popkin, p. 74.

[5] Montaigne, in Popkin, p. 72.

[6] Malebranche, *Dialogues on Metaphysics*, [1688] in Richard H. Popkin, ed., *The Philosophy of the 16th and 17th Centuries*. (New York: The Free Press, 1966) p. 294.

[7] Malebranche, *Eclaircissment sur la recherché de la verite*, [1675], in Popkin, 1966, p. 343n.

[8] John Locke, *An Essay Concerning Human Understanding*, (1690) Book IV, Chap. I, sec. 1.

[9] George Berkeley, "Three Dialogues Between Hylas and Philonous, In Opposition to Skeptics and Atheists," (1713); reprinted in *The Empiricists*. p. 254.

[10] Berkeley, "Three Dialogues," in *The Empiricists*. p. 259.

[11] "Three Dialogues," in *The Empiricists*. p. 257.

[12] Berkeley, *Three Dialogues*, in Locke, Berkeley, Hume, *The Empiricists*, (Anchor Books) p. 274, 303, 305, 253.

[13] Berkeley, "Three Dialogues," in *The Empiricists*. p. 253.

[14] David Hume, *A Treatise of Human Nature*, [1740] Book I, Part IV, section II, edited by L. A. Selby-Bigge 1888, second edition, revised by P. H. Nidditch, (Oxford: Clarendon Press, 1978) p. 193.

[15] Hume, *Treatise*, Book I, Part IV, Section II, in Selby-Bigge ed., p. 191.

[16] Hume, *An Enquiry Concerning Human Understanding,* [1748] Section XII, part I, 118-119, in Selby-Bigge ed., pp. 152f.

[17] Hume, "Scepticism with Regard to the Senses," *Treatise of Human Nature,* [1739] Book I, Part IV, Sect II, in Selby-Bigge ed., pp. 212f.

[18] Hume, *Treatise,* Book I, Part IV, Sect II, in Selby-Bigge ed., pp. 210f.

[19] *Treatise,* Book I, Part II, Sect IV, in Selby-Bigge ed., p. 67.

[20] Hume, *Treatise,* "Scepticism Regarding the Senses," Book I, Part IV, Sect II, in Selby-Bigge ed., p. 189.

[21] Hume, *Enquiry Concerning Human Understanding,* Section XII, part I, 118-119, in Selby-Bigge ed., p. 152-153.

[22] David Hume, "Abstract of the Treatise," *A Treatise of Human Nature,* [1740], edited by L. A. Selby-Bigge 1888, second edition, revised by P. H. Nidditch, (Oxford: Clarendon Press, 1978) p. 650.

[23] Hume, *Treatise,* Book I, Part IV, Sect. VI, in Selby-Bigge ed., p. 89.

[24] *Treatise,* "Conclusion of this Book," Book I, Part IV, Sect. VII, in Selby-Bigge ed., p. 268-269.

[25] "Conclusion of this Book," Book I, Part IV, Sect. VII, in Selby-Bigge ed., p. 270.

[26] *Treatise,* Book I, Part IV, Sect. VII, in Selby-Bigge ed., p. 269.

[27] *Treatise,* Book I, Part IV, Sect. VII, in Selby-Bigge ed., p. 270.

[28] Book I, Part IV, Sect. VII, in Selby-Bigge ed., p. 268.

[29] *Treatise,* in Selby-Bigge ed., p. 269.

[30] *Treatise,* in Selby-Bigge ed., p. 267-268.

[31] *Treatise,* Book I, Part IV, Sect II, in Selby-Bigge ed., p. 218.

[32] Hume, *Enquiry,* Section IV, Part I, 26, in Selby-Bigge ed., p. 31.

[33] Immanuel Kant, *Critique of Pure Reason,* Bxl.

[34] Kant, *Critique of Pure Reason,* B519.

[35] Kant, *Prolegomena to Any Future Metaphysics.* 13, Note II.

[36] Kant, *Critique of Practical Reason,* Part I, Book I, Chap. I, sec. II, 55.

[37] *Critique of Pure Reason,* A385.

[38] *Critique of Pure Reason,* B45.

[39] Kant, *Critique of Pure Reason,* A370.

[40] *Critique of Practical Reason,* Part I, Book I, Chap. I, sec. II, 54.

[41] *Critique of Pure Reason,* B520.

[42] B235.

[43] *Prolegomena to Any Future Metaphysics,* Part One, Remark II, 288-289.

[44] *Critique of Pure Reason,* A494/B522.

[45] *Prolegomena to Any Future Metaphysics,* Part One, Remark II, 288-289.

[46] *Critique of Pure Reason,* A484/B512.

[47] A507/B535.

[48] *Critique of Pure Reason,* A492/B520.

[49] Kant, *Critique of Pure Reason,* A126.

[50] A383.

[51] *Critique of Pure Reason,* A380.

[52] Kant, *Critique of Pure Reason,* Bxxx.

[53] G. E. Schulze, *Aenesidemus,* [1792] 94, translated by George di Giovanni and H. S. Harris, eds., *Between Kant and Hegel,* revised edition, (Hackett Publishing, 2000), pp. 105-106

[54] Fichte, *The Vocation of Man,* (1800) Book III, ed. and trans. Roderick Chisholm, (Bobbs-Merrill, 1956) p. 83.

[55] J. G. Fichte, "First Introduction to the Science of Knowledge," I 421, in *Science of Knowledge,* translated by Peter Heath & John Lachs, (Appleton Century Crofts, 1970) p.4.

[56] F. W. J. Schelling, *System of Transcendental Idealism,* 1800, translated Peter Heath (Charlottesville, University Press of Virginia, 1978) p. 34-35.

[57] Russell, "On Scientific Method in Philosophy," in *Mysticism and Logic,* (New York: Longmans, 1918) p. 123.

[58] Russell, "Knowledge by Acquaintance," in *Mysticism and Logic*, (New York: Longmans, 1918) p. 214.

[59] Quine, *Ontological Relativity and Other Essays,* (Columbia University Press, 1969), p. 72.

[60] Putnam, *Realism with a Human Face,* (Harvard University Press, 1990) p. 28.

[61] Putnam, *Realism and Reason,* p. viii.

[62] Davidson, 1983 essay, "A Coherence Theory of Truth and Knowledge," reprinted in *Subjective, Intersubjective, Objective,* (Oxford University Press, 2001) p. 144.

[63] Davidson, 1997 essay "Indeterminism and Anti-realism," reprinted in *Subjective, Intersubjective, Objective,* (Oxford University Press, 2001) p. 83.

[64] Davidson, *Subjective, Intersubjective, Objective,* (Oxford University Press, 2001) p. 219-220.

[65] Rorty, "John Searle on Realism and Relativism," *Truth and Progress,* (Cambridge University Press, 1998) p. 63.

[66] Rorty, "De Man and the American Cultural Left," *Essays on Heidegger and Others,* (Cambridge University Press, 1991) p. 129.

[67] Rorty, *Truth and Progress,* (Cambridge University Press,1998) p. 72.

[68] Rorty, "Reply to Conant," in Robert Brandom, ed., *Rorty and His Critics,* (Blackwell, 2000), pp. 342-343.

[69] Rorty, Nov. 18, 2003 lecture: "Putnam, Pragmatism, and Parmenides."

[70] Rorty, *Philosophy and the Mirror of Nature,* p. 170.

[71] *Philosophy and the Mirror of Nature,* p. 10.

[72] *Philosophy and the Mirror of Nature,* p. 170.

[73] Rorty, "John Searle on Realism and Relativism," *Truth and Progress,* (Cambridge University Press, 1998) pp. 71-72.

[74] Rorty, "Pragmatism and Romanticism," in *Philosophy as Cultural Politics,* (Cambridge University Press, 2007) p. 112.

[75] *Philosophy as Cultural Politics,* (Cambridge University Press, 2007) p. 109.

[76] Rorty, *Objectivity, Relativism, and Truth,* Philosophical Papers, vol. 1 (Cambridge: Cambridge University Press, 1991) p. 13.

[77] Rorty, *Objectivity, Relativism, and Truth,* Philosophical Papers, vol. 1 (Cambridge: Cambridge University Press, 1991) p. 39.

[78] "Pragmatism and Romanticism," in *Philosophy as Cultural Politics,* (Cambridge University Press, 2007) p. 107.

[79] Rorty, *Objectivity, Relativism and Truth,* (Cambridge University Press, 1991) pp. 38-39.

[80] Rorty, *Contingency, Irony, and Solidarity,* (Cambridge University Press, 1989) pp. 176-177.

[81] "Hilary Putnam and the Relativist Menace," *Truth and Progress,* (Cambridge University Press, 1998) p. 45.

[82] Rorty, "The Quest for Uncertainty," in *Take Care of Freedom and Truth Will Take Care of Itself: Interviews with Richard Rorty,* edited by Eduardo Mendieta, (Stanford University Press, 2006) p. 15.

Bibliography

[1] Galileo, 1632, Francois Arago, *Biographies of Distinguished Scientific Men*, (Boston: Ticknor & Fields, 1859) p. 365.

LaVergne, TN USA
04 August 2010
192053LV00005B/74/A